TEST ANXIETY

Applied Research, Assessment, and Treatment Interventions

2nd Edition

Marty Sapp

University Press of America,® Inc.
Lanham • New York • Oxford

Copyright © 1999 by
University Press of America,® Inc.
4720 Boston Way
Lanham, Maryland 20706

12 Hid's Copse Rd.
Cumnor Hill, Oxford OX2 9JJ

Library of Congress Cataloging-in-Publication Data

Sapp, Marty.
Test Anxiety : applied research, assessment, and treatment
interventions / Marty Sapp. —2nd ed.
p.   cm.
Includes bibliographical references and indexes.
l. Test anxiety—Research—Statistical methods. 2. Social
sciences—Statistical methods. I. Title.
LB3060.6.S27 1999 371.26'01'9—dc21   99—22530 CIP

ISBN 0-7618-1386-1 (cloth: alk. ppr.)

To my students

Preface to First Edition

This text is divided into three parts. Part I deals with applied research design and statistical methodology frequently occurring in test anxiety literature. Part II focuses on theories and methods of assessing test anxiety using standardized instruments. Part III extensively describes and provides treatment scripts for test anxiety. In addition to advanced undergraduate and graduate students in the social sciences, this text is designed to attract two audiences—the quantitatively oriented professors teaching statistics and research methodology courses and counseling psychology professors teaching counseling and social sciences research courses. Essentially, the purpose of this text is to present a conceptual understanding of test anxiety within a research context.

On a semester system it is possible to cover all eleven chapters within two semesters. It seems plausible, since this is an innovative applied research textbook on test anxiety, that chapters can be adjusted to fit a professor's specific objectives. For example, the treatment scripts could be used in a counseling fieldwork or practicum course, while the research section would be appropriate for a research methods or statistics course in which the instructor could edit or expand upon the topics presented.

Preface to Second Edition

Over the last five years, the nature of test anxiety research has been influenced greatly by structural equation modeling. One purpose of the second edition of this text is to introduce researchers to the logic of structural equations and to show how the EQS, structural equation program, can easily perform structural equations modeling. Another purpose of this second edition is to synthesize more than 100 studies that have been published on test anxiety since 1993. Moreover, researchers generally view test anxiety as existing of factors such as Sarason's four-factor model or Spielberger's two-factor model. All of these models of test anxiety can be easily analyzed by EQS; therefore, this second edition provides an entire chapter on structural equation modeling.

The features that made the first edition popular, such as applied research, assessment, and treatment interventions, are retained in the second edition; however, a chapter on measurement issues—item response theory and generalizability theory—was added to the second edition. In addition, control lines are provided for the SAS statistical software. Moreover, nested designs, both the univariate case and multivariate case, are covered in this edition. Comments from students, faculty, and researchers at various institutions indicated that their institutions had at least one of these major statistical packages; therefore, readers will have the option of two packages.

Test Anxiety: Applied Research, Assessment, and Treatment Interventions, Second Edition, like the previous edition, is directed toward students in the social sciences because it integrates statistical methodology and research design with actual research situations that occur within the test anxiety area. The current edition will draw from two major audiences—the quantitative professors who teach statistics and research methodology courses and others who teach counseling psychology and related courses.

In closure, the current edition is a brief, applied text on research, assessment, and treatment interventions for test anxiety. Moreover, the current edition demonstrates how to conduct test anxiety research, and it provides actual empirically based treatment interventions. Finally, this edition presents the two most-employed statistical packages, and illustrations of EQS for structural equations modeling and confirmatory factor analysis are provided.

Preface
To Students and Social Scientists

This text was designed to give you the courage and confidence to understand and conduct test anxiety research; however, the research skills employed in test anxiety are those generally employed in the social sciences. By combining research methods and design with applied research statistics, this text offers a perspective not found in any other texts on applied research that this writer is aware of; therefore, this text would be useful for applied social scientists.

Students taking an introductory or intermediate statistics or research methods course will find this text a useful supplement. Unlike other texts, example after example of applied research situations are described along with an adequate sample of exercises followed by detailed solutions. In contrast to traditional texts with statistical exercises, this text provides solutions following every exercise so that students and social scientists can obtain instant feedback. Possibly, the most useful feature of this text for advanced level students and applied researchers are the complete control lines for running statistical analyses on the SPSSX and SAS computer software. Many statistical analyses that are usually covered in introductory, intermediate, and advanced statistics courses are discussed along with the exact codes for running them on SPSSX and SAS.

In summary, a text on test anxiety that combines applied research, assessment, and treatment interventions has not heretofore been available; neither has one offering clear procedures for assessing test anxiety. In order to demonstrate how to assess test anxiety, the reproduction of several commonly used self-report measures of test anxiety are provided. Finally, it is hoped that this text will facilitate your development as an applied researcher in test anxiety or in social science research.

Acknowledgments

Now it is time to thank individuals who helped facilitate bringing this work into press. First, I would like to thank Daniel Bieser for running many of the statistical exercises for the first edition and Khyána Pumphrey for running many of the exercises for the second edition. Second, June Lehman deserves thanks for proofreading this entire text. In addition, I offer thanks to Cathy Mae Nelson for bringing this text into camera-ready condition. I am grateful to the Literary Executor of the late Sir Ronald A. Fisher, F.R.S., to Dr. Frank Yates, F.R.S., to Longman Group, Ltd., London, and to Oliver and Boyd, Ltd., Edinburgh for permission to reproduce statistical tables B and J from their book, *Statistical Tables for Biological, Agricultural and Medical Research.* Thanks goes to Helen Hudson and James E. Lyons for their continued support and encouragement. I would like to also thank my department at the University of Wisconsin-Milwaukee and the following individuals at the University of Cincinnati. First, Dr. James Stevens, who taught me research design and statistics. Second, Dr. Patricia O'Reilly, the chairperson of my doctoral committee. And third, Dr. Purcell Taylor, Dr. Judith Frankel, and Dr. Marvin Berlowitz, all of whom served on my doctoral committee. Finally, I would like to thank Dr. David L. Johnson who served as my doctoral internship supervisor.

In closing, it is hoped that this text will help students and social scientists learn to understand and conduct test anxiety research. Social scientists and students in social sciences will find that this is an excellent applied research reference book with many exercises and examples. Note that careful studying of the research chapters is necessary to facilitate one's understanding of the social science research. Comments or discussions concerning this text—both positive and negative—are encouraged. My address is The University of Wisconsin-Milwaukee, Department of Educational Psychology, 2400 E. Hartford Avenue, Milwaukee, WI 53211. My telephone number is (414) 229-6347, my e-mail address is Sapp@uwm.edu, and my Fax number is (414) 229-4939.

Marty Sapp

Contents

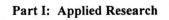

Part I: Applied Research

Chapter 1

CONTENTS

Variables Employed In Test Anxiety Research:

1.1 VARIABLES

A **variable** is any condition in a scientific investigation that may change in quantity and/or quality. For example, a self-report measure of test anxiety is a variable that can change due to many factors. Specifically, test anxiety changes in individuals over time (Anastasi, 1988). Often test anxiety increases as an evaluative situation approaches, such as an examination in a course. In summary, from a practical standpoint weight, height, room temperature and time of day are variables or conditions that can vary in quantity. Confounding, independent, dependent, moderator, control, intervening, and suppressor are the common variables employed in test anxiety research.

1.2 CONFOUNDING VARIABLES

Confounding variables are variables that affect the internal validity of a study. That is, to what extent are the results of a study attributable to flaws in the research design? When a variable obscures the effects of another variable, it is said to be a confounding variable. Chapter 2 provides a discussion of confoundment and threats to internal validity.

1.3 INDEPENDENT VARIABLES

Independent variables are those variables which are manipulated or selected by a researcher, therapist, or clinician for study. These are presumed causes of change on the dependent variable(s). For test anxiety, independent variables are treatments such as supportive counseling, relaxation therapy, systematic desensitization, cognitive-behavioral hypnosis, and so on. Furthermore, classrooms of students selected for studying test anxiety would also represent independent variables.

1.4 DEPENDENT VARIABLES

Dependent variables are measures of some behavior, or the presumed effects of the independent variables. A common dependent variable for test anxiety is the Test Anxiety Inventory (Spielberger, 1980). One can probably infer that measures on a dependent variable are dependent upon the values of an independent variable (a treatment), which results in changes on the dependent variable. Let us take a simple example of one treatment—relaxation therapy. Suppose we decided to have two levels of this treatment. For simplicity, let us assume that we had a class of students suffering from test anxiety and we decided to randomly divide them into two groups. We could treat one group and use the other as a referent or control group. *Thus, the independent variable would have two levels—treatment and control.* Moreover, measures on the dependent variable is dependent upon the value or level of the independent variable. Thus, we would expect students in the treatment group to have lower levels of test anxiety than the control group. In summary, dependent variables are dependent upon the levels of an independent variable which theoretically always has at least two levels.

1.5 MODERATOR VARIABLES

Moderator variables are special types of independent variables that moderate the effect between the primary independent and dependent variables. Moderator variables are factors that are measured, manipulated, or chosen for study to determine if they modify the relationship between the primary independent and dependent variables. Levels of motivation and intelligence are moderating variables that can affect the results of test anxiety research. Another example of a moderator variable is what Rotter (1982) calls a **generalized expectancy**, which is an expectation that one generally applies in a variety of related experiences. Of course, this is an individual's subjective expectancy that occurs in a variety of related situations. Specifically, an example of a generalized expectancy that is important to consider as a moderating variable in test anxiety research is locus of control. **Locus of control** is how an individual generally perceives the source of his or her outcomes. These outcomes can be positive or negative. For example, suppose you receive an "A" in a psychology course. Is this result luck or ability? Internal locus of control means that an individual's reinforcements and punishments are the results of his or her abilities, while external locus of control means that an individual's reinforcements and punishments are attributed to outside or external events.

1.6 CONTROL VARIABLES

Control variables are independent variables that the researcher does not want to affect the results of a research design. Moreover, control variables are confounding variables that a researcher must take into account in a research investigation. A researcher usually wants to hold a control variable constant. Commonly, levels of test anxiety are held constant. For example, we usually want subjects or clients with high levels of test anxiety. This can be accomplished by screening for or retaining subjects with high test anxiety scores.

1.7 INTERVENING VARIABLES

Intervening variables or mediating variables are theoretical variables; unlike independent variables, they cannot be seen, measured, or manipulated. They can influence the relationship between the primary independent and dependent variables. One's familiarity with theory will suggest which factors can theoretically affect the observed test anxiety phenomenon. The effect of an intervening variable must be inferred from the effects of the independent and moderating variables on the observed phenomenon. In this case it is, of course, test anxiety. Learning styles are often intervening variables in test anxiety research. Learning is a theoretical construct that cannot be directly seen, measured or manipulated but can be indirectly measured and inferred to have existed.

1.8 SUPPRESSOR VARIABLES

Suppressor variables are independent variables that are often used in regression analysis, and they conceal, obscure, or suppress the relationship between variables. Suppressor variables are correlated with other independent variables, but they are uncorrelated with the dependent variable. When a suppressor variable is removed from a study, irrelevant variance is eliminated, and the correlation between the residual independent variables and dependent variable is increased.

1.9 EXERCISES

For the following examples, identify the independent variables, the corresponding levels, and the dependent variables.
1. Cognitive-behavioral hypnosis, relaxation therapy, and supportive counseling was used to reduce the worry and emotionality components of test anxiety.
2. A researcher found a significant correlation between educational status, undergraduate and graduate, and the reduction of test anxiety.

Answers to Exercises
1. The treatment has three levels (cognitive-behavioral hypnosis, relaxation therapy, and supportive counseling) and is the independent variable; worry and emotionality test anxiety are the dependent variables.
2. Educational status, undergraduate and graduate, is the independent variable, and test anxiety is the dependent variable.

1.10 SUMMARY

In test anxiety research there are two very important variables, the treatments for test anxiety-independent variables and measures of test anxiety-dependent variables. Moderating and control variables are special types of independent variables that can affect test anxiety results. Finally, intervening variables are factors which can theoretically affect the relationship between a treatment for test anxiety and a measure of test anxiety.

References

Anastasi, A. (1988). *Psychological testing* (6th ed.). New York: Macmillan.

Rotter, J. B. (1982). *The development and application of social learning theory*. New York: Praeger.

Spielberger, C. D. (1980). *Test anxiety inventory*. Palo Alto, CA: Consulting Psychology Press.

Chapter 2

CONTENTS

2.1 THREATS TO INTERNAL VALIDITY

Internal validity answers the following question: Did the treatment actually make a difference? More formally, did the independent variable cause a change on the dependent variable? There are many possible threats to internal validity in test anxiety research. However, only nine will be discussed. These threats are history, maturation, pretest sensitization, selection, statistical regression, experimental mortality or attrition, instrumentation, statistical error, and expectation. Each term will be defined followed by a vignette which will help illustrate the concept through a practical example.

External validity focuses on whether results obtained from an experiment can apply to the actual world or to other similar programs, situations, and approaches (Tuckman, 1978). Generally, as a researcher controls internal validity, he or she decreases the probability of external validity. In essence, internal validity answers the question of whether a treatment for test anxiety makes a difference, while external validity answers the questions whether or not the results obtained from a study can be generalized to other situations, subjects, or settings.

2.2 HISTORY

History occurs when something happens to research groups during the treatment period which can cause the groups to differ on the dependent variables. Suppose 30 test-anxious subjects were recruited for a test anxiety study, and they were randomly assigned to a cognitive-behavioral counseling group and a Hawthorne control group. After 8 weeks of treatment, we decide to evaluate the effectiveness of the cognitive-behavioral counseling in comparison to the control group. Let us assume we are doing a posttest on both groups in separate rooms. During the posttest measure for the treatment group a small fire occurs. Now, we measure both groups on the Test Anxiety Inventory once the fire is under control. It is clear from this vignette that the fire could have had unusual effects for the treatment group. Hence, it is doubtful that the impact of the fire will not influence the responses to test anxiety for the treatment group. It is extremely probable that the test anxiety scores for the treatment group may be higher or statistically equal to the control group due to the stress of the fire.

2.3 MATURATION

Maturation are developmental changes that occur in subjects during the treatment period which affects the dependent variables. Let us assume we have identified 50 third grade children for a test anxiety study. We test them for test anxiety during the beginning and toward the end of the school year to determine if our treatment interventions had made a difference. The point to remember from this example is the fact that with young children, over the course of a school year, there will be developmental changes that can affect measures such as achievement, as well as test anxiety.

2.4 PRETEST SENSITIZATION

Pretest sensitization is where pretesting influences or sensitizes subjects to the dependent variable. Let us return to the maturation example, but for this instance, we will assume we are using the same instrument for both the beginning and end of the school year assessments of test anxiety. On many measures, such as self-report, using the same individuals on both pretest and posttest measures tend to affect the correlation between the two points in time. When the same self-report questionnaire is employed, this increases the correlation due to repeated measures from point one to point two. Primarily, this results from subjects remembering responses from the pretest and report similar responses on the posttest, which can lead to spurious results.

2.5 SELECTION

Selection is a process where the research groups differ or are unequal on some dependent variables before treatment begins. Suppose we recruit a group of 20 high school students for test anxiety and we divide the high test anxiety students in one group and separate the low test anxiety in another group. Now, we decide to treat each group with covert desensitization therapy. We noticed that after treatment, the low test anxious students improved more than the high test anxiety students. These results can be attributed to the fact that the groups differed initially on the test anxiety variable and the results are not due to the treatment.

2.6 STATISTICAL REGRESSION

Statistical regression is a statistical fact that extremely high or low scores regress towards the arithmetic mean. Let us assume we are able to select 30 college students who scored above the 90th percentile on the

Test Anxiety Inventory. Students are given six sessions of relaxation therapy combined with study skills counseling. After the treatment session, we again measure the subjects on test anxiety and find that the mean percentile is now at the 50th. With extreme scores, there is a tendency for regression towards the mean. If the scores are high, the regression will be downward towards the mean which occurred in this case. If the scores are low, the regression will be upward towards the mean. It should be noted that on the Test Anxiety Inventory the mean is the 50th percentile which is what occurred with this example.

2.7. EXPERIMENTAL MORTALITY OR ATTRITION

Experimental mortality or **attrition** is the differential loss of subjects from research groups. If one starts off with 20 subjects in a treatment and control group and after four weeks 12 subjects withdraw from the control group, this clearly indicates attrition or experimental mortality, the systematic withdrawal of subjects from experimental groups.

2.8 INSTRUMENTATION

Instrumentation is error in measurement procedures or instruments. That is, the differences between or among research groups is the product of the dependent variables employed. Suppose Jack, a new Ph.D. in counseling, decides to construct a new test anxiety instrument and he administers it to 50 subjects. He randomly selects 20 for research purposes in which 10 are in a hypnosis group and 10 are in a covert modeling group. Towards the end of treatment, he finds a significantly lower treatment mean for the hypnosis group. Jack concludes that his treatment reduced test anxiety. The difficulty with this example lies in the fact that Jack did not use a standardized instrument with adequate reliability and validity.

2.9 STATISTICAL ERROR

Statistical error is an error that can occur in a statistical analysis as a result of the null hypothesis being rejected when it is true. The null hypothesis simply states that the group means are equal. Suppose Jill decides to conduct a two-group MANOVA (multivariate analysis of variance) to determine if rational emotive behavior therapy is more effective in reducing test anxiety than a placebo control group.

Let us assume that Jill conducts a MANOVA and finds multivariate significance and decides to conduct ten univariate tests and finds one significant. This significance is spurious because one would expect one significant univariate test out of ten to be significant just simply due to change alone—especially if the difference was not predicted a priori.

2.10 EXPECTATION EFFECTS

Expectation effects can occur and are due to influences of the experimenter or the subjects. The experimenter can unconsciously influence the results of a research project; in contrast, subjects can determine the research hypothesis and give the experimenter the responses needed to support a hypothesis.

The expectation effect is extremely problematic when the experimenter knows which subjects are receiving treatments and also gathers data after the treatment. It is not uncommon for an experimenter to fit the responses into a certain theoretical framework. Good corrections for this bias are double blind studies or **interrater measures of consistency** or other measures of reliability included within a study.

2.11 DOUBLE AND SINGLE BLIND CONTROLS FOR EXPECTATION EFFECTS

In a **double blind study**, neither the experimenter nor the subjects are aware of who is receiving the treatment or the experimental manipulations. A **single blind study** is a control procedure in which the experimenter measuring the behavior does not know whether the subject is a member of the treatment or control group. Here a research assistant could make this possible by keeping track of subjects' experimental status. Another example of a single blind study is where subjects are ignorant of the purpose of study or to the specific treatments they are receiving. A single blind study can control for the experimenter expectancy bias; similarly, double blind procedures control for expectancy bias in both the experimenter and subjects.

2.12 EXERCISES

Identify the potential threats to internal validity.
1. Suppose 10 high test-anxious students are assigned to a cognitive-behavioral hypnosis group, and 10 low test-anxious students are assigned to a relaxation therapy group. After treatment, students

from the relaxation group scored significantly lower on test anxiety than the cognitive-behavioral hypnosis group.

2. A researcher takes one item from Test Anxiety Inventory, a standardized test anxiety measure, to determine if a sample of 50 participants experienced test anxiety. The researcher used this item to diagnose students with test anxiety.

Answers to Exercises
1. Selection.
2. Instrumentation.

2.13 SUMMARY
In terms of test anxiety research, internal validity allows one to determine if a given treatment resulted in a decrease in test anxiety. The shortcomings of test anxiety research can be evaluated by investigating and ruling out threats to internal validity. Finally, in essence, internal validity allows a researcher to establish causal inferences within a certain confidence limit.

Reference
Tuckman, B. W. (1978). *Conducting educational research.* New York: Harcourt Brace Jovanovich.

Chapter 3

CONTENTS

3.1 EXTERNAL VALIDITY

External validity examines if results obtained from a given experimental investigation apply to situations outside of the initial experimental setting. Essentially, external validity answers the question of whether the results obtained from a study generalize to other situations, subject, or settings. External validity falls into two broad categories: population validity-generalization of the results to other subjects and ecological validity-generalization of the results to similar settings. The difficulties that occur with true experimental designs are often related to sources of threats to external validity. The difficulties with test anxiety that follow are often associated with threats to external validity.

3.2 DIFFICULTIES WITH TEST ANXIETY RESEARCH

There are many difficulties that can occur with test anxiety research; however, only the following will be discussed: Hawthorne Effect, demand characteristics, evaluation apprehension, social desirability, placebo effect, controlling the Hawthorne Effect, reactivity, pretest/posttest sensitization, and generalization of results.

3.3 HAWTHORNE EFFECT

The **Hawthorne Effect** is particularly problematic for behavioral researchers. It can easily confound the effects of treatments for test anxiety. This effect makes it difficult to partial out from a dependent variable for test anxiety that which is the result of treatment interventions, and that which is the consequence of the Hawthorne Effect. The Hawthorne Effect explains how a subject's knowledge of participating in an experiment can influence the outcome or results in a study. There are at least four features associated with the Hawthorne Effect, and they are demand characteristics, evaluation apprehension, social desirability, and the placebo effect.

3.4 DEMAND CHARACTERISTICS

Demand characteristics are the subtle cues and nuances that subjects detect from an experiment which may convey the purpose of a study. The mere fact that subjects know that they are participating in an experiment can have a significant influence on their behavior. The demand characteristics account for the fact that subjects can determine the research hypothesis and thereby produce the desired results.

3.5 EVALUATION APPREHENSION

Evaluation apprehension is especially detrimental for test anxiety research. With pre- posttest test anxiety research designs, the initial pretest may be extremely high due to evaluation apprehension or the anxiety of participating in an experiment.

3.6 SOCIAL DESIRABILITY

Social desirability, which is related to the demand characteristic, is the subject's motivation to produce socially acceptable results. This is the motivation the subject has to please the experimenter. For example, if a subject discovers that it is socially desirable to report less test anxiety after a certain treatment intervention. This may well be the outcome.

3.7 PLACEBO EFFECT

Placebo effects are extremely prevalent when blind studies are not employed in test anxiety research, which is often the case with practical research adventures. The placebo effect are changes in a subject's behavior due to expectations of treatment effectiveness. The subject's tendency to believe in the effectiveness of a particular treatment for test anxiety can influence the results on the dependent(s) in an experiment.

In summary, the mere fact that subjects are participating in a study can change measured behavior. It is important to be aware that subjects' beliefs, expectations, perceptions, attitudes, and values can influence behavior in an experiment.

3.8 CONTROLLING THE HAWTHORNE EFFECT

Rosenthal and Rosnow (1984) recommend several strategies to combat the Hawthorne Effect. One strategy is to employ field experiments and quasi-experimental designs that use nonreactive measures. Nonreactive measures will not alert the subject to the fact that he or she is participating in an experiment. Another helpful technique for countering the Hawthorne Effect is not telling subjects the purpose of an experiment until it is over. In addition, it can be stated to subjects that it is important for them not to attempt to figure out the purpose of a given study. Also, a Hawthorne control group, a control group that receives attention, is a good control for this effect. Finally, self-monitoring can serve as an attentional procedure, and when the experimenter interacts with participants, this reduces the Hawthorne effect.

3.9 REACTIVITY

Reactivity is the notion that tests, inventories, rating scales, and even observing subjects' behavior can change the events that a researcher is attempting to measure. Since test anxiety research often involves the administration of tests, reactivity becomes a concern. Whenever possible, **nonreactive measures** should be employed. These are items that are normally part of a subject's environment. For example, school enrollment records are usually nonreactive or passive measures. Whenever reactive measures are employed in test anxiety research, the researcher can control this confoundment by controlling in the research design for the testing effect.

3.10 PRETEST AND POSTTEST SENSITIZATION

Pretest posttest sensitization indicates that the pretest and/or posttest affects the results on the dependent variable. The pretest and/or the posttest can sensitize subjects to the effects of a treatment. Pretests, as well as posttests, can facilitate learning by helping subjects determine what effects they should be getting from a given treatment. It is important to remember that pretests and posttests can serve as a learning experience for subjects and thereby influence the results of a treatment.

3.11 GENERALIZATION OF RESULTS

One of the goals of test anxiety research is to **generalize** the results from a sample to some clearly defined population. Random selection or selecting subjects who are representative of a population facilitates the researcher's ability to generalize results.

Similarly, randomly assigning subjects to groups is another factor that contributes to generalization of results. Finally, a researcher must consider the limitations of his or her results in respects to the experimentally accessible population and the population in which he or she wishes to generalize the results. In essence, since no study can sample the entire universe, every study will inevitably have limited generalizability in some respect.

3.12 SUMMARY

Many difficulties can occur with test anxiety research. Subject-experimenter artifacts and the lack of external validity can contribute to systematic error in test anxiety research. The mere fact that subjects are participating in an experiment can result in the Hawthorne Effect, reactivity, and pretest and posttest sensitization.   Due to sampling limitations, external validity or generalization of results are also a necessary restriction of research that a researcher must consider.

Reference

Rosenthal, R., & Rosnow, R. (1984). *Essentials of behavioral research.* New York: McGraw-Hill.

Chapter 4

CONTENTS

4.1 ONE-GROUP DESIGNS

One-group designs involve the observation of a single group of subjects under two or more experimental conditions. Each subject serves as his or her own control by contributing experimental and control group scores (Matheson, Bruce, & Beauchamp, 1978). One-group designs can serve as useful experimental designs when random sampling is employed and the independent variable is manipulated.

The simplest of the one-group designs is the one-shot case study. Schematically, this design is depicted as: X O.   The X denotes a treatment, while the O indicates an observation or dependent variable measure. This is not an experimental design and should not be used under any circumstances because there is not a pretest or a comparison group.

Before-After Designs

One-group **before-after designs** consists of observing subjects before treatment and after treatment. The data are analyzed by comparing before and after measurements. Schematically, this design is: O1 X O2. The O1 is the before treatment observation, while O2 is the after treatment observation and the X indicates a treatment.

Function

This design can be used when one knows that an experimental condition will occur. Essentially, one is able to observe subjects before and after the occurrence of a treatment or experimental condition. The experimental condition can be designed naturally. For example, it could be possible to observe the attitudes of teachers to a new teaching method. Suppose this new method is one of teaching math. Teachers are measured on a dependent variable before and after receiving the new method of teaching math. The teachers are serving as their own control.   In summary, this means additional subjects are not needed for a control group.

Advantages

The one-group before-after design is an improvement over one-shot case studies.   This design is useful for descriptive or correlational research. *It is not helpful in making causal conclusions.*

Limitations

This design leaves a number of variables uncontrolled. Any outside influences that occur between the two observations may account for observed differences **(history effect)**. If the time between the two observations is more than a few days, the intervening effects of learning and maturational processes can change behavior **(maturational effect)**. The process of collecting the pretest may alert subjects to the experimental condition and can change behavior (pretest sensitization). Finally, if subjects are not selected at random, any observed differences may be due to unknown factors.

Statistical Analysis

The appropriate analysis for this design is the dependent measures t-test or analysis of variance for repeated measures.

4.2 INDEPENDENT TWO-GROUP DESIGNS

Independence—the probability of each subject being assigned to a group—is not affected in any way by the nature of the other members of each group. In the independent two-group design, subjects are equivalent on all variables except the independent one(s). This equivalence is achieved by randomly assigning subjects to groups.

Advantages

1. The observations on the two groups can be made at the same time, so that time-related variables such as aging, maturation, history, and so on are controlled.

2. In a one-group, before-after design, the pretest can affect the posttest observations. In a two-group design, this sequence effect can be eliminated by not using a pretest or is controlled by using the pretest on both groups. Below, in Figure 4.3, is the schematic representation of a randomized pre-post two-group design. The X corresponds to the treatment and the dashed line "-" represents the control procedure.

Figure 4.3 Randomized Pre-Posttest Two-Group Design

Schematically, this design can be depicted as:

Assignment	Group	Pretest	Treatment	Posttest
R	Experimental	O1	X	O2
R	Control	O1	-	O2

Due to randomization, this is a true experimental design since the experimenter randomly assigns subjects to the two groups. The pretest, or before measure, allows one to test the initial equivalence of the two groups.

Advantages
Pretests provide a check for the effectiveness of random assignment.

Limitations
The pretest can sensitize subjects to the treatment. Similarly, it can interact with the treatment and affect the posttests (dependent variables).

Statistical Analysis
Analysis of covariance.

4.3 RELATED TWO-GROUP DESIGNS
Related two-group designs involve the observation of an experimental group and a control group that have been matched on some variables. The matching helps each individual in the experimental group to be identified with his or her counterpart in the control group on some measure. The dependent variables, which in this case would be some measure of test anxiety, such as the Test Anxiety Inventory can be thought of as occurring in pairs, with each matched subject contributing one-half of a pair under each condition. Matching minimizes between group variability or error at the onset of the experiment. Related two-group designs employ the same statistical analysis as one-group before-after designs, the t-test for related or correlated measures. If random assignment can be employed, individual differences can be controlled. In summary, the combination of matching and random assignment of

matched pairs to experimental conditions results in a more precise statistical analysis of the effects of treatment interventions for test anxiety than does random assignment alone.

4.4 MULTIPLE TREATMENT DESIGNS

Multiple treatment designs involve more than two levels of an independent variable or more than one independent variable in a single experiment. In a sense, multiple treatment designs or multilevel designs involves several two-group designs run simultaneously. Suppose subjects suffering from test anxiety were randomly assigned to a study skills counseling group, relaxation therapy group, nondirective counseling group, and a hypnosis group. This is an example of a multiple treatment design in which four treatments are used to treat test anxiety. The statistical analysis for such designs is the one-way ANOVA (analysis of variance) or F test for independent samples.

Factorial Designs

Factorial designs also represent another type of **multiple treatment design**. Factorial designs employ two or more independent variables simultaneously in one experiment. It is the combination of all levels for two or more independent variables on a dependent variable. The factorial design permits an experimenter to test the **interaction effect** of two or more independent variables upon a dependent variable. That is, factorial designs determine the effect that one independent variable has on one or more other independent variable(s). In factorial designs, each independent variable is called a **main effect**. Schematically, the effects of both levels of B under both levels of A is called an interaction effect. Similarly, *the fact that the effect of one variable depends on all the levels of another also represents interaction.* In a diagram form, interaction for a two-way design can be represented as:

Figure 4.4 Factorial Design

	B					Treatments	
		B1	B2			B1	B2
A	A1	I	II	Sex	M	21	33
	A2	III	IV		W	29	28

The As and Bs correspond to **independent variables**, while the Roman numerals represent **different levels**. A factorial design can be used to control for a **moderating variable**. The design above is sometimes called a 2 X 2 factorial design because there are two rows and two columns. *The effect of one independent variable on the dependent variables is not the same for all levels of the other independent variable; this is another example of interaction.*

Notice in Figure 4.4 that the best treatment dependents on the moderating variable, sex. Men had higher scores with treatment B2, while women had higher scores with treatment B1. A 3 X 2 factorial design would have three rows and two columns. Factorial designs can employ more than two independent variables such as three-way (three independent variables) and four-way (four independent variables) factorial designs. In essence, a factorial design allows a researcher to study the effects of two or more factors at once. This design allows a researcher to observe the separate effects of each independent variable and the interaction effects of several independent variables interacting simultaneously. The statistical analysis for these types of designs is the analysis of variance. In summary, multiple treatment designs can become complex by being either independent group designs or related or dependent group designs, with or without some type of factorial combinations.

Solomon Design

The **Solomon design** in its exact form is not common in test anxiety research, but a discussion of it is important for two reasons. First, the Solomon design is a **factorial design**; second, it can control for the pretest sensitization threat to external validity.

Test Anxiety: Applied Research

The Solomon design usually occurs as a four-group design or some factor times four. As previously stated, it is used to determine the effects of pretesting on the dependent variable. The Solomon four-group design conceptually is a combination of a two-group pretest-posttest control group design and a two-group posttest only control group design.

The Solomon designs are **true experimental designs**, since it involves randomization or randomly assigning subjects to groups. Specifically, the Solomon four-group designs involve two independent variables, a treatment with two levels, and a pretest with two levels. This results in a 2 X 2 design or a two-way analysis of variance (ANOVA) design. Schematically, this design can be depicted as:

Group 1	R	0_1	X	0_2
Group 2	R	0_3		0_4
Group 3	R		X	0_5
Group 4	R			0_6

R = random assignment
X = a treatment
0_1 and 0_3 = pretests
0_2 0_4 0_5 0_6 = posttests

In the schematic presentation of this design, the first two groups correspond to a pretest-posttest control group design; in contrast, the last two groups are equivalent to a posttest-only control group design. Similarly to the first example of a factorial design, the Solomon four-group design can be diagramed as:

		Treatment	
		Yes	No
	Yes	0_2	0_4
Pretest	No	0_5	0_6

The Solomon four-group design is analyzed like any 2 X 2 factorial design by means of a two-way analysis of variance (ANOVA) on the four groups' posttest scores. Note that pretest scores are not part of the statistical analysis.

Since Solomon designs employ randomization, they control for all threats to internal validity. In addition, after performing a factorial ANOVA on the posttest, if there is a significant interaction between the pretest and the treatment, this suggests pretest sensitization. In other words, treatment effectiveness varies as a function of pretesting. When one finds a significant pretest by treatment interaction, an examination of the simple main effects can be obtained by comparing the posttest scores of O_2 versus O_4 and O_5 versus O_6. If there is a significant difference between posttest scores in O_2 versus O_4 and not a significant statistical difference between posttest scores in O_5 versus O_6, this indicates that pretesting affected the treatment groups but not the control groups. In conclusion, if there is pretest sensitization, one cannot generalize findings to nonpretested subjects, thus limiting external validity. Finally, the major limitation of this design is the large number of subjects needed in order to randomly form four separate groups.

4.5 QUASI-EXPERIMENTAL DESIGNS

Cook and Campbell (1979) discuss 14 variations of quasi-experimental designs. Three designs will be discussed in this text: time series, nonequivalent control group, and equivalent time-samples.

Quasi-experimental designs have some of the features of "true" experimental designs, such as control groups (and multiple testing). In essence, they do not control all sources of threat to internal validity. In the educational world, where it is often impossible to have complete experimental control, quasi-experimental designs become extremely useful. In summary, when an experimenter cannot randomly select subjects, nor randomly assign them to experimental situations, considerations should be given to quasi-experimental designs.

Time-Series Designs

This is an extended version of the one-group before-after design. Multiple observations before and after treatment are compared. Schematically, this design is: O1 O2 O3 X O4 O5 O6. **The time-series design** is used to measure changes in subjects' behavior under at least 3 observations at fixed time intervals. Once a baseline or trend has been established, the treatment is introduced and observations are continued. Any changes in observations after treatment is attributed to the independent variable. At least two things can happen with observations. First, the before measures or pretests may consistently change. Second, the before measures and after measures may maintain a consistent trend.

One method of strengthening the basic interrupted time series design is to add a second interrupted time series design with nonequivalent dependent variables. This is similar to a nonequivalent control group design (Figure 4.7) and it reduces the **historical threat** to internal validity.   The interrupted times series design with nonequivalent dependent variables is exactly the same as the simple interrupted times series design; however, as opposed to one set of dependent variables, with the interrupted times series design with nonequivalent dependent variables, there are two sets of dependent variables. Schematically, this design is:

Week 2	Week 4	Week 6	Week 8	Week 10
Pretest	Pretest	Treatment	Posttest	Posttest

Figure 4.6 Interrupted Times Series Design with
Nonequivalent Dependent Variables

$$O_{A1} \ O_{A2} \ O_{A3} \ X \ O_{A4} \ O_{A5} \ O_{A6}$$

$$O_{B1} \ O_{B2} \ O_{B3} \ X \ O_{B4} \ O_{B5} \ O_{B6}$$

O_A represent the first set of dependent variables and O_B represent the second set of dependent variables.

Advantages

Fewer subjects are required, since subjects are serving as their own control. Also, multiple observations reduces the chance of erroneous observations which provides measurement of maturational and learning effects. The maturational effects can be controlled statistically by measuring the departure from the established trend set by the pretests before treatment with those created by the posttest measures.

Limitations

The major limitation of these designs is the lack of control for history effects. Even though the interrupted times series design with nonequivalent dependent variables and the interrupted times series with a nonequivalent no-treatment control group minimize all threats to internal validity, unlike experimental designs these threats are not totally eliminated. Another difficulty with time-series designs is the difficulty that sometimes occurs in determining which scores to analyze. When there is a changing trend in scores, Cook and Campbell (1979) suggested comparing the before and after trend at the point where the treatment occurred. Graphical information on discontinuity may help in determining which scores to analyze. If data consist of a constant baseline and a different posttest level of performance, averaging scores may be adequate for data analysis.

Statistical Analysis

The average before and after scores can be compared. Essentially, data can be analyzed with a slope analysis technique. A straight line is fitted to the average before and average after measurements. The slopes of the lines are tested to determine if they are reliably different from each other. The *SPSSX User's Guide* (3rd ed.) has a section on the Box-Jenkins procedure. It can be used to fit and forecast time series data by means of a general class of statistical models (*SPSSX User's Guide* [3rd ed.], 1988, pp. 385-395). In summary, school settings where certain behavior occurs periodically are excellent settings for time-series designs. Finally, Cook and Campbell (1979) give more complete descriptions, applications, and analyses of time-series designs.

Figure 4.7 Nonequivalent Control Group Design

Schematically, this design can be depicted as:

O1	X	O2
O3	-	O4

O1 is a pretest for the treatment group. The dashed lines indicated that subjects were not randomly assigned to groups, thus this is an intact group design. O2 is the posttest or dependent variable for the treatment group. O3 is the pretest for the control group, while O4 is the posttest or dependent variable for the control group.

This is similar to the pretest-posttest independent two-group experimental design except for the lack of random assignment of subjects to groups. Thus, the nonequivalent control group design is not as good as the pretest-posttest independent two-group experimental design, but it is extremely superior to the one-group before-after design. Unless the assumptions of analysis of covariance are met, the correct statistical analysis is a repeated measures analysis and not a gain score analysis. Statistically, gain scores (pretests minus posttests) analyses are less precise than repeated measures analyses.

Figure 4.8 Equivalent Time-Samples Designs

The time series design can be modified into an **equivalent time-samples design**. This design does control for the history bias. This design looks like this:

```
O1 XO O2 X1 O3 XO O4 X1 O5 XO O6 X1 O7
```

X1 is a treatment, while XO is some control experience that is available in the absence of the treatment. When a single group of subjects are available for study, an equivalent time-samples design can be employed to control for the history threat of internal validity; however, this design lacks external validity. This suggests that the treatment can be different when it is continuous as opposed to being dispersed, which makes the results sample specific. Moreover, subjects often adapt to the repeated presentation of a treatment. This makes it difficult to make conclusions concerning the continuous effect of a given treatment. The foregoing discussion underscores the limited external validity of the equivalent time-samples design.

Function

Like the one-group time series design, the equivalent time-samples design is used with a single group of subjects. This design, like the time series design, is a repeated measures one-group design.

Advantages

Similarly, to the time series design, the equivalent time-samples design uses fewer subjects, since subjects serve as their own control. This design controls for threats to internal validity, including historical bias.

Limitations

The major weakness of the equivalent time-samples design is in the area of **external validity**. This is especially problematic when the effect of the independent variable is different when continuous than when dispersed, which makes it difficult to generalize to other independent samples. Similarly, often with equivalent time-samples design, subjects tend to adapt to the independent variables; thus, lessening external validity of this design. In summary, the major weakness of the equivalent time-samples design is its lack of external validity.

Statistical Analysis

The equivalent times-samples design can be analyzed by a repeated measures analysis of variance, if pretests or covariates are used, as was the case with the present example. Winer (1971, pp. 796-809) recommends combining analysis of covariance with repeated measures analysis of variance. Essentially, a two-factor analysis of covariance with repeated measures can be constructed to analyze equivalent time-samples designs.

4.6 COUNTERBALANCED DESIGNS

An experimenter may consider incorporating **counterbalancing** techniques with one-group designs or time series designs. In counterbalanced designs subjects are given treatment one then observation one is made. Next, treatment two is given followed by observation two. This procedure is repeated with treatment two given again followed by an observation, which is the third one. The procedure is repeated with treatment one. That is, treatment one is given again followed by observation four. It should be noted that two observations are obtained under treatment one and two. Schematically, this design is:

Figure 4.9 Counterbalanced Design

```
Treatments    X1 X2 X2 X1
After-
O1 O2 O3 O4
Observations
```

For two treatments, the sequence of treatment is ABBA. Three treatments would yield the following sequence: ABCCBA.

The ABBA sequence is often referred to as a 1221 sequence. The 1s and 2s refer to the treatments. Counterbalanced means balanced sequences or orders of treatments. For example, with the 1221 sequence, the sequence of treatments is 1,2 in that order followed by 2,1. The counterbalanced design can be referred to as a posttest-posttest-posttest-posttest design, or an after-after-after-after design.

Function
The counterbalanced design is used to control the **order effect** when employing several treatments. More thorough counterbalancing can be achieved with the ABBA sequence by having half of the subjects serve under the 1221 sequence while the other half experience 2112. The counterbalanced design controls for any peculiar order effect.

Advantages
Counterbalanced designs, using one group of subjects, require fewer subjects than two-group experiments. Like other one-group designs, subjects serve as their own control. Time related variables such as maturation, learning, outside events, frustration, and fatigue are controlled by the data collection sequence. Finally, the counterbalanced design requires fewer observations than the time-series design.

Limitations
Sufficient time must be allowed between observations. If sufficient time is not allowed, there will be carry-over effects from the previous trials. Another difficulty with counterbalanced designs is the assumption of linearity among all time related variables. That is, one is assuming the effect of change from trial one to trial two is the same as between all other

adjacent trials. Finally, the last difficulty to consider with counter-balanced designs is the possibility of multiple treatment interactions.

Statistical Analyses

Matheson, Bruce, and Beauchamp (1978) recommended the analysis of variance procedure for the counterbalanced design. Essentially, the average performance under treatment one is compared with the average performance of treatment two to determine the differential effect of the two treatments.

4.7 NESTED DESIGNS

Factorial designs involve the complete crossing of all levels of a given factor with each level of the other factor. A factor is completely nested in another factor if each level of one factor occurs at only one level of another factor (Honeck, Kibler, & Sugar, 1983).

For example, a 4 X 2 factorial design would be depicted as follows:

	B1	B2
A1		
A2		
A3		
A4		

Suppose two treatments for reducing test anxiety (B1 and B2) combined with four classrooms (A1, A2, A3, A4) produced the following design:

	B1	B2
A1	A1 B1	
A2	A2 B1	
A3		A3 B2
A4		A4 B2

It is apparent that all levels of one factor do not occur under all levels of the other factor; hence, this is a nested design.

Factor A has four levels (A1, A2, A3, and A4), and Factor B has two levels (B1 and B2). A1 and A2 occur at B1, forming the combinations A1B1 and A2B1, and A3 and A4 occur at B2, forming the combinations A3B2 and A4B2. It can be said that factor A is nested completely within factor B. Nested designs are also called incomplete or asymmetrical designs because every cell does not contain scores or data. In addition, Bryk and Raudenbush (1992) refer to these designs as hierarchical linear models, multilevel linear models, mixed-effects models, random-effects models, random-coefficient regression models, and covariance component models. Finally, A(B) is used to denote that Factor A is nested with Factor B.

Another example of a nested design is the evaluation of two treatments for test anxiety with six schools. Suppose schools 1, 2, and 3 are confined to Treatment 1, and schools 4, 5, and 6 are restricted to Treatment 2. Again, when effects are confined or limited to a single level of a factor, nesting has occurred. This design can be depicted schematically as follows:

In addition, this design can also be represented as follows:

Treatment 1			Treatment 2		
School 1	School 2	School 3	School 4	School 5	School 6
n	n	n	n	n	n

Finally, a common nesting situation that occurs with educational research is students nested within classes, and classes nested within schools.

Advantages

Nested designs provide a smaller and more appropriate standard error than between group designs (i.e., one-way designs). This increases statistical power; however, there are some disadvantages or limitations of these designs.

Limitations

One major limitation of these designs is that they do not permit a researcher to test interactional effects. Moreover, it is not uncommon, within educational settings, for researchers to ignore class and school effects and to just analyze the data as a one-way or between-subjects design. Careful thought has to go into interpreting the results of nested designs, and a researcher must determine the appropriate error terms to use. Finally, the analysis and interpretation of unbalanced designs, an unequal number of each treatment combination, is complex.

Statistical Analysis

Lindman (1991) provides the computational formulas for analysis of variance for nested designs. Moreover, Wang (1997) describes how to analyze nested designs using the mixed procedure of Statistical Analysis System (SAS). Wang uses a Hierarchical Linear Model (HLM) approach in contrast to analysis of variance for nested designs. Bryk and Raudenbush (1992) developed a statistical program called Hierarchical Linear Models (HLM) to analyze complex nested or hierarchical designs. Finally, whenever variables such as city, county, state, and so on are located within other variables, the variables are said to be nested and the appropriate statistical analysis is analysis of variance for nested designs or HLM.

4.8 EXERCISES

1.   Suppose we were interested in how males and females responded to relaxation therapy and cognitive-behavioral hypnosis in reducing test anxiety. Describe and schematically sketch this design.

2.   A researcher investigated the effects of hypnosis in reducing test anxiety and improving achievement with introductory psychology students. Participants were pretested simultaneously within the hypnosis and control groups. After the pretesting, the hypnosis group received hypnosis, and the control group served as a comparison group. Describe this design and schematically sketch it out.

Answers to Exercises

1.   This is a 2 X 2 factorial design. Gender has two levels—males and females—and the treatment variable has two levels—relaxation therapy and cognitive-behavioral hypnosis. Schematically, this design would be depicted as:

Treatments

		1	2
Gender	Males		
	Females		

2.   This is a quasi-experimental design called a nonequivalent control group design, and it can be depicted as the following:

0_1 X 0_2 0_1 - pretests on test anxiety
0_1 – 0_2 0_2 - posttests on test anxiety
                          X - hypnosis treatment
                          – - control group

4.9 SUMMARY

This chapter covered common research designs that are employed in test anxiety research. Many of these designs can be viewed as an extension of the one-group before-after design. This design involves measuring subjects before and after treatment. When randomization is impossible and a control group is available, the one-group before-after design can be improved by adding a control group that also receives a pretest and posttest simultaneously with the treatment group. Such a design is called a nonequivalent control group design and falls within the category of quasi-experimental designs.

If randomization can be added to the nonequivalent control group design, this improves internal validity and results in a randomized pretest posttest two-group design. The construction of useful research designs involves ingenuity and extensive thought. Finally, once one understands the methodology underlying applied research designs, it is possible to construct designs that answer important questions in the area of test anxiety.

References

Bryk, A. S., & Raudenbush, S. W. (1992). *Hierarchical linear models.* Newbury Park, CA: Sage Publications

Cook, T. D., & Campbell, D. T. (1979). *Quasi-experimentation: Design and analysis issues for field settings.* Chicago: Rand McNally.

Honeck, R. P., Kibler, C. T., & Sugar, J. (1983). *Experimental design and analysis.* Lanham, MD: University Press of America.

Lindman, H. R. (1991). *Analysis of variance in experimental design.* New York: Springer-Verlag.

Matheson, D. W., Bruce, R. L., & Beauchamp, K. L. (1978). *Experimental psychology: Research design and analysis* (3rd ed.). New York: Holt, Rinehart and Winston.

Wang, J. (1997). Using SAS PROC mixed to demystify the hierarchical linear model. *The Journal of Experimental Education, 66*(1), 84-94.

Winer, B. J. (1971). *Statistical principles in experimental design.* New York: McGraw-Hill.

Chapter 5

CONTENTS

Measures of Central Tendency

5.1 AVERAGES

There are three commonly used **averages** in univariate statistical methodology. These measures of central tendency are the **mean, mode,** and **median.** First, the mode and median will be discussed, since they are less often used in statistics than the mean. In addition, they lack the necessary properties that are needed for advanced statistics. The mode is the most occurring score in a frequency distribution. It is the score with the greatest frequency. The mode is not a very stable measure of central tendency. For example, a distribution of scores can be bimodal, trimodal, or multimodal. Let us assume the following distribution of scores existed.

Figure 5.1 Frequency Distribution

X = some score	F-frequency of a score
3	10
2	9
1	8

The highest frequency in the above distribution is "10," indicating that the **mode** is 3. By definition, the median is the middle value in a distribution of scores ordered from lowest to highest or from highest to lowest. With the median, half of the scores fall above it and half fall below it. Let us take another example, with the following distribution of scores.

X
10
9
8
7*
6
5
4

The **median** for the above distribution is 7, since three scores fall above "7" and three scores fall below "7." The median is sometimes called the fiftieth percentile. The mean is the most used measure of central tendency. It is the summation or addition of a group of scores, divided by the total number of scores. The following is the formula for the sample mean:

$$\text{Mean } (\bar{X}) = \frac{\Sigma X}{N}$$

Where: X is some score in a distribution.
        ΣX is the summation or addition of every score in a distribution.
        N is the number of scores.

5.2 CHARACTERISTICS OF THE MEAN

The mean has **six** very important characteristics. **First,** changing a score in a distribution will change the mean.   **Second,** adding or subtracting a constant from each score in distribution will have the same effect on the mean. If a constant value is added to every score in a distribution, the same will be added to the mean. Similarly, subtracting a constant value from every score in a distribution will result in the constant being subtracted from the mean.

Third, multiplying or dividing each score in a distribution by a constant will result in the mean being changed in the same way. Fourth, the mean is a balance point. It is known that by definition the mean defined as "X bar" is:

$$\bar{X} = \frac{\Sigma X}{N}$$

If one were to cross multiple, the result would be

$$\Sigma X = N\bar{X}.$$

Suppose we had the following simple distribution of scores:

$$
\begin{array}{cc}
X & X-\bar{X} \\
3 & 3-2 \\
2 & 2-2 \\
1 & 1-2 \\
\end{array}
$$
$$\Sigma(X-\bar{X}) = 0$$

If the

$$\Sigma(X-\bar{X}) = 0,$$

we can employ the distributive property and get

$$\Sigma(X-\bar{X}) = \Sigma X - N\bar{X}.$$

By definition, the summation of a constant is N times the constant. So

$$\Sigma(X-\bar{X}) = N\bar{X} - N\bar{X} = 0.$$

The summation of

$$X = N\bar{X},$$

due the previous mentioned cross multiplication. The summation of a a constant (ΣK) can be shown with the distribution below by adding a constant of "2" to each score in the distribution.

```
X   K
3   +2
2   +2
1   +2
    ΣK=NK, or 3x2=6
```

The above example arithmetically shows how the mean is a **balance point** in a distribution, since scores are deviated from a mean in distribution and the sum of the deviation scores equals zero. **Fifth**, the mean is that point in a distribution about which the sums of squares deviations is at a **minimum**. When the sum of the deviation scores are calculated using the mean, the sum of the squares of these values is smaller than if it had occurred with any other point or score. This is demonstrated using simple algebra and summation notions below.

**Demonstration that the Sum of the
Deviation Scores Are at a Minimum**
Arithmetically, $\Sigma(X-P)^2$ = a minimum, when

$$P = \bar{X}.$$

Let Z be some point about which the deviations are to be taken, it differs from the mean by, a:

so $Z = \bar{X} + a$.

Then,

$$\Sigma(X-Z)^2 = \Sigma[X-(\bar{X}+a)]^2$$
$$= \Sigma[(X-\bar{X})-a]^2$$
$$= \Sigma[(X-\bar{X})^2 - 2a(X-\bar{X})+a^2]$$
$$= \Sigma[X-\bar{X})^2 - 2a\Sigma(X-\bar{X})+na^2]$$

Apparently, $\Sigma(X-\bar{X}) = 0$, so

$$\Sigma(X-Z)^2 = \Sigma(X-\bar{X})^2+na^2$$

Therefore, observation of the right side of the above equation shows that

$$\Sigma(X-Z)^2$$

is smallest when a=0. From the definition of a, if

$a=0, Z=\bar{X}$.

It is apparent that the sum of square is at a minimum value when deviations are taken from the mean.

   Sixth, the sample mean has some important sampling properties. The random sample mean of some distribution is the **best linear, unbiased estimate** of the population mean for that distribution. This property of the sample mean allows one to make generalizations from a sample to some population of interest.

5.3 WHEN TO USE THE MODE
   The mode can be used with **nominal scaled data**. Nominal scales of measurement are just the naming or classification of events. For example, if one observed the number of students entering or leaving the rest rooms on campus, this would correspond to a nominal scale of measurement. The number of men and women represent discreet categories used for discriminating two separate classes of gender. In addition to gender, psychiatric classification, and the number of football players or even basketball players are other examples of nominal data. Nominal scales of

measurement are the weakest level of measurement. In essence, this scale is the naming or assigning of numbers to classify behavioral categories.

5.4 WHEN TO USE THE MEDIAN

The median is used on **ordinal level scales** or observations rank ordered from least to most on some attribute. Individuals rated on beauty during beauty contests, body building contests, or the order of finish for stock racing drivers are examples of ordinal scaled data. One can possibly infer that ordinal scales are also nominal; however, these ordinal scales do not tell one the distance apart for units of measurement. The median is also a good measure for skewed distributions.

5.5 SKEWED DISTRIBUTIONS

A distribution can be **positively** or **negatively** skewed. On a positively skewed distribution, the tail of the distribution goes towards the right and the mean is greater than the median. With a negatively skewed distribution, the tail of the distribution goes towards the left and the mean is less than the median. Since the mean is affected by extreme scores, this makes the median a more appropriate measure for skewed distributions.

Figure 5.2 Negatively Skewed Distribution

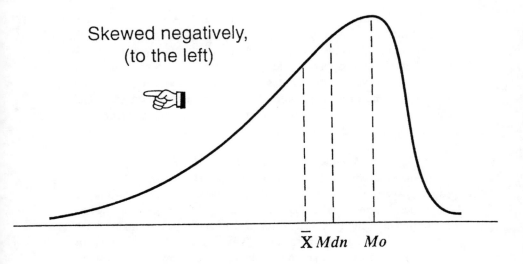

Skewed negatively,
(to the left)

$\overline{X}$ *Mdn*   *Mo*

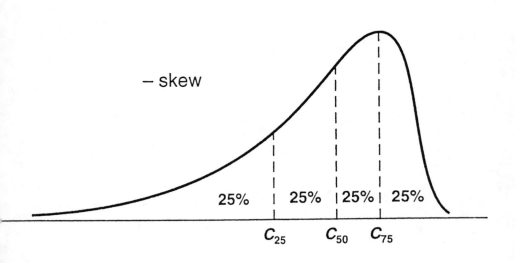

− skew

25%   25%   25%   25%

C_{25} C_{50} C_{75}

Figure 5.3 Positively Skewed Distribution

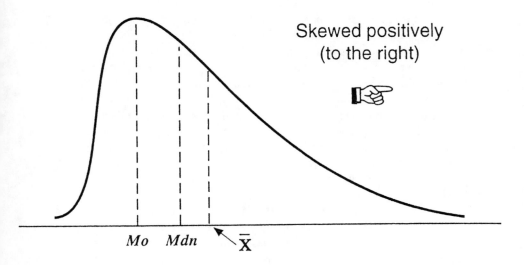

Skewed positively
(to the right)

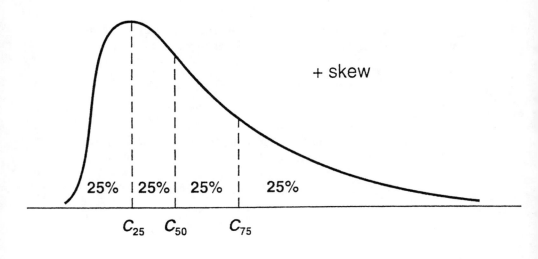

+ skew

5.6 WHEN TO USE THE MEAN

The mean is used with interval or ratio scales. **Interval scales of measurement** includes nominal and ordinal information along with an arbitrary zero point. Unlike ordinal scales, with interval scales, the distance between units can be measured. Essentially, interval scales permit one to measure the distance values are apart. **Ratio scaled data** includes the properties of nominal, ordinal, and interval scales. In addition, it has an absolute zero point. Ratio scales pertain mostly to physical measurements such as inches, centimeters, pounds, miles per hour and so on. If one were doing research on learning errors or the number of correct scores on a learning task, a perfect score or zero errors would be the nonarbitrarily real zero point. This is another example of a ratio scale of measurement.

5.7 MEASURES OF VARIABILITY:
STANDARD DEVIATION AND VARIANCE

Measures of variability determine how much scores vary or disperse from the mean. Essentially, they measure how far scores spread out from the mean. There are measures of variability that do not fit this property of spread-outedness; however, these measures will not be discussed since they seldom occur in test anxiety research. The **standard deviation** is the most widely used measure of variability. By definition, the **variance** is the sum of squares divided by the degrees of freedom, and the **standard deviation** denoted by S is the square root of the variance. The following relationships hold for S and S^2.

$$S^2 = \frac{\Sigma(X-\bar{X})^2}{N-1} = \frac{\text{Sum of Squares}}{\text{Degrees of Freedom}} \qquad S=\sqrt{S^2}$$

Similarly, the standard deviation is the square root of the **second moment** (m_2). For example, the first and second moments are:

$$m_1 = \frac{\Sigma(X-\bar{X})}{N} = 0 \qquad m_2 = \frac{(X-\bar{X})^2}{N}$$

If we make an adjustment on the population variance by replacing N with N-1, or the degrees of freedom, this formula becomes the sample variance. The square root of this sample variance or moment is the standard deviation. Let us take a simple example of 3 scores that were used for calculating the mean.

X	$\Sigma(X-\bar{x})$	$\Sigma(X-\bar{x})^2$
3	1	1
2	0	0
1	-1	1
		$\Sigma(X-\bar{x})^2 = 2$

$$S = \sqrt{\frac{\Sigma(X-\bar{X})^2}{N-1}} = \frac{\sqrt{2}}{2} = \sqrt{1} = 1$$

By substitution the standard deviation is $\sqrt{2}/2 =$ the square root of "1" or 1. Similarly, the variance is 1 squared or 1. Like the mean, the standard deviation has some interesting properties. I will mention two properties of the standard deviation. First, adding or subtracting a constant to each score in a distribution will not change the standard deviation. Second, multiplying or dividing each score in a distribution by a constant results in the standard deviation being multiplied or divided by the same constant.

Traditionally, many textbooks present the sum of squares,

$$\Sigma(X-\bar{X})^2$$

using computational formulas. With summation operations, we will define a computational formula for the sums of squares.

Steps	Algebraic Expression	Reason
1.	$\Sigma(X-\bar{X})^2$	Definition of sum of squares
2.	$\Sigma(X^2-2X\bar{X}+\bar{X})^2$	Expansion of a polynomial
3.	$\Sigma X^2-2\Sigma X\bar{X}+\Sigma\bar{X}^2$	Distribution of a summation sign
4.	$\Sigma X^2-2N\bar{X}^2+\Sigma\bar{X}^2$	Substitution, since $\Sigma X=N\bar{X}$. Thus, $$2\Sigma X\bar{X}=2(N\bar{X})\bar{X}=2N\bar{X}^2$$
5.	$\Sigma X^2-2N\bar{X}^2+N\bar{X}^2$	Effects of summation over a constant
6.	$\Sigma X^2 - \dfrac{N(\Sigma X)^2}{N^2}$	Definition of a mean
7.	$\Sigma X^2 - \dfrac{(\Sigma X)^2}{N}$	Combination of terms

Finally, the sum of squares can be expressed as a definitional formula,

$$\Sigma(X-\bar{X})^2$$

or as a computational formula, $\Sigma X^2 - \dfrac{(\Sigma X)^2}{N}$.

The difficulty with computational formulas, and there are a variety of them, is they do not define or explain the operations one needs to perform; therefore, we will only emphasize definitional formulas.

5.8 COMPUTER EXAMPLES FOR MEASURES OF CENTRAL TENDENCY AND MEASURES OF VARIABILITY

The SPSSX statistical package will be used to illustrate an analysis of some actual test anxiety scores in which we would like to obtain measures of variability and measures of central tendency. The following are data from a treatment and control group measured on the Test Attitude Inventory (TAI). The TAI has a mean of 50 and a standard deviation of 10, which corresponds to what statisticians call t-scores.

1	50	2	65
1	51	2	56
1	45	2	32
1	53	2	50
1	55	2	51
1	47	2	53
1	46	2	50
1	61	2	47
1	55	2	47
1	53	2	44

The "1s" correspond to TAI scores of group one (treatment group), while the "2s" are for group two (control group).

SPSSX Computer Example

The following are the control lines for finding measures of central tendency and variability for the actual data listed above.

Example 1

Title "Measures of Central Tendency and Measures of Variability"
Data List/GPID 1 TAI 3-4
Begin Data
1   50
1   51
1   45
1   53
1   55
1   47
1   46
1   61
1   55
1   53
End data

Frequencies Variables=TAI/
    Statistics=All

Example 2
Title "Measures of Central Tendency and Measures of Variability"
Data List/GPID 1 TAI 3-4
Begin Data
2   65
2   56
2   32
2   50
2   51
2   53
2   50
2   47
2   47
2   44
End data
Frequencies Variables=TAI/
    Statistics=All

5.9 SPSSX RELEASE 4.0
SPSSX is a relatively easy statistical software package to use. It can run in an interactive or batch mode; however, the options and statistics commands only work in the batch mode.   The SPSSX commands provided in this text are designed for the batch mode operation. If one is using SPSSX interactively, any control lines in this text employing the options or statistics commands must be replaced with new subcommands and key words which are found in *SPSSX User's Guide* [3rd ed.] (1988, pp. 1027-1044). SPSSX's interactive mode allows one to execute each command immediately; whereas with the batch mode one submits a file of SPSSX commands for execution. The batch mode is the preferred method for using SPSSX. It allows one to perform the same analysis repeatedly, and it is less tedious and error prone when one is performing detailed analyses. Batch processing also allows a file to be saved, retrieved, and edited. After running the numerous computer examples provided in this text, the reader should purchase the SPSSX manual and be able to follow it without too much difficulty. SPSSX consists of commands and subcommands. All commands must start in column one,

while all subcommands must be indented at least one space. There are four commands that are common to all SPSSX computer runs. These are the **title, data list, begin data,** and **end data** commands.

The **Title** command specifies the text for the first line of each page of SPSSX display. The **Title** can be up to 60 characters long. The second command used in this SPSSX control language is the **Data List** command, placed before the **variable definitions** which in the previous examples were **GPID**-group identification and **TAI**-Test Attitude Inventory. The **"1"** after **GPID** indicated that groups were identified in column one. The **3-4** after **TAI** indicated that data for this variable occurred in **columns three to four**. It should be noted that a **"List"** command can be inserted before the **Begin Data** command in order to get a listing of the data. This is a good idea in terms of checking for data entry errors.

The **Begin Data** command informs SPSSX that lines of data will follow, while the **End Data** command tell SPSSX that it has read all the data. The **frequency** command works through subcommands. As previously stated, all SPSSX subcommands must be indented one space.

Variables is a subcommand of the **frequency** command. With the two previous examples, it named the variables that were analyzed, which were **TAI**. Names of variables can only be eight characters or less. Other examples of **variables** are **Y1, y2, x1, x, and y**. It should be clear to the reader that in order to use SPSSX one must be familiar with one's computer software or hardware system. It should also be noted that on a personal computer that some minor modification of the control lines may be necessary to complete a run, such as adding a period to each control line. Many of the control lines in this text will run on SPSS/PC+ if a period is added at the end of each line; however, other control lines may need additional modification according to the SPSS/PC+ manual.

Figure 5.4 Selected Output Example 1

Selected PrintOut From SPSSX Runs			
Page 1 Measures of Central Tendency and Variability for Treatment Group			
TAI Value Label			
Mean 51.600	Median 52.000	Mode 53.000	*Multiple modes exist. The smallest value is shown.
Std dev 4.881	Variance 23.822		

Figure 5.5 Selected Output Example 2

Page 1 Measures of Central Tendency and Variability for Control Group			
TAI Value Label			
Mean 49.500	Median 50.000	Mode 47.000	*Multiple modes exist. The smallest value is shown.
Std dev 8.475	Variance 71.8333		

It was demonstrated earlier that the mean and standard deviation can be calculated using simple arithmetic. The mean =

$$\frac{\Sigma X}{N} = \frac{516}{10} = 51.600 \text{ for the treatment group.}$$

$$\text{The variance} = \frac{\text{Sum of Squares}}{N-1} = \frac{214.4}{9} = 23.822.$$

If we take the square root of the variance, the standard deviation is 4.881. It will be left to the reader to do the same arithmetic for the control group data.

Statistical Analysis System (SAS)

SAS consists of statements or instructions that must end in a semicolon. As we saw with SPSSX, runs consist of commands-data list, begin data, and end data. The SAS codes consist of three statements: (1) statements for setting up data, (2) statements indicating where the data are located (input statement), and (3) procedure statements (PROC) that tell the computer which statistical analysis to perform.

To reiterate, all SAS statements have to end in a semicolon. This is the most common error. SAS codes must start with a data statement that tells the computer about your data and where variables are located. A cards statement is placed before data are entered. The PROC or procedure statement tells SAS which statistical analysis to perform.

Finally, variable names must start with a letter, cannot exceed 8 characters, and cannot contain blanks or special characters such as commas or semicolons.

SAS Control Lines for Example 1

```
Data Example1;
Input gpid 1  TAI 3-4
cards;
1    50
1    51
1    45
1    53
1    55
1    47
1    46
1    61
1    55
1    53
Proc print;
    Title "Measures of Central Tendency and Measure of Variability";
Proc univariate;
    Var TAI;
```

SAS Control Lines for Example 2

```
Data Example2;
Input gpid 1   TAI 3-4;
cards;
2    65
2    56
2    32
2    50
2    51
2    53
2    50
2    47
2    47
2    44
Proc print;
    Title "Measures of Central Tendency and Measure of Variability";
Proc univariate;
    Var TAI;
```

**SAS Generated Frequency Distribution and Bar Graph
for Example 1**

```
Data Example1;
Input gpid 1  tai 3-4;
cards;
1    50
1    51
1    45
1    53
1    55
1    47
1    46
1    61
1    55
1    53
Proc print;
Proc Freq;
     Tables tai;
     Vbar tai;
```

5.10 APPLICATIONS OF THE MEAN AND STANDARD DEVIATION TO THE NORMAL CURVE

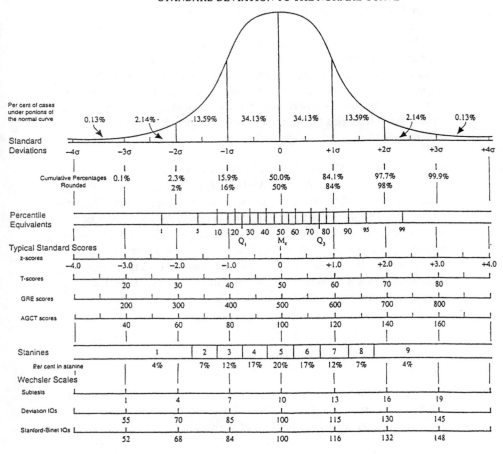

Unlike other measures of central tendency and variability, the mean and standard deviation can be applied to the normal curve. The normal curve is a theoretical probability distribution. If we take the previous computer exercise for example 1, and look at the TAI scores of subjects five and nine which is 55, it is clear that these subjects' scores are 1/2 standard deviation above the mean, since the TAI has a mean of 50 and a standard deviation of 10.

As one can see from the normal curve, 34% of all cases fall within 1 standard deviation and the mean. Furthermore, 34% + 14% or 48% of all cases fall within 2 standard deviations above the mean. Finally, as is apparent, 50% of all cases fall within 3 standard deviations above the mean. In summary, on a normal curve the mean, median, and mode are located at the same position or center of the normal curve, hence measures of central tendency.

5.11 MOMENTS: MEASURES OF SKEWNESS AND KURTOSIS

A moment is the sum of the deviation scores raised to some power. We mentioned earlier that the standard deviation is the square root of the second moment. The two printouts from the SPSSX computer runs provide two pieces of information that relate to the normal curve and moments. Similar information can be found from the SAS runs. First the printouts provide a measure of skewness, which is measured by the third moment. By definition the third moment is:

$$\frac{\Sigma(X-\bar{X})^3}{N}$$

The value on the SPSSX printout has a positive value for skewness, indicating a positively skewed curve; however, the value is not large therefore there is not a large amount of skewness.

Kurtosis

The second statistic that is related to moments reported on the SPSSX printout is kurtosis, which is measured by the fourth moment defined by the following formula:

$$\frac{\Sigma(X-\bar{X})^4}{N}$$

Kurtosis measures how much peakedness that exist within a distribution. Below are indications of leptokurtic, mesokurtic, and platykurtic distributions. The closer the values of skewness and kurtosis are to zero the less skewness and kurtosis.

Test Anxiety: Applied Research

Figure 5.7 Graphs of Kurtosis

A=Leptokurtic
B=Mesokurtic
C=Platykurtic

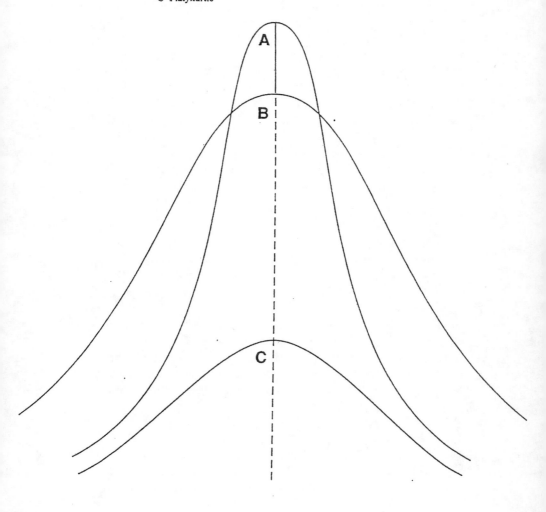

Specifically, if the measure for skewness is positive, the distribution is positive; however, if it is negative, the distribution is negatively skewed. Similarly, a zero measure of skewness indicates a lack of skewness, or a normal distribution. In terms of kurtosis, if the measure for kurtosis is zero the shape of the distribution is mesokurtic. When the measure of kurtosis is negative, the distribution is platykurtic and when the measure is positive, the distribution is leptokurtic. For those who are interested, the precise formulas for skewness and kurtosis are the following:

$$\text{Skewness} = \frac{m_3}{m_2 \sqrt{m_2}}$$

$$\text{Kurtosis} = \frac{m_4}{m_2^{\,2}} - 3$$

m_2 = the second moment
m_3 = the third moment
m_4 = the fourth moment

Skewness is the third moment divided by the second moment times the square root of the second moment. Kurtosis is the fourth moment divided by the second moment squared minus three.

To summarize, the first moment equals 0, the second moment is the population variance, the third moment is used to measure skewness, and the fourth moment measures kurtosis.

5.12 SUMMARY
Measures of central tendency and measures of variability represent the foundations of statistical reasoning, because most applications for advanced statistical methodology involve means and variances. In this chapter, it was demonstrated that skewness and kurtosis are also measures of variability, corresponding to approximately the third and fourth moments, respectively. Finally, it was demonstrated how SPSSX and SAS can be easily employed to find measures of central tendency and variability and to estimate deviations from an ideal normal curve.

5.13 EXERCISES

1. The following is the frequency distribution for the previous exercise.
    Run the data using the previously given control lines. What is the
    value for skewness and kurtosis?

    (skewness=.418, kurtosis=.052).

Value	frequency
45	1
46	1
47	1
50	1
51	1
53	2
55	2
61	1

2. With the data of exercise one, what is the minimum and maximum
    value? (minimum=45 and maximum=61).
3. What would be your best estimate of kurtosis for exercise 1?
    (mesokurtic, since the value is very close to 0).
4. The following statistics are the results of the TAI for three groups of
    subjects. Compute the mean and standard deviation for the three
    groups combined.

Figure 5.8 Calculations of Grand Mean and
Averaged Standard Deviation

	mean	standard deviation	N
Group 1	66	12.02	5
Group 2	44	9.00	7
Group 3	59.89	4.31	9

The actual data for this example are listed on the next page. Run this data
using SPSSX.

1	55	2	50	3	61
1	60	2	47	3	67
1	57	2	47	3	55
1	78	2	44	3	67
1	80	2	56	3	58
		2	32	3	58
		2	32	3	58
				3	58
				3	57

(Overall mean=56.05 and standard deviation=11.95)

The reader should have noticed that the means and standard deviations cannot be averaged. The formula for averaging means is the summation of the weighted means (each mean multiplied by its group size) divided by the total N. The reader remembers that the formula for the mean =

$$\frac{\Sigma X}{N}$$

Therefore, the $\Sigma X = \bar{X}(N)$.

This is the weighted mean formula. To find the grand mean the formula is

$$= \frac{\Sigma \bar{X}(N)}{N_t}$$

Where N_t=the total sample size. Only when common group sizes exist can the mean be averaged without using the weighted formula.

Standard deviations cannot be averaged using the weighted formula. The following is the formula for averaging three standard deviations.

$$S_t = \sqrt{\frac{N_1\ (\bar{X}_1^2 + S_1^2)\ +\ N_2\ (\bar{X}_2^2 + S_2^2)\ +\ N_3\ (\bar{X}_3^2 + S_3^2)}{N_1 + N_2 + N_3} - \bar{X}_t^2}$$

Where $\sqrt{}$ = the square root of the expression

N_1, N_2, N_3 = the number of individuals in each of the three groups

$\overline{X}_1$, $\overline{X}_2$, $\overline{X}_3$ = the means for the three groups

$\overline{X}_t$ = the weighted means of the three groups combined

S_1, S_2, S_3 = standard deviations for the three groups.

Substitute the corresponding values into the above formula and see how close your answer comes to the answer listed. Your answer may be off by a few decimal points due to rounding error.

Chapter 6

CONTENTS

6.1 HYPOTHESIS TESTING

Before the t-test can be discussed, it is important to define the following seven terms related to hypothesis testing: null hypothesis, alternative hypothesis, type I error, type II error, power, one-tailed tests, and two-tailed tests. The possible outcomes of hypothesis testing are presented in figure 6.4.

The **null hypothesis (H_o)** states that the independent variable had no effect on the dependent variable, hence the population means are equal. The H_o is an actual or theoretical set of population parameters or values that would occur if an experiment was performed on an entire population, where the independent variable had no effect on the dependent variable. The alternative hypothesis (H_1), scientific or research hypothesis, is the opposite of the null hypothesis. This hypothesis states that the treatment had an effect on the dependent variable; therefore, the population means or parameters are not equivalent. In sum, both H_o and H_1 are statistical hypotheses.

Type I error is where the null hypothesis is rejected when it is actually true. One is saying that group differences exist when there are not any. Type I error is also called the alpha level, symbolized by the Greek letter alpha α. This level is often set at .05 in the social sciences. It determines how much risk one is willing to take in committing a type I error. When statistical significance is reached, the alpha is the level of significance for the statistical test. Some researchers like to control type I error by testing statistics at stringent levels such as .01, .001, or .0001. The difficulty with controlling type I error by using such small α levels is the fact that as type I error decreases, type II error increases. Therefore, these two errors are inversely related.

Type II error, symbolized by the Greek letter ß (Beta), is the probability of accepting the null hypothesis when it is actually false. One is saying the groups do not differ when they do.

Power of a statistical test is the probability of rejecting a false null hypothesis. This is the probability of making a correct decision. Power is defined as 1 minus type II error or 1-ß. Stevens (1990, p. 84) points out that power is dependent on at least five factors: α level, sample size, effect size (the amount of difference the treatment makes), the statistical test used, and the research design employed (Heppner, Kivlighan, & Wampold, 1992).

A one-tailed test, or directional test, states the statistical hypothesis as either an increase or decrease in the population mean value. In a **two-**

tailed test, the statistical hypothesis is stated as the null hypothesis. One-tailed tests are more powerful than two-tailed tests, but they result in an increase of type I error.   Similarly, they must be stated before an experiment is conducted and should be based on theory. This means one cannot start an experiment with a two-tailed test and fail to find statistical significance and later decide to use a one-tailed test because it can result in statistical significance. This is why many researchers consider one-tailed tests invalid, since the null hypothesis can be rejected when differences between population means are relatively small. Graphically, with two-tailed tests, the alpha level is divided between the two tail ends of a normal curve. For example, if $\alpha=.05$, 2.5% of the α is distributed on each tail of the normal curve. With a one-tailed test the total alpha value is placed on the right or left tail of a normal curve. Figure 6.1 graphically presents a two-tailed test and Figures 6.2-6.3 present one-tailed tests.

Figure 6.1 Two-Tailed Test $\alpha=.05$

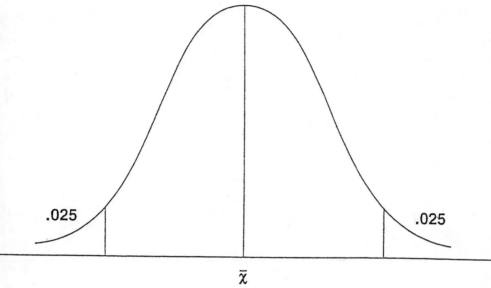

Test Anxiety: Applied Research

Figure 6.2 One-Tailed Test α=.05

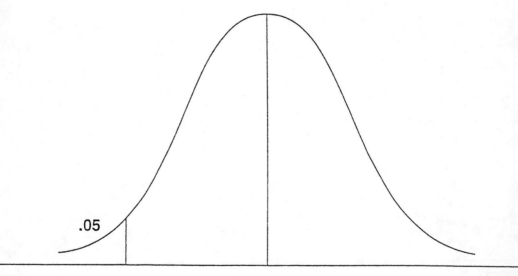

Figure 6.3 One-Tailed Test α=.05

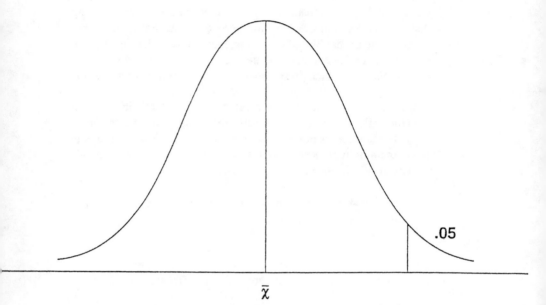

Steps in Hypothesis Testing

1. State the null and alternative hypothesis.
2. Choose a statistical test.
3. Select an alpha level or level of significance.
4. Calculate the test statistic—this is just performing the statistical analysis.
5. Compare the test statistic with the critical value of its sampling distribution. Sampling distributions provide values that a statistic can take and the probability of obtaining each value under the H_o. For example, if the t-test were calculated, one could find the critical value of t from a table which presents values for the sampling distribution of t.
6. Make a decision. If the absolute value of the test statistic is greater than the critical value, reject the null hypothesis at the set alpha level. If the test statistic is not greater than the critical value, one fails to reject the null hypothesis; and, therefore report the failure to obtain statistical significance.

Figure 6.4 Possible Outcomes of Hypothesis Testing.

State of Reality

Decision	H_o True No Treatment Effect	H_o False Treatment Effect
Retain H_o	Correct Decision $1-\alpha$	Type II Error ß
Reject H_o	Type I Error α	Power Correct Decision $1-$ß

6.2 t-TEST FOR INDEPENDENT GROUPS
Sampling Distribution of the Mean

The **sampling distribution of the mean** permits one to employ inferential statistics. Suppose we had a computer that contained only TAI scores from individuals suffering from test anxiety. Now, imagine randomly drawing samples or groups of TAI scores with various values from the computer. Suppose we decide to record each score. Let us assume we kept drawing samples of 100, 200, and so on of TAI scores and we decided to record each score value for every sample.

Now we can calculate the mean TAI score for each sample. Suppose we kept drawing random samples, until we got an infinitely large number of samples. Again, we calculate the sample means for each sample of TAI scores drawn. For example, we calculate the mean TAI score for sample one, two, and so on. We can treat each sample mean of TAI scores as a raw score. From these raw scores or **sample means** for TAI scores, we can construct a frequency distribution of sample means. This frequency distribution would tell how many times each sample mean occurred. This sampling distribution of TAI means is a theoretical distribution of sample means for TAI scores. (The shape of 30 or more TAI means randomly drawn this distribution of TAI means will be approximately normal.) The mean of the sampling distribution of TAI means is the population mean for all TAI scores. This sample mean would result in the same value obtained if every TAI score from the computer were added and divided by the number of scores on the computer.

Remember, from chapter 5, that in the long run the **averages** of the **sample means** will equal the **population mean**. The standard deviation for the sample means of TAI scores is called the **standard error** of the mean. It provides a measure of how much the sample mean varies from the population mean. Additionally, it provides information about the amount of error likely to be made by inferring the value of the population TAI mean from the sample TAI mean. The greater the variability among sample means, the greater the changes that the inference made about the population TAI mean from a single sample TAI mean will be in error.

The standard error of the mean for TAI scores is a function of the population standard deviation for all TAI scores and the sample size. As the number of cases for TAI scores increase, the standard error for TAI scores decreases.

Central Limit Theorem

The previous observations lead us to the central limit theorem. If **random samples** of a fixed number of cases are drawn from any population, regardless of the shape of the distribution, as the number of cases get larger, the distribution of sample means approaches **normality**, with an overall mean approaching the population mean, and the **variance** of the sample means equals $\sigma^2{}_{\bar{x}}$. The standard error equals the population standard deviation divided by the square root of the number of cases. The formula is: $\sigma/\sqrt{N}$.

t-Distribution

The t-distribution is a **family of distributions** that changes with the degrees of freedom. A different sampling distribution exits for every degree of freedom. As the degrees of freedom increases, the t-distribution gets closer in shape to a normal z-distribution. The z-distribution is less variable because the standard error of the mean is constant. That is, the **standard error** will not vary from sample to sample because it is derived from the population standard deviation. The standard error for the t-distribution is not constant, since it is estimated. It is based on a sample standard deviation which varies from sample to sample. As the number of cases increase, the variability of t decreases and gets closer and closer in shape to the z-distribution. *The differences between the t-distributions and the z-distribution becomes negligible when a sample becomes large, such as 30 or more cases.*

Assumptions of Independent t-test

The independent t-test is used to compare the difference between two independent sample means. There are three important assumptions of the t-test for independent samples.
1.   Normality—the variables are normally distributed in each population.
2.   Homogeneity of variance—the variances of the two populations are equal.
3.   Independence—the observations are independent.

Robust Assumptions of Independent t-test

A test statistic is said to be **robust** when a given assumption is violated and the results are still fairly accurate. The independent samples t-test is robust to the assumption of **normality**. Similarly, the **homogeneity of variance** assumption can be ignored, if the two sample sizes are equal. If the sample sizes are fairly equal, that is, the larger group size is < 1.5 times greater than the smaller, the test is still robust. Specifically, if the group sizes are approximately equal,

$$\frac{\text{Larger group size}}{\text{Smaller group size}} < 1.5$$

the t-test statistic is still robust to the violation of the homogeneity of variance assumption (Welkowitz, Ewen, & Cohen, 1982, p. 163).

Violations of the Homogeneity of Variance Assumption
for t-test for Independent Samples

There are two conditions to be aware of in terms of violating the homogeneity assumption. That is, a researcher should be aware of what happens to the test statistic when the homogeneity of variance assumption is violated. First, we have to present two definitions concerning alpha levels (levels of significance).

A **nominal alpha level** (level of significance) is the level set by an experimenter. If the assumption concerning homogeneity of variance is met, the actual alpha level equals the nominal level. The **actual alpha level** is the percent of time one is rejecting the null hypothesis falsely when one or more assumptions are violated; therefore, when one says the t-test is robust, this means that the actual alpha level is close to the nominal alpha level. For example, for the normality assumption, the actual alpha level is close to the nominal because of the central limit theorem. It states that the sum of independent observations having any shape distribution (skewed, rectangular, and so on) approaches normality as the number of observations increase. Remember, when the group sizes are equal the t-statistic is robust to heterogeneous variances. That is as long as the group sizes are approximately equal. For instance, if the largest group size divided by the smaller size is less than 1.5, the t-test is robust to the homogeneity assumption.

When the group sizes are sharply unequal and the population variances are different, what happens to the actual alpha level? If the larger sample variance is associated with the smallest group size, the t-test is **liberal**. This means we are rejecting the null hypothesis falsely too often. To illustrate, the actual alpha level > the nominal alpha level.

An experimenter may think he or she is rejecting falsely 5% of the time (nominal alpha), but in reality may be falsely rejecting the null hypothesis at an actual alpha of 11%. When the larger variance is associated with larger group size, the t-statistic is **conservative**. This means the actual alpha level is less than the nominal. You may not think this is a serious problem, but the smaller alpha level will decrease statistical power (the probability of rejecting a false null hypothesis). This conservative test statistic results in not rejecting the null hypothesis as often as it should be rejected, thus leading to what is called a type II error.

If the normality assumption is tenable, the homogeneity assumption can be tested by the **Hartley's F-Max test**, which is:

$$F\text{-Max} = \frac{S^2 \text{ (largest)}}{S^2 \text{ (smallest)}}$$

df = (k, n) k is the number of variances and n is the average group size if there are equal n's or the harmonic mean (see Section 6.9 for the harmonic mean formula) if the n's are unequal. Critical values of F-Max are found in Table F. Suppose, F-Max = 44.8/1.6 = 2.8 for three variances with an n of 20. The critical value of F-Max with (3,20) degrees of freedom is 2.95 at α=.05; hence, the absolute value of the test statistic is not greater than the critical value; therefore, we fail to reject the null hypothesis. This indicates that the homogeneity assumption is tenable or the population variances are equal. The reason it is important to ensure that the normality assumption is not violated before performing the F-Max test is that all tests of homogeneity, other than the **Levene's test**, are extremely sensitive to violations of normality. That is, the null hypothesis can be rejected due to violations of normality. In summary, the Levene's test, found on SPSSX version 4, is not as sensitive to nonnormality as other tests of homogeneity of variance. If the homogeneity of variance assumption is violated, it is possible to perform **nonparametric statistics** such as the **Mann-Whitney U** (Siegel, 1956, pp. 116-127) or the **Kruskal-Wallis** one-way ANOVA (Siegel, 1956, pp. 184-193) which do not make any assumptions about populations variances; however, these tests are not as powerful as their parametric counterparts, the t-tests for independent samples, and the one-way ANOVA, respectively. Stevens (1990) recommends the Welch t statistic for heterogenous variances and unequal group sizes. Monte Carlo studies have shown that the Welch t statistic provides better control of Type I error, and it provides greater power than the nonparametric alternatives. In chapter 7, under the regression section, we discuss how to handle assumption violations by using data transformation strategies.

The Assumption of Independence for the Independent t-test

The most important assumption of the t-test is the independence assumption. A small violation of this assumption has a considerable impact on both the level of significance and the power of the statistical test. A small amount of independence among observations causes the actual alpha level to be several times greater than the nominal alpha level. The **intraclass correlations** measures dependence among observations. The formula is R=MSW-MSB/MSB + (n-1)MSW. MSB is the numerator of the F statistic, while MSW is the denominator of the F statistic. n is the number of subjects per group.

Let us take an example with a moderate amount of dependence. Using certain statistical tables, with moderate dependence, n=30, for a two group situation, and an intraclass correlation = .30, it can be determined that the actual alpha level is .59. Now we will take an example with a small amount of dependence. With a small amount of dependence, n=30 and the intraclass correlation=.10, for a two group situation, the actual alpha level is .34, whereas the experimenter would assume it is .05.

The moral of the story is for a very small amount of dependence, the actual alpha level is essentially several times greater than the nominal alpha level.

The **dependence** previously discussed is sometimes called **statistical** dependence. There is another form of dependence called linear dependence where one or more **vectors** of a matrix (columns or rows) is a linear combination of other vectors of the matrix. Suppose we have a vector $a'=[1,2]$ and vector $b'=[2,4]$. The vectors are dependent, since $2a'=b'$. The correlation coefficient between the two vectors is 1.00, hence one vector is a function of the other.

A matrix is also dependent when the determinant is zero. For example, the determinant of the following matrix formed by transposing and joining the previous given two vectors has a **determinant** of zero since:

$$\begin{vmatrix} 1 & 2 \\ 2 & 4 \end{vmatrix} = 1(4) - 2(2) = 0$$

which is the determinant of the matrix. This suggests that vectors Y_1, Y_2....Y_n of the same order are linearly dependent, if there exists scalars S_1, S_2.....S_n not all zero, such that $S_1Y_1 + S_2Y_2.....S_nY_n=0$. Vectors are linearly independent when the preceding equation is only satisfied when all the scalars are zero (Kirk, 1982, p. 784). In summary, for **linear independence**, one vector cannot be a linear combination of the other. In addition, as Rummel (1970, p. 66) notes, statistical independence means the intraclass correlation is not significantly different from zero, while in terms of vectors statistical independence implies that the vectors are orthogonal or uncorrelated.

Formula for the Independent t-test

The t-test determines if two groups came from the same population. The null hypothesis states that the population means are equal. Symbolically, $\mu_1=\mu_2$, or $\mu_1-\mu_2=0$. The formula for the t-test is the difference between the group means divided by the standard error. Symbolically, the formula is

$$ t = \overline{X}_1 - \overline{X}_2 / S_{\overline{x}_1 - \overline{x}_2} $$

$\overline{X}_1$ = the mean for group one, while $\overline{X}_2$ is the mean for group two. $S_{x_1 - x_2}$ = the standard error of the mean. The standard error can be rewritten as the variance of group one divided by its group size plus the variance of the second group divided by its group size.

Symbolically, the standard error =
$$ \sqrt{\frac{S_1^2}{N_1} + \frac{S_2^2}{N_2}} $$

$$ t = \frac{\overline{X}_1 - \overline{X}_2}{\sqrt{\dfrac{S_1^2}{N_1} + \dfrac{S_2^2}{N_2}}} $$

with N-2 degrees of freedom.

Symbolically, the null hypothesis is

H_o: $\mu_1 = \mu_2$

H_1: μ_1 is not $= \mu_2$

Let us take a computer example from the measure of central tendency data.

Table 1

SPSSX Control Lines for Independent Samples t-test

The control lines for the t-test is the following:

Title 't-test for independent groups'
Data list free/gpid TAI |1* |
Begin data
1 50 2 65 |2* |
1 51 2 56
1 45 2 32
1 53 2 50
1 55 2 51
1 47 2 53
1 46 2 50
1 61 2 47
1 55 2 47
1 53 2 44
End data
t-test groups = gpid (1,2) |3* |
 Variables = TAI/
|1* | Free on the Data List line indicates that data is in the free format.

|2* | The "1s" and "2s" correspond to the group identification numbers.

|3* | This is the command for the t-test with two levels in parentheses.

Table 2

SAS Control Lines for Independent Samples t-Test

```
Independent Samples t-test
Data TAI;
Input gpid 1 TAI 3-4;
cards;
1    50
1    51
1    45
1    53
1    55
1    55
1    47
1    46
1    61
1    55
1    53
2    65
2    56
2    32
2    50
2    51
2    53
2    50
2    47
2    47
2    42
Proc TTEST;
Class gpid;
Proc Print;
```

Figure 6.5 Selected Printout from t-test for Independent Samples

t-test for independent groups Group 1: GPID Eq 1.00   Group 2: GPID 2.00 t-test for: TAI

	Number of Cases	Mean	Standard Deviation	Standard Error
Group 1	10	51.60	4.88	1.54
Group 2	10	49.50	8.48	2.68
F 2-Tail	Pooled Variance Estimate			
Value Prob. 3.02 .116	t Value	Degrees of Freedom	2-Tail Prob.	
	*.68	**18	***.506	

* = the value of the t-test statistic.

** = the degrees of freedom which is N-2 or 18.

*** is the two-tailed probability which is greater than .05, so the null hypothesis is not rejected. This indicates that the group means did not differ greater than we would expect by chance alone.

The results of the above selected printout can be verified by substituting the appropriate value in the t formula:

$$t = \frac{\overline{X}_1 - \overline{X}_2}{S_{\overline{x}_1 - \overline{x}_2}} = \frac{51.60 - 49.50}{\sqrt{\frac{23.82}{10} + \frac{71.83}{10}}} = \frac{51.60 - 49.50}{3.09} = .68$$

.68 must be compared with its critical value from Table B (critical values of t). With 18 degrees of freedom, the critical value at the .05 alpha level is 2.101. Since the test statistic is not greater than the critical value we fail to reject the null hypothesis at the .05 alpha level. In APA journal form the results are $t(18)=.68$, $p>.05$.

Table 3

Control Lines for Running the Pearson-Product Moment Correlation

```
Title "correlation"
Data list free/TAI1 TAI2
Begin data
50 65
51 56
45 32
53 50
55 51
47 53
46 50
61 47
55 47
53 44
End data
Pearson Corr variables = TAI1 TAI2/ | * |
Option 3  | ** |
```

* = the command for the Pearson correlation, using variables TAI1 and TAI2.

Note: The new SPSSX command for Pearson Corr is Correlations.

** = Option 3 provides a two-tail test of significance.
Note: The new subcommand for a two-tail test for correlations is print=twotail/.

6.3 THE T-TEST FOR RELATED SAMPLES OR CORRELATED GROUPS

The t-test for related samples is sometimes called the t-test for **repeated measure** or the t-test for correlated or paired measures. The formula for the repeated measures t-test is the mean of the differences scores divided by the standard error of the difference. The formula is:

$$\text{repeated } t = \frac{\bar{D}}{\sqrt{S^2/N}}$$
$$\text{measures}$$

D = the mean of the difference scores.

$\sqrt{S^2/N}$ = standard error of the difference scores.

N = the number of pairs and the degrees of freedom.

The repeated measures t-test is used with pretest/posttest designs. Let us take the data provided for the t-test for independent measure and show how the data can be analyzed assuming repeated measures. Suppose one group of 10 matched pairs of subjects on the TAI are randomly assigned by pairs in a pretest and posttest design. Subjects are given guided imagery training to reduce test anxiety. We measure subjects before treatment (01) and after treatment (02).

We would like to know if there are any statistically significant changes from pre-post measures on the TAI. Schematically, the design is: X-is the guided imagery training.

01	X Treatment	02	D = Difference Scores or Gain Scores
50		65	65-50 = 15
51		56	56-51 = 5
45		32	32-45 = -13
53		50	50-53 = -3
55		51	51-55 = -4
47		53	53-47 = 6
46		50	50-46 = 4
61		47	47-61 = -14
55		47	47-55 = -8
53		44	44-55 = -9

D = Mean of difference scores =   -2.1
S = standard deviation of differences scores = 9.386

$$t = \frac{-2.1}{\sqrt{9.386^2/10}} = -2.1/2.968 = -.70 \text{ with N-1 or 9 degrees of freedom}$$

Using Table B for critical values of t, with 9 degrees of freedom the critical value is 2.262 at the .05 level for a two-tailed test. Since the absolute value of the test statistic is not greater than the critical value, we fail to reject the null hypothesis at the .05 level. Therefore, the results in APA journal form is t(9)=-.70, p>.05.

It should be noted that the pretest posttest design when used without careful matching and random assignment leaves a number of threats to internal validity uncontrolled. As discussed in Chapter 4, the one-group before-after design is extremely susceptible to experimental contamination. **This design suffers from maturational, testing, and history threats to internal validity. In addition, the pretesting can sensitize subjects to the treatment. Finally, reactive effects are also left uncontrolled.**

Table 4
SPSSX Control Lines for Repeated Measures t-test

Title 't-test for repeated measures'
Data list/TAI1 3-4 TAI2 9-10
List
Begin data
50   65
51   56
45   32
53   50
55   51
47   53
46   50
61   47
55   47
53   44
End data
t-test Pairs = TAI1 TAI2

Table 5
SAS Control lines for repeated measures t-test

Data Depen;
Input Pre 3-4 Post 9-10;
Diff = Pre-Post;
Cards;
50   65
51   56
45   32
53   50
55   51
47   53
46   50
61   47
55   47
53   44
Proc Print;
Proc Means N Mean Stderr T PRT;
Var diff;

Exercises

1. Using SPSSX and SAS, run the t-test for the data given in the section for the t-test for independent samples.
2. Subtract 10 from each score for the data used in exercise 1 and perform the t-test for independent samples again. Compare your answer from each run.
3. Using SPSSX and SAS, run the data from exercise 1, but this time perform the t-test for repeated measures. What is the mean for the differences scores? Answer (2.10). What is the standard error? Answer (2.968). From the printout, what is the degrees of freedom? Answer (9).
4. It was determined in an earlier example that the t-test for independent samples was .68 and the one for the dependent samples was .71. Why is the dependent measure t-test larger? Also, why does the dependent measures t-test have a smaller standard of error. Answer

(the t-test for repeated measures is more powerful than the t-test for independent samples. The repeated measures t-test reduces error variability due to individual differences, thus leading to a smaller standard of error and hence a more powerful statistical test).

6.4 T-TEST OF A SPECIAL CASE OF CORRELATION OR REGRESSION

The t-test for independent samples is a special case of correlation. It can be shown that the relationship between the Pearson Product Moment correlation and the t-test for independent samples is:

$$t = r \sqrt{N - 2/1 - r^2}$$

r = the Pearson Product Moment correlation.
N = the number of pairs.
N-2 = the degrees of freedom for using the critical values of t.

The formula for transforming critical values of t to critical values of r is the following:

$$r = \sqrt{t^2/N - 2 + t^2}$$

Exercise

Using SPSSX, find the correlation for the data given with the t-test for independent samples. Now, make the appropriate substitution in the formula above. Critical values of the Pearson r are found in Table H. What is your decision in terms of rejecting the null hypothesis at the .05 probability level? Answer (r=.23, p>.05), failure to reject the null hypothesis.

Using the following control lines for SAS, rerun the correlation for the data given for the t-test of independent samples.
Data Relate;
Input TAI1 1-2 TAI2 4-5;
Cards;
Proc Corr;
Var TAI1 TAI2;
Note: the data are inserted between the cards and proc corr statements.

6.5 ONE-WAY ANALYSIS OF VARIANCE

The **one-way analysis of variance** is used to compare two or more group means in order to determine if they differ greater than one would expect by chance. One cannot compare three or more groups with t-tests, because the **overall alpha level** (experimentwise error) becomes several times larger than the level set by the experimenter, for example the .05 level. The point to be remembered is, if one conducts several t-tests, the chances of one yielding significance increases with the number tests conducted. The advantage of the **ANOVA** is that it keeps the risk of a type I error small even when several group means are compared. The one-way analysis of variance or one-way ANOVA has the same three assumptions as the t-test for independent samples. Essentially, the same thing happens to the F-test which is used to calculate ANOVA as what occurs when the assumptions are violated under the conditions of the t-test for independent samples.

Assumptions of ANOVA

1. Normality - the variables are normally distributed in each population. Also, this is equivalent to the errors (e_{ij}) within each population being normally distributed.
2. Homogeneity of variance - the variances of the populations are equal, or the samples are drawn from populations with equal variances.
3. Independence - the observations are independent. This assumption also includes the notion that the numerator and denominator of the F-test are independent. If one suspects independence or correlated observations, calculate the intraclass correlation, and if there is a high correlation among observations, perform statistical tests at a stringent (lower) level of significance. Finally, if observations are correlated within groups, but not across groups, employ the group mean as the unit of analysis. Even though this will reduce the sample size, it will not lead to a substantial decrease in statistical power because the means are more stable than individual observations.

Relationship Among t-test, F-test and
Correlation or Regression

It was just mentioned that ANOVA is calculated using a statistic called an F-test. The t-test squared is an F-test. Also, remember it was stated that t-test is a special case of correlation or regression. This is also the case for the F-test. Since

$$F = \frac{r^2}{\frac{(1-r)^2}{(n-2)}}$$

n = the number of pairs.

It becomes clear that the t-test, as well as the F-test, is a special case of regression or correlation. It should also be noted the one-way ANOVA fits a linear model. Suppose the ith subject is in group j, for a one-way ANOVA the model for a subject's score is:

$y_{ij} = \mu + \alpha_j + e_{ij}$
where: μ = the general effect or grand mean
α_j = the main effect
e_{ij} = the error

Verbally, this linear model states that an observed value of a dependent variable is equal to a weighted sum of values associated with the independent variable(s), plus an error term (Hays, 1981, p. 326).

Formulas for One-way ANOVA

With the one-way ANOVA, we calculate a test statistic called an F-test. This F-test, similar to the t-test, is a ratio. The numerator is called the mean square between groups (MSB), which measures the variability among groups. The denominator is the mean square within or the average variability within groups. Hence, with the ANOVA, we measure variability across groups and variability within groups. Below are the formulas for a one-way ANOVA.

$F = \dfrac{MSB}{MSW}$ called an F-test

The MSB $= \dfrac{SSB}{K-1}$

K-1 is the degrees of freedom between for the term SSB.

$SSB = \Sigma n_i (\bar{X}_i - \bar{X})^2$

formula for sum of the squares between (SSB) which measures the amount of variability each group mean varies about the grand mean. This is a weighted sum of squares, since each separate sum of squares is multiplied by its corresponding group size n_i. Σ (Sigma) indicates the sum of squares for each group is added across groups.

MSW=$\underline{SSW}$ This is the formula for mean square within groups.
        N-K   N-K is the degrees of freedom for the MSW, while K is the
               number of groups.

SSW is the pool within group variability, it measures how much each score deviates from its corresponding group mean. Σ (Sigma) indicates that the deviations or $(\bar{x}-\bar{x})^2$ are pooled or added across each group.

     In summary, MSB and MSW are both variance estimates, so with the F-test we are analyzing the variances, hence the name analysis of variance.

Numerical Calculations of One-Way ANOVA

     Let us take an example to illustrate how the ANOVA is calculated. Later, the control lines for running this analysis on SPSSX and SAS are provided. Suppose we had three groups of subjects randomly assigned to three treatments for test anxiety. Let us assume subjects were randomly assigned to a relaxation therapy, cognitive-behavioral counseling, or study skills counseling group for test anxiety reduction. The dependent variables are the scores from the TAI.

Figure 6.6 Schematic Diagram of One-Way ANOVA

relaxation therapy	cognitive-behavioral counseling	study skills counseling
53	56	55
55	55	53
52	56	54
54	54	55
54	55	52
53	53	54
$\bar{x}=53.5$	$\bar{x}=54.83$	$\bar{x}=53.83$

(Grand mean) $\bar{X}_g$ = 54.05

ANOVA computes and compares two sources of variation (Stevens, 1990).

1. Between group variation—how much the group means vary about the grand mean.
2. Within group variation—how much the subjects' scores vary about their corresponding group means. This variation is due to individual differences, and possibly experimental error.

Between Group Variability

The first term to calculate is the sum of the squares between groups, which is SSB=$\Sigma n(\bar{x}_i-\bar{x})^2$. Σ denotes the summation symbol, n is the number of subjects in a given group, while SSB stands for the sum of the squares between groups. This is the weighted sum of squares in that each deviation is weighted by the number of subjects in a given group.

SSB=$6(53.5-54.05)^2 + 6(54.83-54.05)^2 + 6(53.83-54.05)^2 = 5.78$

Now we need to calculate the mean square between (MSB), which is just simply the SSB/(K-1), where K=the number of groups.

$$MSB=SSB/(K-1)=5.78/2=2.89$$

Within-Group Variability

The next term to calculate is the sum of the square within (SSW) which is:

k

$$SSW = \Sigma(X-\bar{X})^2 + \Sigma(X-\bar{X})^2 + ... \Sigma(X-\bar{X})^2$$

i = 1

where X is the score of a subject in a given group, and X is the group mean of a given group.

$$SSW = (53-53.5)^2 + (55-53.5)^2 + (52-53.5)^2 +$$
$$(54-53.5)^2 + (54-53.5)^2 + (53-53.5)^2 +$$
$$... + (54-53.83)2 = 19.16$$

The sum of the squares within is finding the variability for each group, then totalling the separate variabilities. This is a pool within group variability. In order to get the variance estimate (MSW), we find the sum of squares within (SSW) divided by its degrees of freedom which is the SSW/(N-K), where N is the total number of subjects and K equals the number of groups.

$$MSW=19.16/15=1.28$$

The F-statistic tests a hypothesis that involves populations means, just like the one used for the t-test for independent samples. The null hypothesis is that the population means are equal, or:

H_o: $\mu_1=\mu_2=\mu_3$ or $\mu_1-\mu_2-\mu_3=0$

The F-test is the MSB/MSW=2.89/1.28=2.26 p>.05. Using Table C, the critical value of F with 2,15 degrees of freedom is 3.68 at the .05 level of significance, hence the absolute value of the test statistic is not greater than the critical value, so we failed to reject the null hypothesis.

It should be apparent that, like the t-test, the F-test is a ratio. The numerator reflects the variance among the means taking into account the different samples sizes, while the denominator reflects the average variance of the groups involved. The results of the above example indicates that the means do not differ greater than one would expect by change alone, hence the null hypothesis is not rejected. The $p > .05$ indicates the lack of statistical significance.

Table 6

SPSSX Control Lines for One-Way ANOVA

Title "one way anova"
data list/gpid 1 Y 3-4
begin data
1   53
1   55
1   52
1   54
1   54
1   53
2   56
2   55
2   56
2   54
2   55
2   53
3   55
3   53
3   54
3   55
3   52
3   54
end data
Manova y by gpid (1,3)/   1
power = F (.05)/   2
print cellinfo (means)   3
Signif (efsize)   4

1 - the code name for multivariate analysis of variance, which is used to calculate the one way analysis of variance. The numbers in parentheses indicate the levels of the groups being compared, in this case the levels are 1 through 3. If there were four groups, it becomes gpid(1,4).
3 - yields the cell means and standard deviations.

2 - provides a power estimate at the .05 level.
4 - provides an effect size measure.

Below is the selected printout from the one-way ANOVA computer run.

Table 7
SAS Control Lines for One-Way ANOVA

Data TAI; Input Gpid 1 Y 3-4; Cards; 1   53 1   55 1   52 1   54 1   54 1   53 2   56 2   55 2   56 2   54 2   55 2   53 3   55 3   53 3   54 3   55 3   52 3   54 Proc Means; By gpid; Proc ANOVA; Model Y = gpid; Class Gpid; Means Gpid/Tukey; Proc Print;

Figure 6.7 Selected Printout from One-Way ANOVA
Tests of Significance of Y using unique sum of squares

Tests of Significance of Y using unique sum of squares Source of Variation	SS	DF	MS	F	F sig of F
Within Cells	19.16	15	1.28		
GPID	5.78	2	2.89	2.26	.139*

*Indicates that statistical significance was not reached since the two-tailed probability level is greater than .05. If significance would have been reached, it would be necessary to conduct post hoc tests such as the Tukey (HSD).

For those who are interested in what to do after the F-test is significant with three or more groups should read the section on planned comparisons and the Tukey post hoc procedure.

Figure 6.8 Power Analysis for One-Way ANOVA

Selected Printout Power Analysis for One Way ANOVA			
Source of Variation	Partial ETA Sqd	Noncentrality	Power
GPID	.232*	4.522	.388**

*Cohen (1988, pp. 280-284) notes that eta squared or the correlation ratio is a generalization of the Pearson Product Moment Correlation squared. Stevens (1990, p. 94) characterizes values of eta squared of around .01 as small effect size measures, while values of .06 are as medium effect sizes and values of eta squared of .14 are large effect sizes.

**This is the measure of power or the probability of making a correct decision in terms of rejecting the null hypothesis. Notice that power is low, the effect size is large, and the null hypothesis was not rejected due to a small power level. More will be said about power in Section 6.6.

6.6 SPSSX POWER ESTIMATES
AND EFFECT SIZE MEASURES

Using the MANOVA command and the power subcommand on SPSSX power values between 0 and 1 can be obtained for fixed effects models. Fixed effects means that the inferences are fixed or are only specific to the study of interest. Within fixed effect models, the researcher is not attempting to generalize results beyond the given level of a factor in a particular study. Similarly, effect size, the practical significance of a statistical test, can also be obtained from SPSSX with the **Signif(efsize)/** subcommand. Table 4 presented the control lines for finding power and effect size estimates for a one-way ANOVA. In order to modify the power levels, one can put any expression in hundredth in the power subcommand. For example, if we wanted power at the .15 level, the power subcommand would be: **Power=F(.15)/**.

The effect size obtained from SPSSX is actually the correlation coefficient eta squared. This eta squared is also called the coefficient of determination or the amount of variance accounted for on a dependent variable or set of dependent variables. As previously stated, eta squared of .01 is considered a small effect size, values of .06 are medium values and values of .14 are considered large effect size measures. **In terms of measures of power, Stevens (1990, p. 85) characterizes power values greater than .70 as adequate and values greater than .90 as excellent.**

SPSSX *Users Guide* (1988, p. 602) states that the effect size measures obtained from SPSSX computer runs are actually partial eta squared correlations. Stevens (1990, p. 85) notes that partial eta squared tends to overestimate the actual effect size. The actual value for eta squared can be obtained from the following formula (Stevens, 1990, p. 94).

$$\text{eta squared} = \frac{(K-1) \cdot F}{(K-1) \cdot F + N}$$

The formula for the partial eta squared is:

$$\text{partial eta squared} = \frac{(K-1) \cdot F}{(K-1) \cdot F + (N-K)}$$

K-1 and N-K are the degrees of freedom from the one-way ANOVA. K-1 is the number of groups minus 1, while N-k is the total sample size minus the number of groups. · implies multiplication. When sample sizes are large N > 100, the differences between eta squared and partial eta squared are negligible. The two formulas only differ by -K.

SPSSX Power Analysis for t-test for
Independent Samples ANOVA

```
Title "Power for t-test"
Data list free/gpid TAI
Begin data
1  50      2    65
1  51      2    56
1  45      2    32
1  53      2    50
1  55      2    51
1  47      2    53
1  46      2    50
1  61      2    47
1  55      2    47
1  53      2    44
End data
MANOVA TAI by gpid (1,2)/
 Power = F(.05)/
 Print = Cellinfo (Means)
 Signif(EFSIZE)/
```

SPSSX Power Analysis for One-way ANOVA

Title "Power for One-way ANOVA"
Data list/gpid 1 Y 3-4
Begin data
End data
MANOVA y by gpid (1,3)/
  Power = F(.15)/
  Print Cellinfo (Means)
  Signif (EFSIZE)/

Note: Data are inserted between the begin data and end data commands.

Exercise

The following data represent the results of three treatments for test anxiety. Perform the correct analysis on the data using SPSSX, what are your results? Perform a power analysis at the .05 and .15 levels.

Figure 6.9 Results of Three Treatments for Test Anxiety

relaxation therapy TAI scores	cognitive-behavioral counseling TAI scores	study skills counseling TAI scores
62	63	64
66	59	65
67	58	63
$\bar{x}=65$	$\bar{x}=60$	$\bar{x}=64$

Was statistical significance reached at the .05 level?
(Answer, no, F=4.20, p=.072.)

6.7 TWO-WAY ANOVA

The two-way ANOVA is a factorial design which was discussed in Chapter 4. The factorial ANOVA allows one to answer three specific statistical questions. First, do the row means differ significantly? This is the row main effect. Second, do the column means differ significantly (column main effect)? Finally, is the profile of cell means in row one significantly nonparallel to that of row two? This is called an interaction between factors one and two. In summary, if the profile of cell means for row one crosses with the profile of cell means for row two, this indicates an interaction. Similarly, if the profile of cells means for row one can be extended in such a way that it crosses with the profile of cell means for row two, this also indicates an interaction. When the profiles of cell means are parallel, this indicates a noninteraction. Graphically, Figures 6.10-6.13, below, represent profiles of adjusted cells means for two kinds of two-way interactions and two forms of noninteractions. See Figure 6.15 for the calculations of adjusted cell means.

Figure 6.10 Disordinal Interaction

Nonparallelism

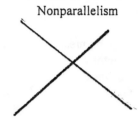

Figure 6.11 Noninteraction

Parallelism

Figure 6.12 Ordinal Interaction

Nonparallelism

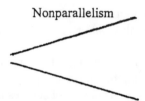

Figure 6.13 Noninteraction

Parallelism

Just like the t-test and the one way anova, the two-way anova is also a linear model. The model looks like this:

$y_{ijk} = \mu + A_i + B_j + O_{ij} + e_{ijk}$

Where:

μ is the general effect or grand mean

A_i is the main effect for factor A

B_j is the main effect for factor B

O_{ij} is the interaction effect

e_{ijk} is the error

Formulas for Two-way ANOVA

$$SSA = nJ \; \Sigma(\bar{X}_i - \bar{X})^2$$

formula for sum of squares for factor A. The subscript i indicates a row.

The nJ is the number of observations each row mean is based upon. The sum of the squares reflects the variability of the row means about the grand mean.

$$SSB = nI \; \Sigma(\bar{X}_j - \bar{X})^2$$

formula for sum of squares for factor B. The subscript j indicates a column.

This reflects the variability of the column means about the grand mean. The nI is the number of observations each column mean is based upon.

MSA = $\underline{SSA}$ formula for mean sum of squares for factor A.
         (I-1), I is the number of rows.

MSB = $\underline{SSB}$ formula for mean sum of squares for factor B.
         (J-1), J is the number of columns.

Error Term

Formula for the sum of the squares of the cells is

$$SSW = \Sigma(X - \bar{X}_{ij})^2.$$

X is a score in a cell, and $\bar{X}_{ij}$ is the mean of a given cell.

SSW is called the error term or the sum of squares within each cell or the pooled within cell variability. For each cell every score is deviated or subtracted from the cell mean and squared. Basically, the sum of squares for each cell is calculated and added across every cell.

MSW = $\dfrac{\text{SSW}}{\text{(N-IJ)}}$ N is the total number of subjects, I is the number of rows, while J is the number of columns.

Next we will provide the interaction sum of squares for the two-way ANOVA.

FORMULAS for TWO-WAY ANOVA
Formula for the Interaction Sum of Squares
SSAB = $n \Sigma 0_{ij}^2$ which is the formula for interaction sum of squares (SSAB), where

$0_{ij} = \bar{x}_{ij} - \bar{x}_i . - \bar{x}._j + \bar{x}$ is the estimated cell interaction effect.

$\bar{x}_{ij}$ is the mean of some cell defined by row i and column j.
$\bar{x}_i$ is the row mean.
$\bar{x}_j$ is the column mean.
$\bar{x}$ is the grand mean.
n is the number of scores or subjects within a cell.
Σ (Sigma) denotes that each interaction effect is added or summed.

The formulas that follow are for main and interaction effects.

Formulas for F-tests Main Effects
F(A) = $\dfrac{\text{MSA}}{\text{MSW}}$

F(B) = $\dfrac{\text{MSB}}{\text{MSW}}$

Formula for Interaction Effect

MSAB = $\dfrac{\text{SSAB}}{\text{(I-1)(J-1)}}$,

F(AB) = $\dfrac{\text{MSAB}}{\text{MSW}}$

where I = the number of rows and J = the number of columns. The expression (K-1)(J-1) is the degrees of freedom for interaction.

In contrast to the one-way ANOVA, the factorial ANOVA is more powerful than the one-way ANOVA. In terms of variation, Stevens (1990, p. 103) notes that there are four sources of variance for the factorial ANOVA and they are:

1.   Variation due to factor 1
2.   Variation due to factor 2
3.   Variation due to factor 1 and 2
4.   Within cell or error variation

The assumptions for the factorial ANOVA are the same as for the one-way ANOVA. That is, normality on the dependent variables in each cell and equal cell population variances.

Let us consider a 2 X 2 design with two scores per cell.

With this design, there are two levels of hypnotic susceptibility and two levels of treatments.

Figure 6.14 2 X 2 Design
Treatments (B)

	1	2	Row Means
(1) High	50, 70 $\bar{x}=60$ high(1) hypnotic susceptibility row A(1)	30, 60 $\bar{x}=45$	Row Mean A(1) $\bar{x}_{1.} = 52.5$
(2) Low	50, 50 $\bar{x}=50$ low(2) hypnotic susceptibility row A(2)	60, 60 $\bar{x}=60$	Row Mean A(2) $\bar{x}_{2.} = 55$
	$\bar{x}.1 = 55$ column mean	$\bar{x}.2 = 52.5$ column mean	$\bar{x}_g= 53.75$ Grand mean

Hypnotic Susceptibility (A)

The scores in this design represent the TAI scores for high and low hypnotic susceptible subjects randomly assigned to two groups: relaxation therapy, and hypnosis. The dot notation above $\bar{x}_1$ indicates rows, while the dot notion in the first part of the subscript indicates columns. We are going to first test the main effects of factor A. The null hypothesis for the row effect is H_o: $\mu_1 = \mu_2 = ...\mu_I$. This indicates that the population means are equal. From the above table $\bar{x}_{1.} = 52.5 = \mu_1$ and $\bar{x}_{2.} = 55$ which are the estimates of the population means for the high and low hypnotic susceptible subjects. The "I" in the above notation indicates rows. The null hypothesis for the B main effect is: H_o: $\mu_{.1} = \mu_{.2} = \mu_{.J}$. This denotes the population column means are equal. Similarly, $\bar{x}_{.1} = 55 = \mu_{.1}$, and $\bar{x}_{.2} = 52.5 = \mu_{.2}$. These are estimates of the population column means. The "J" above indicates columns. Thus, this is a I X J design. That is, there are two levels of A (susceptibility—high and low) and two levels of treatment.

Sum of the Squares for a Balance Factorial Design

Balanced designs mean that there are an equal number of observations per cell. Later, we will provide the SPSSX control lines for running unbalanced designs.

$SSA = nJ \Sigma (\bar{x}_i - \bar{x})^2$ The nJ is the number of observations each row mean is based upon, or 2 X 2. The sum of the squares reflects the variability of the row means about the grand mean. For this example, SSA is: $SSA = 2(2)[(52.5 - 53.75)^2 + (55 - 53.75)^2] = 12.50$

The mean sum of squares for factor A (MSA) is:
$MSA = SSA/ (I-1) = 12.5/1 = 12.5$

$SSB = nI \Sigma (\bar{x}_j - \bar{x})^2$ This reflects the variability of the column means about the grand mean. The nI is the number of observations each column mean is based upon. For our example, it is:
$SSB = 2(2) [(55 - 53.75)^2 + (52.5 - 53.75)^2 = 12.50$

The mean sum of squares of B (MSB) is:
$MSB = SSB/ (J-1)=12.50/1=12.50$

Error Term

The error term is the sum of squares within each cell or the pooled within cell variability. Essentially, for each cell we take each score and deviate it about the cell mean, square the deviation and add these deviations across all cells. Essentially, the sum of squares for each cell is calculated and added across every cell. For our example, the error term (SSW) is: $SSW = \Sigma(x - \bar{x}_{ij})^2$

$SSW = (50-60)^2 + (70-60)^2$ Variability for cell row 1, column 1
$\qquad (50-50)^2 + (50-50)^2$ Variability for cell row 2, column 1
$\qquad (30-45)^2 + (60-45)^2$ Variability for cell row 1, column 2
$\qquad (60-60)^2 + (60-60)^2$ Variability for cell row 2, column 2
$\qquad = 650$

MSW = SSW/ (N-IJ) = 650/(8-4)=162.50. This represents the average of the cell variances.

The Main Effects for the F-Tests

F(A) = MSA/MSW = 12.5/162.50 = .08.(1,4) p>.05. The number in parentheses are the degrees of freedom which is I-1 and J-IJ or 1,4. With (1,4) degrees of freedom the critical value of F at the .05 level is 7.71. Since the absolute value of the test statistic is not greater than the critical value of F, we fail to reject the null hypothesis. F(A) listed above is the way statistics are usually presented in APA journals. The F(B) = MSB/MSW = 12.50/162.50 = .08. The degrees of freedom is J-1, N-IJ or 2-1, 8-2x2 which is (1,4). The critical value for these degrees of freedom at the .05 level is 7.71. The results for F(B) = .08(1,4) p>.05. This indicates that the null hypothesis was not rejected or the population columns means are equal. In sum, for both factors A and B statistical significance was not obtained.

Interaction

One should note that if a significant interaction is found the main effects are ignored, since the interaction is a more complex model for the data. **If a significant interaction is found, it is used to explain the data.** Similarly, after a significant interaction is found one must conduct post hoc test to determine exactly where the differences are located. See Hays (1981) for a discussion of post hoc procedures. Interaction is defined as 0_{ij}.

Where $0_{ij} = (\mu_{ij}-\mu) - (\mu_{i\cdot} - \mu) - (\mu_{\cdot j} - \mu)$
$= \mu_{ij} - \mu_{i\cdot} - \mu_{\cdot j} + \mu$

μ denotes a population mean or the mean of every score in some population. The sum of the squares for the interaction is SSAB = n times $\Sigma\, 0_{ij}^2$, and n is the number of observations within a cell.

Where $0_{ij} = \bar{x}_{ij} - \bar{x}_{i\cdot} - \bar{x}_{\cdot j} + \bar{x}$ is the estimated cell interaction effect. We can obtain this formula, because a sample mean is the best linear unbiased estimate of the population parameter or mean. It is known that the sum of the interaction effects for a fixed effects design equal 0 for every row and column; therefore, it is only necessary to find the interaction effects for cells 0_{11} and 0_{12}.

$0_{11} = 60-52.5-55+53.7 = 6.25$
$0_{12} = 45-52.5-52.5+53.75 = -6.25$
$0_{21} = 50-55-55+53.75 = -6.25$
$0_{22} = 60-55-52.5+53.75 = 6.25$

Figure 6.15
Adjusted Cell Means

		Treatments (B)	
		1	2
Hypnotic Susceptibility (A)	(1) High	$0_{11} = 6.25$	$0_{12} = -6.25$
	(2) Low	$0_{21} = -6.25$	$0_{22} = 6.25$

0_{ij} is also called an adjusted cell mean, *and these values should be used to graph interactions*. It is common practice of many research design and statistics textbook writers to recommend the graphing of observed cell means. Such graphs can lead to the misinterpretation of interaction effects. This is because interaction effects are residual effects in that lower-order effects must be removed. Essentially, interaction effects are the residual (remaining) effects after the row and column effects are removed, especially if they are statistically significant (Harwell, 1998).

Interaction contrasts can be identified and tested if they are not of the following form: $\mu_{ij}-\mu_{ij\bullet}$.

This type of one-way contrast is most appropriate for one independent variable. The following form is appropriate for factorial designs: $(\bar{Y}_{11}-\bar{Y}_{12}) - (\bar{Y}_{21}-\bar{Y}_{22})$.

If we let C_i denote a contrast for a factorial design,
$t = C_i$ divided by the standard error.
$C_i = W_1\bar{x}_1 + W_2\bar{x}_2 \cdots W_k\bar{x}_k = \sum W_i \, \bar{x}_i$, and $W_{ij}W_2 \cdots W_k$ are the coefficients or weights. And $\bar{x}_k$ is the adjusted cell mean or the unadjusted cell mean. These contrasts can be tested by the following t-test:

$$t = \frac{C_i}{\text{standard error}}$$

Where the standard error is:

$$[MSW(\Sigma W_k^2/n)]^{\frac{1}{2}}$$

n = the cell size.

The reader can read the section on planned comparisons in order to understand the rationale for contrasts; however, the calculations for the one-way and the factorial cases are similar. Finally, Kirk (1995) provides an excellent discussion of how to interpret interactions. He noted that whenever two treatments interact this interaction is referred to as a treatment-contrast interaction. And he notes that the follow-up procedures for such designs can be complex, and researchers have different perspectives for handling such designs.

$$SSAB = 2 [(6.25)^2 + (-6.25)^2 + (-6.25)^2 + (-6.25)^2] = 312.50$$
$$MSAB = SSAB/(I-1) (J-1) = 312.50/(2-1) (2-1) = 312.50$$
$$F(AB) = MSAB/MSW = 312.50/162.50 = 1.92$$

The critical value of F for 1,1 degrees of freedom is 161 at the .05 level; hence $F(AB)(1,1) = 1.92$, $p>.05$. The null hypothesis was not rejected. The reader may encounter designs with random factors. That is, the researcher would like to generalize to some population of treatments, if treatments were the factor with various levels. If a researcher wishes to generalize beyond the factors in a given study, this represents a **random factor**. Also, it is possible to have a **mixed model** in which one factor is **fixed** and the other is random. Hays (1981) discusses the correct error term to use in each case; that is, for fixed and random factors, or some combination thereof. The control lines for running a balance factorial anova are provided below. The same control lines are used for an unbalanced design since the unique sum of squares will be provided, which is the default option of SPSSX.

Test Anxiety: Applied Research

Table 8
Control Lines for Running a Two-Way Anova
With Equal n's on SPSSX

```
Title "two-way anova equal ns"
Data list/gpid1 1 gpid2 3 dep 5-6
begin data
1  1  50
1  1  70
1  2  30
1  2  60
2  1  50
2  1  50
2  2  60
2  2  60
end data
Manova dep by gpid1(1,2)                          1
  gpid2(1,2)/
  design/                                         2
List variables=gpid1 gpid2 dep                    3
```

1 - This produces the factorial ANOVA. The numbers in parentheses are the levels being used for each factor.
2 - Specifies the design, which is gpid1, gpid2, gpid1*gpid2/. For a full model, only design/ is needed.
3 - List provides a listing of the data.

Note: This analysis will also run with unequal ns.

Table 9

SAS Control Lines for Two-Way ANOVA

```
Data Twoway;
Input gpid1 1 gpid2 3 dep 5-6;
Cards;
1   1   50
1   1   70
1   2   30
1   2   60
2   1   50
2   1   50
2   2   60
2   2   60
Proc Print;
Proc GLM;
Class gpid1 gpid2;
Means gpid1 gpid2 gpid1*gpid2;
Model dep=gpid1 gpid2 gpid1*gpid2;
```

Table 10

Below is the selected output from the SPSSX run.

Selected Printout Two-Way ANOVA

Tests of Significance for dep using unique sum of squares					

Source of Variation	SS	DF	MS	F	F sig of F
Within Cells	650.00	4	162.50		
Constant	23112.50	1	23112.50	142.23	.000
GPID1	12.50	1	12.50	.08	.795
GPID2	12.50	1	12.50	.08	.795
GPID1 BY GPID2	312.50	1	312.50	1.92	.238

F sig of F are the probability values for each statistic. Because none of the main effects or the interaction was not less than .05, statistical significance was not found for any main effect or the interaction.

6.8 DISPROPORTIONAL CELL SIZE OR UNBALANCED FACTORIAL DESIGNS

For **disproportional cell size** or **unbalanced factorial designs**, the effects are **correlated** or **confounded**. If the correlation is not accounted for, the results can be misinterpreted. When we calculate a one-way ANOVA, the sum of the squares will be partitioned into two independent sources of variations, in which we previously noted were between and within variation.

With a factorial ANOVA, for equal cell sizes, the sum of the squares for all effects are **independent**. That is, the sum of the squares for the main effects, interaction effects and error effects are independent. For an

A X B design, remember that SSA, SSB and SSAB and SSW are independent. SSA corresponds to the A effect, SSB is the B effect, SSAB is the interaction effect, and SSW is the error effect. Similarly, the variance estimates or mean squares will also be independent. Stevens (1990) notes that there are three approaches to unbalanced factorial designs:

Method 1:   Find the unique contribution of each effect. This is adjusting each effect for every other effect in the design which is called the **regression approach**. On SPSSX, this approach is called the unique sum of squares and is the default option.

Method 2:   Estimate the main effects, disregarding the interaction effect. Now estimate the interaction effect, adjusting it for the main effects. This is the **experimental approach**.

Method 3:   Due to previous research and theory, establish an ordering of effects, then adjust each effect for the preceding effects. This is called the **hierarchical approach**. On SPSSX, this is called the sequential sum of squares. Suppose we had effects in the following order: A,B, A*B, B*C, A*C, A*B*C. In the sequential approach, the main effect A is not adjusted. The main effect B is adjusted for by A effect. The interaction effect A*B is adjusted for by each main effect. The interaction B*C is adjusted for by the A*B interaction and the separate main effects A and B.   A*C is adjusted for by the two interaction effects B*C and A*B and the two main effects. Finally, the second order interaction A*B*C is adjusted for by the three first order interactions A*C, B*C and A*B along with the two main effects A and B.

Table 11 is the command used to obtain the sequential sum of squares on SPSSX for the hierarchical approach, and Tables 11 and 12 are the control lines for a three-way ANOVA.

Table 11

Method = SSTYPE (Sequential)/

Table 12
SPSSX Three-way ANOVA

Higher Order Factorial ANOVA 2 X 2 X 2
Below are the control lines for running a three-way ANOVA.
Title "three-way ANOVA"
Data list/gpid1 1 gpid2 3 gpid3 5 dep 7-8
Begin data
1   1   1   52
1   1   1   57
1   1   1   53
1   1   1   52
1   1   1   56
1   1   1   58
1   1   2   61
1   1   2   61
1   1   2   60
1   1   2   55
1   1   2   60
1   1   2   58
2   2   1   55
2   2   1   55
2   2   1   57
2   2   1   60
2   2   1   65
2   2   1   62
2   2   2   63
2   2   2   60
2   2   2   61
2   2   2   62
2   2   2   64
2   2   2   65
End data
Manova dep by gpid1(1,2), gpid2(1,2), gpid3(1,2)/
List variables = gpid1 gpid2 gpid3 dep

Table 13
SAS Three-way ANOVA

```
Title "Three-way ANOVA";
Data Threeway;
Input gpid1 1 gpid2 3 gpid3 5 dep 7-8;
Cards;
1   1   1   52
1   1   1   57
1   1   1   53
1   1   1   52
1   1   1   56
1   1   1   58
1   1   2   61
1   1   2   61
1   1   2   60
1   1   2   55
1   1   2   60
1   1   2   58
2   2   1   55
2   2   1   55
2   2   1   57
2   2   1   60
2   2   1   65
2   2   1   62
2   2   2   63
2   2   2   60
2   2   2   61
2   2   2   62
2   2   2   64
2   2   2   65
Proc Print;
Proc GLM;
Class gpid1 gpid2 gpid3;
Means gpid1 gpid2 gpid3 gpid1*gpid2
Gpid1*gpid3 gpid2*gpid3
Gpid1*gpid2*gpid3;
Model dep=gpid1|gpid2|gpid3;
```

With higher order factorial designs, the major difficulty is that the overall alpha level can become extremely high. For example, with a three-way factorial design, there are 8 or 2^k sources of variation. The sources are the following: A, B and C main effects, AB, AC and BC first order interactions, ABC second-order interaction, and within cell or error variation. Because several sources of variation exist, these increase the probability that one interaction may be significant simply as the result of chance; therefore, significant interactions must be hypothesized a priori. If an interaction is found to be significant and it was not hypothesized a priori it should be tested at a smaller alpha level like the .02. This is obtained by setting alpha at .05 divided by three, the number of statistical tests in a two-way factorial design.

6.9 PLANNED COMPARISONS AND THE TUKEY POST HOC PROCEDURE

A priori or **planned comparisons** are extremely useful statistical tools for conducting research on test anxiety. Both post hoc procedures and a priori procedures are **multiple comparisons**. These procedures permit a researcher to test differences among means. As the name suggests, post hoc comparisons or procedures are performed after an ANOVA test has been found to be significant.

Some statisticians use the term **a posteriori** in reference to post hoc tests. If an F-test is significant, among K groups there are $K(K-1)/2$ possible pairwise comparisons. For three groups there will be three pairwise comparisons. This can be verified by the formula for combinations. For example, when three (n=3) groups taken r=2 at a time, this can be solved by the following formula for a combination which is:

$$\frac{(n)\ n!}{(r)\ r!(n-r)} = \frac{3(2)(1)}{2(1)(1)} = 3$$

! called a factorial. $n! = n(n-1)\ (n-2) \ldots 1$. By definition $0! = 1$.

A Priori or Planned Comparisons

Before one can understand the meaning of pairwise comparisons, it is necessary to define the term contrast. A **contrast** is the difference among means, given the appropriate algebraic signs (Kirk, 1982, p. 90).

C_i denotes a contrast. A contrast can be expressed as a linear combination of means with the appropriate coefficients, such that at least one contrast is not equal to zero and the coefficients sum to zero. Specifically, a contrast can be expressed as:

$$C_i = w_1\bar{x}_1 + w_2\bar{x}_2 + ... + w_k\bar{x}_k = \Sigma w_i\bar{x}_i$$

Where $w_i, w_2 ... w_k$ correspond to the coefficients or weights.
$\bar{x}_k$ = the mean for group k.

Now the concept of a pairwise comparison becomes sensible. If two **coefficients** of a contrast are two opposite integers, such as 1 and -1 and all other coefficients equal zero, the contrast is called a pairwise comparison; otherwise, it is a nonpairwise comparison (Kirk, 1982, p. 91). It should be noted that the F test does not have to be significant in order to perform a priori or planned comparisons.

Post Hoc Procedures
       Post hoc procedures are used to determine which pairs of means differ significantly. In essence, they are follow-up tests to F-tests according to Kirk (1982, pp. 90-133). Huck, Cormier, and Bounds (1974, pp. 68-72) describe the five basic post hoc comparisons and label them from liberal to conservative, as the following: Fisher's LSD (Least Significant Difference), Duncan's new multiple range test, Newman-Keuls, Tukey HSD (Honestly Significant Difference), and Scheffe's test. The Fisher's LSD is the most liberal; the Scheffe's test is on the other side of the spectrum being extremely conservative. Figure 4 depicts this liberal to conservative continuum for post hoc procedures.
Figure 15

Liberal to Conservative Continuum for Five Commonly Used Post Hoc Procedures
LIBERAL   CONSERVATIVE
Fisher's---Duncan's-Newman-Keuls'--Tukey----------------- Scheffe

Liberal post hoc procedures increase the chance that an experimenter will find statistical significance when two means are relatively close together, while conservative procedures will only indicate statistical significance when two means are relatively far apart. Thus, liberal procedures are more powerful than conservative procedures; however, conservative procedures such as the Scheffe test control type I error better than do liberal procedures.

There is another post hoc test, called the Dunnett's test, it can only be used when one has a control group and wishes to compare each treatment group with a control group. The Dunnett's test can be expressed as the following t statistic:

$$t = \frac{\overline{X}_1 - \overline{X}_2}{\sqrt{MSW \left(\frac{1}{n} + \frac{1)}{n_2)}\right)}}$$

df=N-K or the total sample size minus the number of groups. The critical values for the Dunnett test are found in Table G.

Because there is little agreement of which techniques are the most appropriate, the topic of multiple comparisons has engendered great debate among statisticians. This writer supports the position of Kirk (1982, p. 127), who recommends finding a statistical test that controls type I error and simultaneously provides maximum power.

The Tukey's HSD is one post hoc procedure that fits this recommendation, as it allows a researcher to make any or all pairwise comparisons. Later, the control lines for obtaining the Tukey will be provided.

Many post hoc procedures are a modification of an independent t-test. In contrast to post hoc procedures, a priori or planned comparisons are planned before an experiment is conducted. *Unlike post hoc procedures, it is not necessary for the F-test to be significant to employ planned comparisons.* Planned comparisons are used for **theory testing**, whereas post hoc comparisons are often employed in **exploratory studies** to investigate all possible differences among group means. Planned comparisons can be viewed as more **precise tests** than the global post hoc statistical tests. A priori comparison should be strongly based on theory and/or empirical evidence.

Note that planned comparisons are more powerful than post hoc procedures. In fact, planned comparisons are the most powerful means of statistically testing differences among means (Shavelson 1981, p. 468).

In addition to the assumptions of the oneway ANOVA, planned comparisons have the following three assumptions:
1.   Hypotheses or comparisons are planned and justified prior to conducting a study.
2.   The sum of the weights for each comparison equals zero.
3.   K-1, independent comparisons are performed.

With equal n sizes, two comparisons are independent if the sum of the crossproduct of their corresponding weights equals zero. If sample sizes are not equal, the orthogonality or independence of comparisons can be expressed with the following equation:

$$\frac{w_{11}w_{21}}{n_i} + \frac{w_{12}w_{22}}{n_2} + \cdots \frac{w_{1k}w_{2k}}{n_k} = 0$$

w_{ik}-corresponds to a given weight

n_k-is the corresponding n size for a group.

Suppose we are interested in using planned comparisons to test the effects of hypnosis, relaxation therapy and a Hawthorne control group on the reduction of test anxiety. It is possible to perform K-1 or 2 independent comparisons. Suppose theory suggested that hypnosis would be the most effective treatment, followed by relaxation therapy as the second most effective treatment. The following contrasts or comparisons can be established:

	Hypnosis group	Relaxation therapy group	Hawthorne control group
C_1 -1		1	0
C_2 0		-1	1

C_1-corresponds to set of weights

The crossproduct of the comparisons weights are not equal to zero since, C_1

vs $C_2 = -1(0) + 1(-1) + 0(1) = -1$; therefore, the two comparisons are not independent. However, the statistical procedure for both independent and dependent comparisons is the same.

Two questions can be asked of this data.

1.   Is hypnosis more effective than relaxation therapy?

$C_1 \doteq -\mu_1 + \mu_2$

The $-\mu_1$ indicates a reduction in test anxiety for the hypnosis group.

2.   Is the relaxation therapy more effective than a Hawthorne control group?

$C_2 = -\mu_2 + \mu_3$

The $-\mu_2$ indicates a reduction in test anxiety for the relaxation therapy group.

There is a statistical test to determine if a given contrast differ significantly from 0. The null hypothesis can be stated as:

H_o: $C_1 = 0$, while the alternative hypothesis is H_1: C_1 is not=0.

There are two statistical tests for testing the difference of a contrast. One test makes use of a t-test, the other employs an F-test. The corresponding t and F formulas are:

$$t = \frac{C}{\sqrt{MSW\ \Sigma w_i^2 / n_i}}$$

$$F = \frac{C^2 / \Sigma wi^2 / n_i}{MSW}$$

When the group sizes are equal, the simpler formula that follows can be employed used for testing the difference of contrasts.

$$F = \frac{n\ C^2\ /\ \Sigma wi^2}{MSW}$$

Table 14
SPSSX for Testing Contrasts

SPSSX uses the t test to perform contrast. Below are the control lines for running this analysis of SPSSX.

```
Title `A priori Comparisons'
Data List Free/Gpid TAI
Begin data
1 55 1 58 1 58 1 61 1 51 1 59 1 55 1 59 2 66 2 68 2 55 2 62 2
61 2 62 2 73 2 69 3 66 3 57 3 60 3 54 3 57 3 73 3 62 3 63
End data
Oneway TAI by GPID (1,3)/
 Contrast= -1 1 0/
 Contrast= 0 -1 1/
 Statistics= all
```

The following is the annotated printout for this analysis.

A Priori Comparison By GPID					

A Priori Comparison By GPID			Analysis of Variance		
Source	DF	Sum of Squares	Mean Square	F Ratio	F Prob.
Between Groups	2	228.00	114.00	4.38	.0256
Within Groups	21	546.00	26.00		

Tests for Homogeneity of Variances
Cochrans C = Max. Variance/Sum(Variances) = .4652,
p = .537(Approx.)
Bartlett-Box F = 1.395, P = .248

Table 15
SAS for Testing Contrasts

```
Data Compare;
Input gpid TAI @@;
Cards;
1  55      1  58     1  61     1  51     1  59
1  55      2  66     2  68     2  55     2  62
2  61      2  62     2  73     2  69     3  66
3  57      3  60     3  54     3  57     3  73
3  62      3  63
Proc Print;
Proc Means;
 By gipd;
Proc GLM;
Class gpid;
Model TAI = gpid;
Contrast "gpid1 vs. gpid2"
Gpid -1 1 0;
Contrast "gpid3 vs. gpid3"
Gpid 0 -1 1;
```

Table 16
SPSSX Results of Planned Comparisons

	Pooled Variance Estimate*				
	Value	S. Error	T value	d.f.	T prob
Contrast1	7.500	2.55	2.94	21	.008**
Contrast2	-300	2.55	-1.17	21	.252***

*If the homogeneity assumption is not tenable, the separative variance estimates should be used. One can see that this is not the case since the Cochran's tailed probability is greater than .05.

**This indicates that the first contrast is significant, meaning the hypnosis group significantly reduced test anxiety when compared with the relaxation therapy group.

***This indicates that the second contrast was not significant. This means that the relaxation therapy group did not significantly reduce test anxiety more than the Hawthorne control group.

The reader can confirm how the t value of 2.94 was obtained by substituting into the appropriate formulas.

$C_1 = -1(57) + 1(64.5) + 0(61.5) = 7.5$

$C_1^2 = 56.25$

$F = \dfrac{8(56.25)/2}{26} = 8.65$ df=1 and (N-k) or 1, 21

It is known that $t = \sqrt{F} = 2.94$. The df for $t = (N-K)$

It is left to the reader to confirm the calculation for the second contrast.

Tukey HSD

Even though the formulas for the various post hoc procedures will not be provided, the control lines and the formula for obtaining the Tukey Honestly Significantly Difference (HSD) will be provided. For a thorough discussion of the various post hoc procedures, consult Kirk (1982, pp. 90-133).

Formula for the Tukey Procedure

$$HSD = q\sqrt{\dfrac{MSW}{H_n}}$$

q = the value of the studentized range statistic, which is found in Table D by using the within group degrees of freedom and the number of groups (K). Specifically, we use K, N-K as the degrees of freedom for locating q. Winer (1971, p. 216) defines the studentized range statistic as the difference between the largest and smallest treatment means (range) divided by the square root of the mean square error divided by n or the common group size. The studentized range statistic can be defined with the equation that follows. But first, critical values of studentized range statistic can be found in Table D. In Table D Error df corresponds to the within degrees of freedom and "number of means (p)" corresponds to K, the number of groups.

Formula for q-Studentized Range Statistic

$$q = \frac{\overline{X} \text{ largest} - \overline{X} \text{ smallest}}{\sqrt{MSW/n}}$$

n= the common group from a one-way ANOVA. For factorial designs, n is the number of observations a row or column mean is based upon. Provided the homogeneity assumption is tenable, when there are unequal n's, n can be replaced by the **harmonic mean** or with the harmonic mean of the largest and smallest group size. This can be accomplished by replacing the denominator with

$$\frac{\sqrt{MSW/2}}{(\dfrac{1}{n_{largest}}) + (\dfrac{1}{n_{smallest}})}$$

This latter procedure for unequal n's is conservative in the sense of reducing the nominal alpha level of significance. For example, one can set the nominal alpha level at .05 while the actual alpha level is less than .05, possibly .04. This procedure is not recommended since it tends to reduce statistical power. The harmonic mean, for which the formula follows, is recommended instead and will be employed with the Tukey procedure. When the harmonic mean is used, the formula is referred to as the **Tukey-Kramer procedure**.   We will provide simultaneous confidence intervals employing this procedure.

Formula for Harmonic Mean

H_n = the harmonic mean

H_n = the number of groups divided by the reciprocal of the Ns.

$$H_n = \frac{Ng}{1/N_1 + 1/N_2... + 1/N_j}$$

Ng= the number of groups.

Formula for Simultaneous Confidence Intervals for the Tukey-Kramer Procedure

Simultaneous confidence intervals can be obtained with the following formula:

$$\bar{x}_I - \bar{x}_J \pm q \frac{\sqrt{MSW}}{H_n}$$

$\bar{x}_I$ and $\bar{x}_J$ are the means of two groups. If the confidence interval includes 0, we fail to reject the null hypothesis and conclude that the population means are not different. Below are the control lines for running the Tukey-Kramer procedure and harmonic mean on SPSSX.

Table 17

Obtaining the Tukey Procedure and Harmonic Mean on SPSSX

```
Title "One way ANOVA with the tukey procedure"
Data list/gpid 1 dep 3-4
Begin Data
1 50
1 60
1 70
2 55
2 45
2 35
3 30
3 38
3 29
End data
Oneway dep by gpid(1,3)/                    1
    ranges=tukey/                           2
    Harmonic= all/                          3
    statistics= all/                        4
List variables=gpid dep
```

1 - Oneway is the code name for one way ANOVA.
2 - Ranges =tukey is the subcommand for the tukey procedure.
3 - List variables provides a listing of the data.
4 - Provides the harmonic mean.

Obtaining the Tukey Procedure on SAS

```
Data Tukey;
Input gpid 1 dep 3-4;
Cards:
1 50
1 60
1 70
2 55
2 45
2 35
2 30
3 30
3 38
3 29
Proc Means;
By gpid;
Proc ANOVA;
Class gpid;
Model dep = gpid;
Means gpid/Tukey;
Proc Print;
```

Exercises

1. The data below represent TAI scores for three treatment groups. Run the data using SPSSX and SAS.

T1	T2	T3
53	56	55
55	55	53
52	56	54
54	54	55
54	55	52
53	53	54

What is the value of the test statistic? (2.26)
Was statistical significance found? no
Write the result of this analysis in journal form.
$F_{(2,15)}=2.26$, $p>.05$.

2. Rerun number 1, but insert the command for the Tukey post hoc test. Were any group means statistically different? (No).
3. Rerun number 1, and perform the following contrasts:

^	T1	T2	T3
C_1	-1	1	0
^			
C_2	0	1	-1

Discuss the results in terms of test anxiety from the analysis.
The results indicated that neither contrast was significant. Contrast 1 had a t value of 2.043 and a probability value of .059; contrast 2 had a t-value of 1.532 and a probability value of .146. The results indicated that treatment 1 did not significantly reduce test anxiety more than treatment 2, nor did treatment 3, significantly reduce test anxiety more than treatment 2.

4. The data below represents a study of males and females randomly assigned to three treatment conditions. The dependent variable is the TAI. Using SPSSX and SAS, perform the appropriate statistical analysis on the data. Is there a GPID1 by GPID2 interaction? If so, is the interaction significant at the .05 level? (Yes)

GPID1	GPID2	TAI
1	1	66
1	1	67
1	2	63
1	2	59
1	2	58
1	3	65
1	3	63
2	1	56
2	1	60
2	1	58
2	2	61
2	2	58
2	2	58
2	3	62

5. How would you classify the design in number 4?
    (unbalanced 2 X 3 design)
6. Let us consider the calculations for a 2 X 3 design with three scores
    per cell. This time, A(1) and A(2) correspond to the two levels of
    hypnotic susceptibility and B represents the three levels of treatment.

Treatments (B)

	1	2	3	Row Means
	62,66,67	63,59,58	64,65,63	
(1) High	$\bar{x}=65$ high (1) hypnotic susceptibility row A (1)	$\bar{x}=60$	$\bar{x}=64$	Row Mean A (1) $\bar{x}_{1.} = 63$
	56,60,58	61,58,58	62,60,68	
Hypnotic Suscepti- bility (A) (2) Low	$\bar{x}=58$ low (2) hypnotic susceptibility row A (2)	$\bar{x}=59$	$\bar{x}=60$	Row Mean A (2) $\bar{x}_{2.} = 59$
	$\bar{x}_{.1}=61.5$ column mean	$\bar{x}_{.2}=59.5$ column mean	$\bar{x}_{.3}=62$ column mean $\bar{x}=61$ Grand Mean	

The scores in this design represent the TAI scores for subjects who had high and low susceptibility to hypnosis and who were randomly assigned to three groups: relaxation therapy, hypnosis and systematic desensitization. As you remember, the dot notation above $\bar{x}_{1.}$ indicates rows the dot notation in the first part of the of the subscript indicates columns.

Let us go through the steps we used earlier. First, we will test the main effects of factor A. The null hypothesis for the row effect is H_o: $\mu_{1.}$ = $\mu_{2.}$ =...$\mu_{1.}$. This indicates that the population means are equal. From the above table $\bar{x}_{1.}$ =63 = $\mu 1.$ and $\bar{x}_{2.}$ =59 are the estimates of the population means for the subjects with high and low susceptibility to hypnosis. The "I" in the above notation indicates rows.

The null hypothesis for the B main effect is:
H_o: $\mu_{.1} = \mu_{.2} = \mu_{.J}$. This denotes the population are equal. Again,
$\bar{x}_1 = 61.5 = \mu_{.1}$, $\bar{x}_2 = 59.5 = \mu_{.2}$ and $\bar{x}_3 = 62 = \mu_{.3}$. These are estimates of
the population columns. The "J" above indicates the column. Thus, this
is a I X J design. That is, there are two levels of A (susceptibility-high
and low) and three levels of treatments.

Sum of the Squares for a balance factorial design
        Now let us calculate the sum of squares. Remember, that a balanced
design means that there are an equal number of observations per cell. It
is now possible to find the sum of squares of A, which is denoted by the
following notation:

SSA = $nJ \Sigma$ $(\bar{x}_{i.} - \bar{x})^2$ The nJ is the number of observation upon which
each row is based. The sum of the squares reflects the variability of the
row means about the grand mean. For this example SSA is:

SSA =3(3) $[(63 - 61)^2 + (59 - 61)^2] = 72$

Our next step is find the mean sum of squares which is:

MSA = SSA/ (I-1)= 72/1 = 72

Now we can determine the sum of squares for factor B. Again, the SSB
= $nI \Sigma$ $(\bar{x}_{.j} - \bar{x})^2$. This reflects the variability of the column means about
the grand mean. For our example, it is:

SSB =3(2) [$(61.5 - 61)^2 + (59.5 - 61)^2 + (62-61)^2 = 21$

Now, the mean sum of squares of B (MSB) is:
MSB = SSB/ (J-1)=21/2=10.5

Error Term
        It was stated earlier that the error term represents the pooled within
cell variability. Basically, for every cell, we take each score and deviate
it about the cell mean, square the deviation and add the deviations across
all the cells. Using the same formula presented earlier, the error term
(SSW) is:

$SS_w = \Sigma (x - \bar{x}_{ij})^2$
  cells

$SSW = (62\text{-}65)^2 + (66\text{-}65)^2 + (67\text{-}65)^2 \ldots (62\text{-}60)^2 + (60\text{-}60)^2 +$
$(68\text{-}60)2 = 52$

$MSW = SSW/(N\text{-}IJ) = 52/(18\text{-}6) = 4.33$ This represents the average of the cell variances.

The Main Effects for the F-Tests

Now, we can test the main effects for the F-tests.
$F(A) = MSA/MSW = 72/4.33 = 16.63(1,12)$ $p<.05$ The numbers in parentheses are the degrees of freedom which are I-1 and N-IJ or 1,12. The critical value at the .05 level is 4.75. Since the absolute value of the test statistic is greater than the critical value of F, we reject the null hypothesis and assume statistical significance at the .05 level. $F(A)$ listed above is the way statistics are usually presented in APA journals. The $F(B) = MSB/MSW = 10.5/4.33 = 2.42$. The degrees of freedom is J-1, N-IJ or 3-1, 18- 2x3 which is (2, 12). The critical for these degrees of freedom at the .05 level is 3.88. This critical value of F was found in Table C. In summary, the results for $F(B) = 2.42(2,12)$ $p>.05$. This indicates that the null hypothesis was not rejected, or the population columns means are equal.

Interaction

The sum of the square for the interaction is $SSAB = n \Sigma 0_{ij}^2$
Where $0_{ij} = \bar{x}_{ij} - \bar{x}_{i.} - \bar{x}_{.j} + \bar{x}$ is the estimated cell interaction effect.

It is known that the sum of the interaction effects for a fixed effects design equal 0 for every row and column; therefore, it is only necessary to find the interaction effects for cells 0_{11} and 0_{12}.

$0_{11} = 65\text{-}63\text{-}61.5 + 61 = 1.5$ (cell 1 1)
$0_{12} = 60\text{-}63\text{-}59.5 + 61 = -1.5$ (cell 1 2)
$SSAB = 3 [(1.5)^2 + (-1.5)^2 + (-1.5)^2 + (1.5)^2] = 27$
$MSAB = SSAB/(I\text{-}1)(J\text{-}1) = 27/(2\text{-}1)(3\text{-}1) = 13.5$
$F(AB) = MSAB/MSW = 13.5/4.33 = 3.12$

The critical value for 2,12 degrees of freedom is 3.88, hence $F(AB)(2,12)=3.12$, $p>.05$. The null hypothesis was not rejected.

Table 18
Control Line for Running a Two-way ANOVA
with Equal n's on SPSSX

Title "two way ANOVA equal ns"		
Data List/gpid1 1 gpid2 3 dep 5-6		
Begin data		
1	1	62
1	1	66
1	1	67
1	2	63
1	2	59
1	2	58
1	3	64
1	3	65
1	3	63
2	1	56
2	1	60
2	1	58
2	2	61
2	2	58
2	2	58
2	3	62
2	3	60
2	3	58
End data		
Manova dep by gpid1(1,2)		
gpid2(1,3)/ design/		
List variables=gpid1 gpid2 dep		

(annotations in inset box)
1
2
3

1 - This produces the factorial ANOVA. The numbers in parentheses are the level being used for each factor.

2 - Specifies the design, which is gpid1,gpid2,gpid1*gpid2/. For a full
model only design/ is needed.

3 - List provides a listing of the data.

Table 19

Below is the selected output from the SPSSX run.

Tests of Significance for dep using unique sum of squares					
Source of Variation	SS	DF	MS	F	F sig of F
Within Cells	52.00	12	4.33		
Constant	66978.00	1	66978.00	15456.46	.000
GPID1	72.00	1	72.00	16.62	.002*
GPID2	21.00	2	10.50	2.42	.131
GPID1 By GPID2	27.00	2	13.50	3.12	.081

*Indicates that statistical significance is reached since the two-tailed
probability level is less than .05.

Run this design on SPSSX, and compare your results with the ones
listed above from both the computer run and the actual calculations.

6.10 ONE-WAY ANALYSIS OF COVARIANCE

*Earlier it was noted that the analysis of covariance (ANCOVA) is
used for randomized pre-post control group designs.* Suppose 21 test
anxious subjects who scored above the mean of the TAI are pretested and
randomly assigned to a covert modeling group (Treatment 1), systematic
desensitization group (Treatment 2) and a group to monitor study
behavior (Treatment 3). Provided that the assumptions of ANCOVA are

met, ANCOVA would be the appropriate statistical analysis. Schematically, the design is presented below:

Table 20
One-Way Analysis of Covariance

Treatment1		Treatment2		Treatment3	
Pretest	X Posttest	Pretest	X Posttest	Pretest	X Posttest
<u>01</u>	<u>02</u>	<u>01</u>	<u>02</u>	<u>01</u>	<u>02</u>
53	56	54	58	53	56
51	54	55	59	52	57
53	55	55	57	52	57
51	53	54	59	53	57
52	54	53	58	54	58
51	53	51	55	51	55
54	56	52	57	54	57

01 is the covariate or pretest.
02 is the dependent variable or posttest.
X indicates treatment.

ANCOVA blends techniques of regression with ANOVA which permits statistical rather than experimental control of variables. ANCOVA involves the use of a pretest or covariate, which is the variable to be controlled, and a posttest (criterion). The pretest is correlated with the posttest, thereby permitting one variable to predict the other. ANCOVA determines the proportion of the variance of a posttest that existed prior to experimentation, this proportion is removed from the final statistical analysis. ANCOVA is used to adjust the posttest means on the basis of the pretest(covariate) means. Then the adjusted means [$*\bar{y}_i = \bar{y}_i - b(\bar{x}_i - \bar{x}_g)$] are compared to see if they are significantly different from each other. In the above equation for the adjusted mean, $*\bar{y}_i$ equals the adjusted mean of the posttest or dependent variable. $\bar{y}_i$ is the mean of the dependent variable scores for group i, while -b is the slope or regression coefficient. $\bar{x}_i$ is the mean of the covariate scores for group i. Finally, $\bar{x}_g$ is the grand mean of the covariate scores. Like ANOVA, ANCOVA is a linear model with the following structural model: $y_{ij} = \mu + \alpha_j + b(X_i - \bar{x}_g) + e_{ij}$

The only difference between this linear model and that of the one-way ANOVA is the regression expression $+b(X_i - \bar{x}_g)$, which is used to find the regression of Y on X. Also, it is used in the regression equation to predict Y values from X values.

ANCOVA is a statistical method of controlling for the selection threat to internal validity. Note that it is only controlling for covariate(s) within an experiment; therefore, groups could conceivably differ on other variables not used in the experiment. Hence, ANCOVA is not a complete control for the selection threat like randomization. Earlier it was reported that the dependent measure t-test is more powerful than the t-test for independent samples. Similarly, when comparing ANCOVA to ANOVA, ANCOVA is a more powerful test statistic. Like ANOVA, ANCOVA has assumptions; three are the same as those of ANOVA and three are unique.

Assumptions of ANCOVA

1. Normality
2. Homogeneity of variance
3. Independence
4. Linearity—a linear relationship between the covariate and dependent variable.
5. One covariate—the assumption is homogeneity of regression slopes.
   Two covariates—parallelism of regression planes.
   More than two covariates—homogeneity of regression hyperplanes.
6. The covariate is measured without error.

The first three assumptions were discussed with ANOVA; therefore, any violation of the assumptions are the same as those that occurred with ANOVA. Even though this is not an assumption of ANCOVA, Stevens (1990, p. 163) recommends limiting the number of covariates to the extent that the following inequality holds:

$C + (J-1)/N < .10$

C-is the covariate.

J-is the number of groups.

N-is the total sample size.

    If the above inequality holds, the adjusted means are likely to be stable. That is, the results should be reliable and cross-validated (Stevens, 1990, p. 163). The Johnson-Neyman technique is recommended when the homogeneity of regression slopes assumption is violated (Stevens, ibid). Shortly, the control lines for running the ANCOVA on SPSSX will be presented. It is important to check the linearity and homogeneity assumptions from the SPSSX computer printout.

Table 21

Control lines for running one-way ANCOVA

Title "one-way ANCOVA"	1
Data List List/gpid pretest posttest	
Begin data	
1 53 56	
1 51 54	
1 53 55	
1 51 53	
1 52 54	
1 51 53	
1 54 56	
2 54 58	
2 55 59	
2 55 57	
2 54 59	
2 53 58	
2 51 55	
2 52 57	
3 53 56	
3 52 57	
3 52 57	
3 53 57	
3 54 58	
3 51 55	
3 54 57	
End data	
Manova pretest posttest by gpid(1,3)/	2
analysis= posttest with pretest/	3
print=pmeans/	4
design/	5
analysis=posttest/	
design=pretest,gpid,pretest by gpid/	
analysis=pretest/	

5 - The format for this design subcommand is **covariate,grouping variable,covariate by grouping variable**.

1 - List—tells the computer that it will be in order of the data list command. The only requirements of the List format is that data is separated by a space.
2 - The covariate follows the key word with
3 - provides adjusted means
4 - tests homogeneity of regression slopes
5 - this tests if the pretests differ significantly from each other.

Table 22
SPSSX Control Lines for Testing the Homogeneity Assumption
with Two Covariates

For two covariates, the control lines for testing the homogeneity of assumption are as follows:
analysis=posttest/
design=pretest1+pretest2,gpid,pretest1 by gpid+pretest2 by gpid/

Note when multiple covariates (two or more) are employed, simple linear regression is no longer applied. This situation requires multiple regression, a statistical procedure that finds predictors which are maximally correlated with a dependent variable. Logically, the formula for the adjusted means becomes:

$$*\bar{y}_i = \bar{y}_i - b_i(\bar{x}_{ij} - \bar{x}_1) - b_2(\bar{x}_{2j} - \bar{x}_2) - \dots - b_k(\bar{x}_{uj} - \bar{x}_k)$$

b_i are regression coefficients, $\bar{x}_{1j}$ is the mean for covariate 1 in group J, $\bar{x}_{2j}$ is the mean for covariate 2 in group j, and so on. Finally, $\bar{x}_1$ $\bar{x}_2 .. \bar{x}_k$ are the grand means for the covariates.

SAS ANCOVA

```
Data Ancova;
Input gpid pretest posttest @@;
Cards;
1   52  56   1   51  54   1   53  55   1   51  53
1   52  54   1   51  53   1   54  56   2   54  58
2   55  59   2   55  57   2   54  59   2   53  58
2   51  55   2   52  57   3   53  56   3   52  57
3   52  57   3   53  57   3   54  58   3   51  55
3   54  57
Proc Print;
Proc GLM;
Classes gpid;
Model posttest = Pretest gpid gpid*pretest;
Proc GLM;
Model Posttest = Pretest gpid;
LSMeans gpid/PDIFF;
```

Table 23
Selected Output from SPSSX ANCOVA run

Tests of significance for posttest using the unique sum of squares source of variation

	SS	DF	MS	F	Sig of F
Within cells	10.30	17	.61		
Regression	16.56	1	16.56	27.32	.000*
Constant	3.13	1	3.13	5.16	.036
GPID	16.93	2	8.47	13.97	.000**

Test Anxiety: Applied Research

The F ratio for ANCOVA=(SSb*/(K-1))/SSw*/(N-K-C)=MSb*/MSw*

C is the number of covariates, and one degree of freedom for the error term is lost for every covariate employed.

Tests of significance for pretest using the unique sum of squares source of variation

	SS	DF	MS	F	Sig of F
Within+ residual	9.63	15	.64		
Constant	2.88	1	2.88	4.49	.051
Pretest	15.67	1	15.67	24.40	.000
GPID	.83	2	.41	.65	.538
Pretest by GPID	.67	2	.33	.52	.605***

Tests of significance for pretest using the unique sum of squares source of variation

	SS	DF	MS	F	Sig of F
Within Cells	30.00	18	1.67		
Constant	58460.19	1	58460.19	35076	.000
GPID	5.81	2	2.90	1.74	.203****

* This indicates a significant relationship between the covariate and the dependent variable.

**These are the main results of ANCOVA. The results indicate the adjusted population means are unequal, indicating statistical significance.

***This is the test of homogeneity of regression slopes. The slopes are not significantly different; hence, the assumption is tenable.

****This indicates that the subjects on the three pretest did not differ.

Exercises
1. Run the data given with the one-way ANCOVA example. First, run the data as a simple one-way ANOVA, omitting the covariate. On the second run, include the covariate. Compare your results.
2. Use the following equation to verify the adjusted means from the ANCOVA run of exercise 1. $*\bar{y}_i = \bar{y} - b(\bar{x}_i - \bar{x}_g)$. Compare your results.

6.11 POST HOC PROCEDURES FOR ANCOVA
Stevens (1990) and Kirk (1982) recommend the Bryant-Paulson procedure, which is a generalization of the Tukey procedure, as a post hoc test for ANCOVA. There are two formulas for this procedure, one for randomized designs and another for non-randomized designs. The randomized and nonrandomized formulas are given below:

randomized design:

$$\frac{\bar{y}* - \bar{y}*}{\sqrt{Msw*[1+Msb_x/Ms_{wx}]/n}}$$

nonrandomized design:

$$\frac{\bar{y}i* - \bar{y}j*}{\sqrt{Msw*([2/n + (\bar{x}_i - \bar{x}_j)^2/SS_{wx}]/2}}$$

n is the common group size

If the group sizes are unequal, the harmonic mean is used.

Msw* is the error term for the covariance.

Msb_x and Ms_{wx} are the mean between and within sums of squares from the analysis of variance on the covariate only.

Let us conduct three post hoc tests for the ANCOVA example, assuming a nonrandomized design.

Groups 1 and 2

$$\frac{54.89 - 57.08}{(.61[2/7 + (54.43 - 57.57)^2 /30]/2)^{1/2}} = -5.06$$

Group 2 and 3

$$\frac{57.08 - 56.75}{(.61[2/7 + (57.57 - 56.71)^2 /30]/2)^{1/2}} = 1.07$$

Groups 1 and 3

$$\frac{54.98 - 56.75}{(.61[2/7 + (54.43 - 56.71)^2 /30]/2)^{1/2}} = -4.97$$

With an alpha level of .05, one covariate, three groups and 17 (N-J-C) error degrees of freedom, the critical value of the Bryant-Paulson Procedure is 3.68. This value was found in Table E. Therefore, we can conclude that groups 1 and 2 and groups 1 and 3 are significantly different, while groups 2 and 3 are not significantly different.

6.12 SPSSX CONTROL LINES FOR FACTORIAL ANALYSIS OF COVARIANCE

The control lines for factorial analysis of variance are basically a generalization of the ones for one-way ANCOVA and factorial ANOVA; therefore, factorial ANCOVA is a logical combination of factorial ANOVA and the one-way ANCOVA. The following are the control lines for running a factorial ANCOVA design.

Title "Factorial Ancova"
Data List Free/gpid1 gpid2 dep covar
List
Begin data
1   1   95   40
1   1   70   20
1   2   80   30
1   2   40   90
1   3   40   70
1   3   30   90
2   1   50   70
2   1   80   70
2   2   90   70
2   2   35   95
2   3   95   50
2   3   85   35
End data
Manova covar dep by gpid1 (1,2) gpid2 (1,3)/
          Method = SSTYPE (Unique)/
          Analysis dep with covar/
          Print = pmeans/
          Design/
          Analysis = dep/
          Design = covar, gpid1, gpid2, covar by gpid1 gpid2/
          Analysis = covar/

6.13 NESTED DESIGNS

We stated in Chapter 4 that nested designs are called incomplete designs. Usually, one level of one factor is paired with one level of another factor. This is called a completely nested design. Suppose we were interested in the extent that students' test anxiety depended on their schools and teachers. We get three schools to participate in our study, and each school has two teachers who are willing to participate. Next, we are able to randomly assign three students to teachers' classes during an exam phase. We can treat the schools as levels of Factor A and the teachers as levels of Factor B, and we have a 6 X 3 design with three test anxiety scores in each cell. Essentially, students are nested within classes and schools. Schematically, this design can be depicted as:

6 X 3 Nested Design

	A1	A2	A3
B1	70, 68, 64		
B2	69, 70, 70		
B3		64, 68, 64	
B4		62, 62, 59	
B5			63, 66, 63
B6			59, 54, 54

Each level of Factor B is associated or paired with one level of A; in contrast, each level of Factor A is connected with two levels of Factor B. Below are the SPSSX control lines for running this design.

SPSSX Nested Design

Title "Nested design for TAI scores"
Data list free/Teachers Schools dep
List
Begin data

1	1	70
1	1	68
1	1	64
2	1	69
2	1	70
2	1	70
3	2	64
3	2	68
3	2	64
4	2	62
4	2	62
4	2	59
5	3	63
5	3	66
5	3	63
6	3	59
6	3	54
6	3	54

End data
Manova dep by Teachers (1,6) Schools (1,3)/
    Design = Schools, Teachers, Teachers within schools[1]

[1]The within command indicates that teachers were nested within schools.

To summarize, we described a 6 X 3 nested design. The term nested suggested that dependent variables will not be in every cell; hence, these are called incomplete designs. Factor B was nested with Factor A. The design notation for this would be B(A). This means that Factor B is nested within Factor A. The following are the SAS control lines for nested ANOVA, and a discussion of how to calculate the sum of squares is provided.

SAS Nested Design

```
Data Nested;
Input Teachers Schools Dep;
Cards;
Data Lines
Proc ANOVA;
Class teachers--Schools;
Model Dep = Teachers|Schools|Teachers (Schools);
Means Teachers|Schools;
Test H=Teachers Teachers*Schools E=Teachers*Schools (Schools);
```

The sum of squares for a nested factor (SS_{nf}) can be calculated as a residual or through subtraction using the following:

$$SS_{nf} = SS_{cells} - SS_b = SS_t - SS_b - SS_w$$

For example, if $SS_t = 235.00$, $SS_b = 112.50$, and $SS_w = 18.50$, $SS_{nf} = 104$, which is the sum of the squares for the nested factor. For fixed effects models, the nested factor is not a random effect, the means squares within cells is used for post hoc and planned comparisons, and for mixed models, the nested factor is a random effect, the appropriate error term is the means squares for the nested factor. In summary, careful thought must be used in determining the appropriate error term for nested designs.

Finally, nested designs do not allow one to separate main effects from interaction effects. If effects cannot be separated, they are said to be confounded. When a design is not completely cross, some factors will be confounded. The table that follows provides the degrees of freedom for the nested ANOVA.

Degrees of Freedom for Nested ANOVA

Source	Df
A	I-1
B(A)	I(J-1)
Error	N-I

6.14 SUMMARY

In summary, this chapter described three sampling distributions or theoretical probability distributions that are important in order to conduct research on test anxiety. First, we described the normal distribution. It should be understood that the normal distribution is a special case of the t-distribution. For example, using Table A, a z-score of 1.96 cuts off 95% of the area under the normal curve; one of 2.58 cuts off 99% of the area. When 95% of the area under the normal curve is cut off, 5% is equally distributed between the two tails with 2 1/2% on each tail. A similar finding occurs for the z that corresponds to 99% of the area under the normal curve. Using table A, if one located a two-tailed t value with infinity degrees of freedom at the .05 level, it becomes apparent that this value corresponds to the probability of obtaining a z score at the .05 level of significance, which is 1.96. The same thing will occur for a two-tailed critical value of t at the .01 level where the critica' value is 2.58.

In this chapter, the second distribution described that is related to the normal curve is the t-distribution. It was noted earlier that a t value squared equals F. Using table C, if we locate an F value with 1 and 6 degrees of freedom at the .05 level of significance, the value equals 5.99. Now, if we locate a critical value of t with 6 degrees of freedom at the .05 level of significance for a two-tailed test, the value is 2.447, which is the square root of F.

The third distribution described in this chapter was the F-distribution, which is a special case of a distribution called Chi-Square. If a critical value from the F-distribution, with degrees of freedom of the denominator set at infinity is multiplied by the degrees of freedom of the numerator, the result is a critical value of the Chi-Square distribution with the same degrees of freedom as the numerator of the F-distribution. For example, a critical value of F at the .05 level of significance with 6 and infinity degrees of freedom at the .05 level is 2.10. If we multiply 2.10 by 6, the result is 12.6; this is the critical value of Chi-Square with 6 degrees of freedom at the .05 level of significance. The exact value of Chi-Square found in table J is 12.592; but when rounded to the nearest tenth, it equals 12.6. In summary, there is a relationship among the normal, t, F, and Chi-Square distributions. Figure 16 depicts the t distribution, and Figures 17 and 18 illustrate the F and Chi-Square distribution, respectively.

Figure 16
t-distribution
degree of freedom =∞

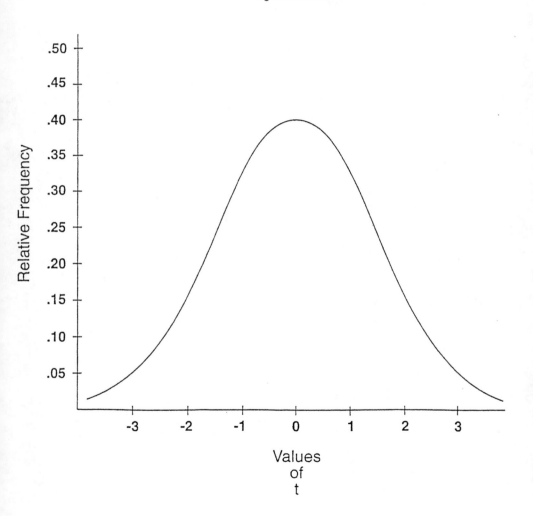

Test Anxiety: Applied Research

Figure 17
F distribution

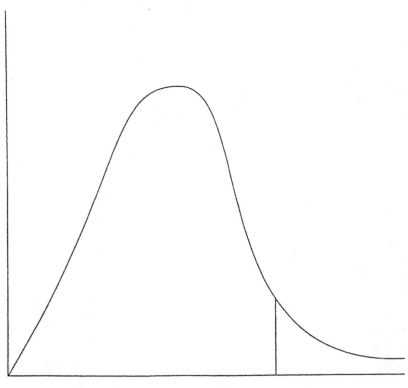

Critical
Value
of
F

Figure 18
Chi Square distribution

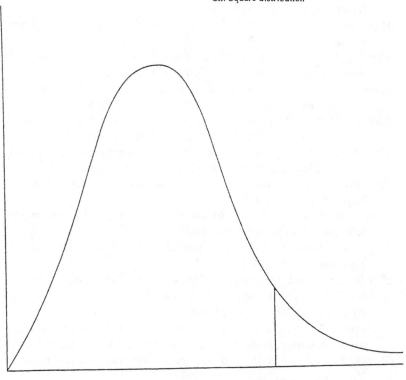

Critical
Value
of
χ^2

References

Cohen, J. (1988). *Statistical power analysis for the behavioral sciences* (3rd ed.). New York: Academic Press.

Harwell, M. (1998). Misinterpreting interaction effects in analysis of variance. *Measurement and Evaluation in Counseling and Development, 31*(2), 125-136.

Hays, W. (1981). *Statistics* (3rd ed.). New York: Holt, Rinehart and Winston.

Heppner, P. P., Kivlighan, D. M., & Wampold, B. E. (1992). *Research design in counseling*. Pacific Grove, CA: Brooks/Cole.

Huck, S. W., Cormier, W. L., & Bounds, W. G. (1974). *Reading statistics and research*. New York: Harper and Row.

Kirk, R. (1982). *Experimental design: Procedures for the behavioral sciences* (2nd ed.). Pacific Grove, CA: Brooks/Cole.

Kirk, R. (1995). *Experimental design: Procedures for the behavioral sciences* (3rd ed.). Pacific Grove, CA: Brooks/Cole.

Rummel, R. J. (1970). *Applied factor analysis*. Evanston, IL: Northwestern University Press.

Shavelson, R. J. (1981). *Statistical reasoning for the behavioral sciences*. Boston: Allyn and Bacon.

Siegel, S. (1956). *Nonparametric statistics for the behavioral sciences*. New York: McGraw-Hill.

SPSSX User's guide (3rd ed.). (1988). Chicago: SPSS, Inc.

Stevens, J. P. (1990). *Intermediate statistics: A modern approach*. Hillsdale, NJ: Lawrence Erlbaum.

Welkowitz, J., Ewen, R. B., & Cohen, J. (1982). *Introductory statistics for the behavioral sciences* (3rd ed.). New York: Academic Press.

Winer, B. J. (1971). *Statistical principles in experimental design*. New York: McGraw-Hill.

Chapter 7

CONTENTS

Multivariate Research Statistical Methodology Using SPSSX Computer Software:

7.1 ONE-GROUP REPEATED MEASURES ANOVA

The **one-group repeated measures ANOVA (analysis of variance)** can be viewed as an extension of the repeated measures t-test. With the repeated measures t-test, one group of subjects is measured repeatedly at two points in time. With the repeated measures ANOVA, however, one group of subjects is measured at three or more points in time. Just as the repeated measures t-test is more powerful than the independent measures t-test, the repeated measures ANOVA is more powerful than the ANOVA for k independent groups. The reader should note that sometimes K independent group designs are referred to as between-group designs. Note that there are many names for the repeated measures ANOVA, including **Linquist Type I, blocked designs, split-plot ANOVA, within-subjects design with repeated measures on one factor, two-way ANOVA with repeated measures on one factor, treatments-by-subjects designs, and mixed designs.**

In many situations, the repeated measures design is the only design of choice. For example, the repeated measures ANOVA is useful for measuring educational performance over time. Similarly, with clinical populations where subjects' availability is limited, repeated measures designs are the ones of choice. Unlike between-subjects or completely randomized designs, repeated measures designs require fewer subjects because the same subject serves as his or her own controls. Not only is this beneficial in reducing the number of subjects required, but it also reduces within-group variability or individual differences among subjects.

Essentially, with the repeated measures ANOVA, variability due to *individual differences is removed from the error term*. This is what makes the repeated measures design more powerful than a between-groups design or a completely randomized design, where different subjects are randomly assigned to different treatments.

7.2 ASSUMPTIONS OF REPEATED MEASURES ANOVA

The three assumptions of the repeated measures design are as follows:
1. Independence of observations
2. Multivariate normality
3. Sphericity or circularity-homogeneity of variance for the difference scores for all pairs of repeated measures, or equality of variances for all difference variables. This statistic is found on the SPSSX and SAS printout as the Greenhouse-Geisser Epsilon. This assumption

is tenable if the **Greenhouse-Geisser Epsilon** equals one. The worst possible violation of the sphericity assumption occurs when the value of the Greenhouse-Geisser Epsilon = $1/(k-1)$, where k is the number of repeated measures (Greenhouse & Geisser, 1959; Keppel, 1982; Stevens, 1990).

The reader can recall that the first assumption, independence of observations, was discussed in chapter 6. It was noted that this is a serious violation. The same holds true for a repeated measures ANOVA. Also, recall from chapter 6 that the independent t-test and the independent k group ANOVA are robust to the violation of the normality assumption. Shortly, the reader will notice a similar finding for the repeated measures ANOVA. In terms of multivariate normality, Stevens (1986, p. 205) and Johnson and Wichern (1988, pp. 120-168) stated three necessary conditions for its tenability. *First*, each variable must approach normality. *Second*, linear combinations of any variables are normally distributed. *Third*, all subsets of variables have a multivariate distribution. That is, all pairs of variables must be bivariate normal. Do not be concerned with the multivariate normality assumption since Stevens (1986, p. 207) and Bock (1975, pp. 104-163) presented evidence that the repeated measures ANOVA is robust to the violation of this assumption, which is the same thing that occurred in chapter 6 with the t-test for independence and the F-test for k independent groups (Stevens, 1996).

7.3 VIOLATIONS OF THE SPHERICITY ASSUMPTION

If the **sphericity assumption** is violated, the type I error rate of the repeated measures ANOVA is **positively biased**. That is, the null hypothesis is rejected falsely too often. When this assumption is violated, Huynh and Feldt (1976) and Stevens (1986, p. 413) recommend adjusting the degrees of freedom of the numerator and denominator from $(k-1)$ and $(k-1)(n-1)$, respectively, to $ê(k-1)$ and $ê(k-1)(n-1)$. Where k is the number of repeated measures or the number of treatments; n is the number of subjects within a treatment, while ê is the Greenhouse-Geisser Epsilon statistic obtained from the SPSSX printout. These new degrees of freedom are used to locate the critical value of F to test for statistical significance.

Other tests of sphericity can be obtained from SPSSX; however, Stevens (1986, p. 414) and Kesselman, Rogan, Mendoza, and Breen (1980) argue that these tests, like their univarite counterparts, are sensitive to violations of multivariate normality; therefore, these tests are not recommended.

7.4 CONTROVERSY IN CALCULATIONS OF GREENHOUSE EPISILON STATISTICS

It should be noted that recently a controversy occurred in terms of the calculation of the Greenhouse-Geisser Epsilon statistic. In the *Journal of Educational Statistics*, Le Countre (1991, p. 371) reported that the routine formula that is used to calculate the Greenhouse-Geisser Epsilon statistic, when the condition of circularity is not fulfilled, may lead to a substantial underestimation of the deviation from circularity, especially when the number of subjects is small. Similarly, he reported that this routine formula, which is the one used by SPSSX is erroneous in the case of two or more groups. Therefore, he recommended the following corrected formula when the number of groups (g) $\geq$ 2: Greenhouse-Geisser Epsilon = ϵ'

$$\epsilon' = \frac{(N-g+1)r\hat{e}-2}{r(N-g-r\hat{e})}$$

Where r is the orthogonal (uncorrelated) normalized variables associated with each within-subject factor and their interactions

$$\text{Where } \hat{e} = \frac{k^2(\bar{s}_{ii} - \bar{s})^2}{(k-1)(\sum\sum s_{ij}^2 - 2k\sum\bar{s}_i^2 + k^2\bar{s}^2)}$$

k is the number of levels for the within variable
s is the mean of all entries in the covariance matrix S
s_{ii} is the mean of entries on the main diagonal of S
s_i is the mean of all entries in row i of S
s_{ij} is the ijth entry of S

Clearly the repeated measures ANOVA requires fewer subjects than does a k independent group design. Similarly, the repeated measures ANOVA removes individual differences from the repeated measures F-test; however, there are disadvantages such as carry-over effects from one treatment to the next, which can make interpretations difficult. From

Chapter 4, the reader can remember that **counterbalancing** is a method of handling carry-over effects in one-group designs. Suppose we wanted to know the effects of four treatments supportive counseling, relaxation therapy, systematic desensitization, and hypnosis on reducing test anxiety in a group of five subjects. Schematically, this one-group repeated measures design can be depicted as:

Table 1

One-Group Repeated Measures Design

Subjects	Treatments for Test Anxiety				
	1	2	3	4	Row Means
1	50	48	36	54	47
2	34	38	30	42	36
3	44	40	38	50	43
4	58	54	40	64	54
5	46	48	34	50	44.5
Column Means	46.4	45.6	35.6	52	

Grand Mean = 44.9
Overall Standard Deviation = 8.86

Completely Randomized Univariate Repeated Measures Analysis

SS_b = Sums of squares for the column means or the between-group sum of squares.

SS_b = $S[(46.4-44.9)^2 + (45.6-44.9)^2 + (35.6-44.9)^2 + (52-44.9)^2 = 698.2$

SS_w = $(50-46.4)^2 + (34-46.4)^2 + ... (46-46.4)^2$ Treatment 1
$+ (48-45.6)^2 + (38-45.6)^2 + ... (48-45.6)^2$ Treatment 2
$+ (36-35.6)^2 + (30-35.6)^2 + ... (34-35.6)^2$ Treatment 3
$+ (54-52)^2 + (42-52)^2 + ... (50-52)^2$ Treatment 4
= 793.60

SS_{bl} or the sum of squares for blocks $= K\Sigma(y_i-\bar{y})^2$ and K is the number of repeated measures.

SS_{bl} can be views as a quantity obtained by finding the sum of squares for blocks, because we are blocking on the participants. Error variability can be calculated by segmenting variability into three parts, SS_w, SS_{bl}, and SS_{res}.

SS_{res} is called the sum of squares residual, and SS_w can be partitioned into SS_b plus SS_{res}; therefore, $SS_w = SS_{bl} + SS_{res}$, and $SS_{res} = SS_w - SS_{bl}$.

The calculation for the sum of squares for blocks is as follows:

$$
\begin{aligned}
SS_{bl} &= K\Sigma(y_i-\bar{y})^2 \\
&= 4[(47-44.9)^2 + (36-44.9)^2 + (43-44.9)^2 + (54-44.9) + (44.5- \\
&\quad 44.9)^2 \\
&= 680.80
\end{aligned}
$$

SS_{res} = SS_w-SS_{bl} = 793.60 - 680.80 = 112.80

MS_{res} = $SS_{res}/(n-1) (K-1)$, where n equals the number of participants, and K is the number of repeated measures; therefore, MS_{res} = 112.80/4(3) = 9.40.

F = MS_b/MS_{res} = 232.73/9.40 = 24.76, and the degrees of freedom are (K-1)=3 and (n-1) (K-1) = 12. This test statistic is significant beyond the .01 level and is about 5 times larger than the F one would obtain from a between-groups or completely randomized design.

Table 2
Control Lines for Running One Group Repeated Measures
Design on SPSSX

Title `Repeated Measures ANOVA'
Data List/TAI1 1-2 TAI2 4-5 TAI3 7-8 TAI4 10-11
List
Begin data

50	48	36	54
34	38	30	42
44	40	38	50
58	54	40	64
46	48	34	50

End data

MANOVA TAI1 to TAI4/

Wsfactor=TAI(4) | 2 |
Wsdesign=TAI/ | 3 |

Print=transform cellinfo(means)error(cor) signif(averf)/
 Analysis(repeated)/
Below is the annotated printout from SPSSX for the repeated measures
ANOVA.
1 - Gives the listing of the data
2 - Lets the computer know there are four levels of the within factor
3 - Specifies the design used

SAS Repeated Measures ANOVA

```
Title "Repeated Measures ANOVA";
Data Repeated;
Input gpid1 1 gpid2 2 TAI 4-5;
Cards;
Data Lines
Proc Print;
proc GLM;
Class gpid1 gpid2;
Model TAI=gpid1 gpid2;
```

Table 3
Greenhouse-Geisser Epsilon Statistic

Mauchly Sphericity Test, W =	.18650	
Chi-Square Approx.=	4.57156 with 5 D.F.	
Significance=	.470	
Greenhouse-Geisser Epsilon=	.60487	This corresponds to ê, indicating a moderate departure from sphericity
Huynh-Feldt Epsilon=	1.00000	
Lower-Bound Epsilon=	.33333	

Table 4
Multivariate Tests of Significance
Effect TAI

Test Name	Value	Approx	Hypoth DF	Error DF	Sig. of F
Pillais	.98	28.41	3.00	2.00	.034*
Hotelings	42.62	28.41	3.00	2.00	.034*
Wilks	.022	28.41	3.00	2.00	.034*
Roys	.97707				

Table 5
Univariate Tests of Significance

	Averaged Test of Significance for TAI Using Unique Sums of Squares				
Source of Variation	SS	DF	MS	F	Sig of F
Within Cells	122.80	12	9.40	24.76	.000**
TAI	698.20	3	232.73		

Table 6
Notations from Annotated Output for
One Group Repeated Measures ANOVA

*Corresponds to the multivariate tests, which are significant at the .05 level.

This is the univariate test. We must adjust the degrees of freedom. The adjusted univariate test is .60487(3) and .60487(3)(4), or 1.8 and 7.25844 degrees of freedom. Rounding to whole numbers, we have 2 and 7 degrees of freedom. The critical value of F with 2 and 7 degrees of freedom at the .05 level is 4.74, which indicates that the adjusted univariate test is still significant at the .05 level. Note: the subcommand **Signif (AVERF UNIV GG HF)/ provides this adjusted univariate test.

7.5 TUKEY POST HOC PROCEDURE FOR ONE-GROUP REPEATED MEASURES DESIGN

If the F-test for a repeated measures ANOVA is found to be significant and sphericity assumption is tenable, a modification of the Tukey HSD can be used to make pairwise comparisons.

As with the K group ANOVA, the Tukey procedure can be modified to obtain **simultaneous confidence intervals**. In contrast to the K group

Tukey procedure, with the one sample repeated measures design, the MSW is replaced with MS_{res}. This is the error term for the repeated measures ANOVA, and n is still the common group size or the number of subjects.

7.6 TUKEY CONFIDENCE INTERVALS FOR ONE-GROUP REPEATED MEASURES ANOVA

For the one-group repeated measure ANOVA, simultaneous confidence intervals can be obtained with the following formula:

$$(\bar{X}_i - \bar{X}_j) \pm q.\alpha = .05;k,(n-1)(k-1) \frac{\sqrt{MS_{res}}}{n}, \text{ df for error } = (n-1)(k-1)$$

$\bar{x}_i$ and $\bar{x}_j$ are the means of two groups. If the confidence interval includes 0, we fail to reject the null hypothesis and conclude that the population means are not different.

Using Table D, if alpha is set at .05, q=4.2 with df=k,(n-1)(k-1)=(5-1)(4-1) + 4,12. The following confidence intervals can be established:

$$(\bar{X} - \bar{X}) \pm 4.20 \sqrt{\frac{9.40}{5}} = 5.76$$

TAI1 vs TAI3   5.04---------16.56
                    lower   upper
                    limit   limit
(45.4 - 35.6) =   10.8 ± 5.76
                    10.8 + 5.76 = 5.04
                    10.8 - 5.76 = 16.56

TAI2 vs TAI3   4.24----------15.76
                    lower   upper
                    limit   limit

(45.6 - 35.6) =   10 ± 5.76
                    10 + 5.76 = 15.76
                    10 - 5.76 = 4.24

TAI3 vs TAI4   -10.64------- -22.16
                         lower   upper
                         limit   limit

$(35.6 - 52) =$ -16.4 ± 5.76
                         $-16.4 + 5.76 = -10.64$
                         $-16.4 - 5.76 = -22.16$

All three confidence limits are significant, since 0 is not included in the intervals.

7.7 ONE-GROUP REPEATED MEASURES ANOVA EXERCISES

1. How many nonredundant confidence intervals can be established for the data given at the beginning of this chapter for the repeated measures ANOVA?
    (Answer $[K(K-1)/2=6]$)

2. With the data given for the repeated measure example, establish a confidence interval for TAI1 vs TAI2. What is the decision in terms of the null hypothesis?
    (Answer: The null hypothesis is not rejected since 0 is included in the confidence interval.)
    TAI1 vs TAI2 -4.96---------6.56
    $(46.4-45.6) =$ $.8 \pm 5.76$
                        $.8 + 5.76 = 6.56$
                        $.8 - 5.76 = -4.96$

3. With the same data, establish a confidence interval for TAI1 vs TAI4.
    (Answer: -11.36--------.16)
    $46.4-52 =$ -5.6 ± 5.76
                    $-5.6 + 5.76 = .16$
                    $-5.6 - 5.76 = -11.36$

4. Run the following repeated measures design on SPSSX and perform the appropriate post hoc procedures. Which group means are significantly different?

	TAI1	TAI2	TA3
1	50	48	54
2	34	38	42
3	44	40	50
4	58	54	64
5	46	48	50

(Answer: The univariate F test is 12.67, p=.003. The adjusted univariate test is significant at the .05 level, since the adjusted degrees of freedom is ê(k-1) and ê(k-1)(n-1)=.66564(3-1) and .66564(3-1)(5-1)=1.33128 and 5.32512. The critical value of F with 1 and 5 degrees of freedom is 6.61. Post hoc tests indicate the following differences: TAI3 differed from TAI1 and TAI3 differed from TAI2.)

Solutions for exercise 4
If α = .05, q.05, df=3,8=4.041

$4.041\sqrt{MS_{res}/n}$ = $4.041\sqrt{4.80/5}$ = 4.041(.09797959) = 3.9593552 = 3.96

TAI1 and TAI3
(46.4-52) ±3.96
    -5.6 + 3.96 = -1.64
    -5.6 - 3.96 = -9.56
TAI3 and TAI2
(52-45.6) ± 3.96
    6.4 ± 3.96
    6.4 + 3.96 = 10.36
    6.4 - 3.96 = 2.44

Using Table C, if alpha is set at .05, q=4.041 with df=k=3, and (n-1)(k-1)=(5-1)(3-1) = 8. Confidence intervals can be established with the following formula:

$$\overline{X}_i - \overline{X}_j \pm 4.041\sqrt{4.8/5} = 3.96$$

7.8 MULTIPLE REGRESSION

The reader can consult Sapp (1997) for a detailed discussion of univariate correlational techniques and regression. And the reader should note that regression is a special case of structural equation modeling. Chapter 9 will provide an introductory discussion to structural equation modeling.

With **multiple regression**, one is interested in using **predictors** (Xs also called independent variables) to predict some criterion or dependent variable (the Y's) (Pedhazur, 1982). Essentially, a set of X values is used to predict a **dependent variable.** For a one predictor case, the mathematical model is:

$Y = bX + C$

b = the slope, which can be expressed as $Y_2 - Y_1/X_2 - X_1$

C = the Y-intercept

The above equation for Y' is called a regression equation (Pedhazur, 1982, p. 45). The values of X are **fixed** (predictors); the values of Y are subject to vary.

We are interested in finding a line that best fits the relationship between Y and X; hence, this is called the regression of Y on X. The graph below represents the regression of Y on X.

Regression of Y on X

For the SPSSX computer example that will follow, we will only consider the two-predictor case; however, one can easily make generalizations to the k-predictor case. The mathematical model for a two-predictor case is (Pedhazur, 1982, p. 46):

$$Y = b_1X_1 + b_2X_2 + C$$

b_1 is the slope of the dependent variable (Y) with predictor X_1, while the second predictor X_2 is held constant. Similarly, b_2 is also the slope of Y, with predictor X_1 held constant.

C = the Y intercept

Below is a schematic design for a two predictor case.

Table 7

Schematic Design for Two-Predictor Case

Schematically, the design for the two predictor case is:		
X_1 X_2		Y
52 51		58
53 52		57
53 52		58
54 53		55
55 54		54
55 55		55
55 56		53
57 58		55
58 59		53
58 60		52

The Xs are the **predictors**, and Y is the **dependent variable**. For this example, X_1 represents measures of stress, X_2 are measures of worry, and Y is the dependent variable, the TAI.

The **two-predictor case** can also be expressed using matrix algebra and parameters or population values. For example, for the two predictor case, the model using matrix notation is:

$$y = B_0 + B_1 X_1 + B_2 X_2 + e_1$$

Where B_0 is the regression constant or Y intercept,

B_1 and B_2 are the parameters to be estimated, and

e_1 is the error of prediction.

If we let **y** be a column vector, **XB** the product of two matrices and e_1 a column matrix, the traditional matrix equation for multiple regression can be established:

$$y = XB + e$$

Using differential calculus, it can be shown that the least squares estimates of the B's is (Finn, 1974, p. 135):

$$B' = (X'X)^{-1} X'y$$

Note that the least squares criterion minimizes error in prediction. This is done by finding a linear combination of the Xs, which is maximally correlated with y. And this is why there is **shrinkage**, or drop-off of prediction power with regression equations and the reason they must be cross-validated.

7.9 STEPS FOR CROSS-VALIDATING REGRESSION EQUATIONS

There are four steps to cross-validation (Huck, Cormier, & Bounds, 1974, p. 159). *First*, the original group of subjects for whom the predictors and criterion scores are available are randomly split into two groups. *Second*, one of the subgroups is used to derive a regression equation. *Third*, the regression equation is used to predict criterion scores for the group that it was not derived from. *Fourth*, the predicted criterion scores are correlated with actual criterion scores. If there is a significant correlation, this indicates there was not shrinkage in predictive power.

7.10 NUMBER OF RECOMMENDED SUBJECTS PER PREDICTOR FOR REGRESSION EQUATIONS

When several predictors are employed in regression with a minuscule sample size, the result will yield a poor prediction for an independent sample of subjects. If the number of predictors approximate the sample size, R will produce a value close to or equal to 1, even if none of the predictors correlate with the criterion (Borg & Gall, 1983, pp. 602-603).

In order to have a reliable regression equation, Stevens (1986, p. 58; 1996) recommends approximately 15 subjects per predictor. He suggests that an n/k ratio of 15/1 is needed to have a regression equation that cross-validates. The n corresponds to the sample size and k is the number of predictors. In chapter 6, it was noted that analysis of variance was a special case of regression. Below is the analysis of variance table for regression.

Table 8

Analysis of Variance Table for Regression

Source	SS	df	MS	F
Regression	SS_{reg}	k	SS_{reg}/k	MS_{reg}/MS_{res}
Residual or Error	SS_{res}	n-k-1	$SS_{res}/(n-k-1)$	

Table 9

Multiple Regression Broken Down into Sums of Squares

sum of squares about the mean	sum of squares about regression	sum of squares due to regression
$\Sigma(Y - \bar{Y})^2$ df=n-1	$\Sigma(Y_i - Y)^2$ df=n-k-1	$\Sigma(Y' - \bar{Y})^2$ df=k

7.11 RELATIONSHIP AMONG R^2, Y AND F

The squared multiple correlation R^2 can be expressed as the ratio of the sum of squares due to regression divided by the sum of squares about the mean. The following is the algebraic formula for R^2:

$$R^2 = \Sigma(Y'-\bar{Y})^2/\Sigma(Y-\bar{Y})^2$$

R^2 is called the coefficient of determination, or the proportion of variance accounted for on Y by a set of predictors. Bock (1975, p. 184) demonstrated a more direct relationship between R^2 and F. The equation is:

$$F = \frac{R^2/k}{(1-R^2)/(n-k-1),}$$

with df + k and (n-k-1)

7.12 ASSUMPTIONS OF MULTIPLE REGRESSION

The assumptions of multiple regression are as follows:
1. Linearity
2. Homoscedasticity of variance
3. Normality
4. Independence of error

Normality and Independence of Error

Normality and independence of error were discussed in chapter 6. As was the case with the independent t-test and F-test, multiple regression is robust to the assumption of normality. In terms of the independence of error assumption, however, a violation creates severe problems as it did in chapter 6 with the independent t-test and F-test. As was the case in chapter 6, independence implies that subjects are responding independently of each other. Moreover, the independence of error assumption suggests that residual values $e_1=\Sigma(Y_i-Y')$ are independent and normally distributed with a mean of zero and constant variance. Stevens (1986, p. 87; 1996) noted that the residuals are only independent when n is large relative to the number of predictors; however, residuals do have different variances. Since the last two assumptions were covered extensively in chapter 6, attention will only be given to the first two assumptions.

Linearity

Linearity is a linear relationship between the predictors and the dependent variable. Scatter diagrams can be used to investigate this assumption. If linearity is violated, other regression techniques must be employed such as ones for curvilinear relationships. An example of such a statistic is the coefficient eta, also called the correlation ratio.

Homoscedasticity

Homoscedasticity of variance, or constant variance, means the variances for columns are equal, and the variances for rows are equal. This implies that, within a distribution, the scatter is the same throughout; or there is uniformity in spread about the regression line. This assumption suggests that if data is sectioned into columns, the variability of Y is the same from column to column. Similarly, if data is sectioned into rows, the variability of Y would be the same from row to row. Figures 1-3 illustrate equal variability among rows, equal variability among columns and violations of homoscedasticity, respectively. Tables 11-15 graphically illustrate how to ascertain assumption violations with scatter plots from SPSSX.

Figure 1
Equal Variability among Rows

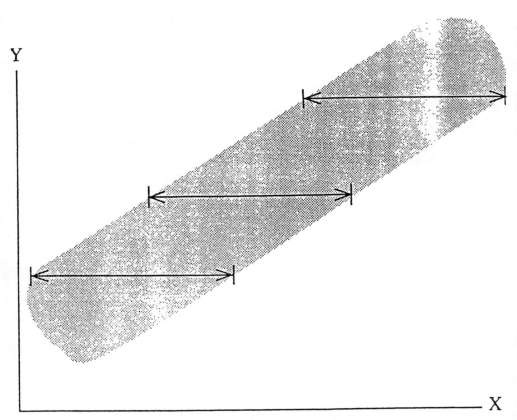

Equal variability among the rows

Figure 2
Equal Variability Among Columns

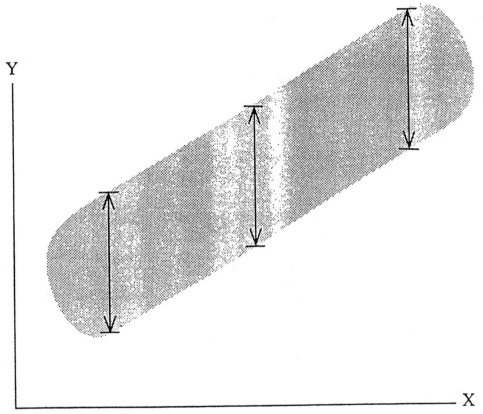

Equal variability among the columns

　　　　　　　Test Anxiety: Applied Research

Figure 3
Violation of Homoscedastic Relationship

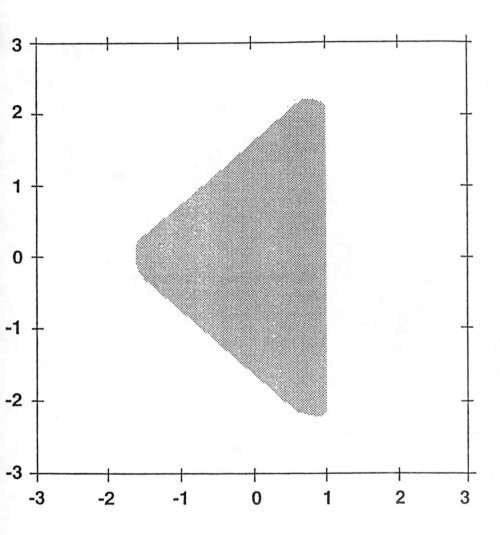

Regression assumptions can be checked by using a scatter plot of the e_i's standardized (standardized or studentized residuals) with Y's (predicted values of Y). If no systematic pattern or clustering of residuals occur, one can assume that the assumption is tenable. To standardize residuals, we divide each residual $[e_i = \Sigma(Y - Y')]$ by the standard deviation of the residuals, which is the standard error of estimate for the residuals. It can be expressed by the following (Pedhazur, 1982, pp. 28, 36):

$$S_{Est} = \sqrt{\Sigma(Y - Y')^2/N - k - 1} = S_y\sqrt{1 - R^2}$$

Where $S_y =$

$$\sqrt{\text{sum of the squares/degree of freedom}}$$

$$= \sqrt{\Sigma(Y - Y')^2/N - k - 1}$$

R^2 = the squared multiple correlation coefficient or the Pearson Product-Moment Correlation between a set of predictors and a dependent variable.

S_y = the standard deviation of Y
N = the sample size
K = the number of predictors.

Therefore, the standardized residual (e_i standardized) =

$$e_i/\sqrt{\Sigma(Y - Y')^2/N - k - 1} = e_i/S_y\sqrt{1 - R^2}$$

Technically, residuals can be adjusted in two ways. That is, by means of standardized residuals and studentized residuals. Standardized residuals have a mean of 0 and a standard deviation of 1. A studentized residual is a residual divided by an estimate of its standard deviation. This is the reason that standardized and studentized residuals can take on different values with the same data set; however, usually standardized and studentized residuals are close in value.

Residuals are plotted to test the normality assumption. In addition, the studentized residuals should randomly scatter about the horizontal line defined by 0 which is found on the SPSSX printout. The control lines for obtaining residual scatter plots are provided with control line for the backward regression example that will soon follow.

7.13 WHEN REGRESSION ASSUMPTIONS
APPEAR TO BE VIOLATED

Rarely are the assumptions of regression not violated in one way or another. Usually the correction for the violation of one assumption will also correct other violations; however, this is not the case for the independence assumption. In terms of equal variances, if the homogeneity assumption is violated, often the variance stabilizing techniques will also correct violations of normality. When the assumptions of regression appear to be violated, a data transformation of variables may stabilize variance and achieve normality. Transformation may be on the independent variables, dependent variables, or both. The three most common transformations is the square root, logarithm to the base 10, and the negative reciprocal. If there is a moderate violation of assumptions, the square root may be an adequate transformation.

When there is a strong violation of assumptions, the logarithm to the base 10 provides a better transformation; however, if there are extreme violations of assumptions, the negative reciprocal provides the strongest transformation of data. The negative reciprocal is recommended over the reciprocal, since it preserves the order of observations. Commonly, when residual plots are positively skewed, the logarithmic transformation may be helpful. Nevertheless, the square root transformation is common for negatively skewed distributions.

SPSSX Users Guide 3rd edition (1988, pp. 109-140) discusses numeric transformations. Many complicated transformations can be performed on SPSSX. SPSSX uses the **COMPUTE** command to perform data transformations. For example, to obtain the square root of a variable called **Y1**, the command is: **Compute X=SQRT(Y1)**. In this example, the transformed variable is called **X**.

7.14 SIX COMPUTER METHODS OF SELECTING
PREDICTORS AND REGRESSION MODELS

SPSSX (1983, p. 604) describes six methods the computer can use for selecting predictors. The reader should be aware that these are six methods to build regression equations. Even with the same data, each method can lead to a different regression equation. This will be illustrated later by applying the forward, backward, and stepwise methods to the same data. The six methods on SPSSX are forward entry, backward elimination, stepwise selection, forced entry, forced removal, and test.

Forward Entry or Selection

With the forward entry method, predictor variables are entered into the regression equation one at a time. At each step, the predictors not in the regression equation are examined for entry. Basically, the first predictor to enter the regression equation is the one with the largest correlation with the criterion. If this predictor is significant, the predictor with the largest semipartial (a variant of a partial correlation or the correlation of several variables with one or more variables held constant) correlation with the criterion is considered. The formula for the partial correlation is:

$$r_{12.3} = \frac{r_{12} - r_{13}r_{23}}{\sqrt{1-r_{13}^2}\ \sqrt{1-r_{23}^2}}$$

$r_{12.3}$ denotes the correlation between variables 1 and 2, with 3 held constant. The formula for the semipartial correlation which is used with R^2 is:

$$r_{12.3(s)} = \frac{r_{12} - r_{13}r_{23}}{\sqrt{1-r_{23}^2}}$$

or

$r_{1(2.3)}$

The semipartial corrleation, also known as the part correlation, can be denoted as $r_{1(2.3)}$. This notion states that Variable 3 has been partialed out from Variable 2 but not from Variable 1; hence, this is the correlation between Variables 1 and 2 once Variable 3 has been held constant from Variable 2 and not Variable 1.

Once a predictor fails to make a significant contribution to predictions, the process is terminated. The difficulty with forward entry is that it does not permit the removal of predictors from a regression equation once they are entered. In contrast, stepwise regression, a modification of forward entry, permits predictors to be entered and removed from regression equations at different steps in the process.

Backward Elimination

Backward elimination is the reverse of the forward entry selection process. With the backward elimination, one starts with the squared multiple correlation of Y and all k predictors in the regression equation. The predictor that contributes least to the regression sum of squares when entered last is deleted, and a new value of R^2 with the remaining k-1 predictors is calculated. Now, the predictor that contributes least to the regression sum of squares when entered last is deleted and a new value of R^2 using only k-2 predictors is calculated. The process continues until k predictors have been retained. In summary, the backward elimination process starts with a regression with all the predictors and attempts to eliminate them from the equation one at a time.

Stepwise Selection

Stepwise selection is a variation of the forward entry process; however, at each stage a test is made to determine the usefulness of a predictor. Hence, a predictor that was earlier selected can be deleted if it loses its usefulness.

Forced Entry

With forced entry, predictors are entered that satisfy a tolerance criterion. Specifically, predictors can be forced into a regression equation in a specific order. For example, using the enter subcommand on SPSSX, one can enter variables in a specific order in a regression equation. If one wanted to enter variable **X1** followed by **X2**, the SPSSX subcommands are: **Enter X1/Enter X2/**.

For SAS, if we had a two-predictor case, the control line for forcing predictors X1 and X2 into a prediction equation is: **Model Y = X1 X 2/Include=2 Selection=Stepwise**.

Forced Removal

Forced removal is the exact opposite of the forced entry process; however, predictors are removed from a regression equation in a specific order.

Test

Test is a process used to test various regression models. For example, it is used for model testing or for finding the "best" model for a data set.

Test is an easy way to test a variety of models using R^2 and its test of significance as a gauge for the "best" model.

SAS Stepwise Regression

```
Data Regress;
Input X1 1-2 X2 4-5 Y 7-8;
Cards;
Data Lines
Proc Reg Simple Corr;
Model Y = X1 X2/Include = 2 Selection = Stepwise;      1
```

1 - Include forces X1 and X2 into the prediction equation.

Table 10
7.15 SPSSX Control Lines for Running the
Backward Elimination Process

```
        The control lines for running multiple regression are similar for
each selection process.  Essentially, the changes needed in the
subcommand are:
dependent=dependent variable/selection procedure key word.

Title `Backward elimination with two predictors'
Data list/X1 1-2 X2 4-5 Y 7-8
Begin data
52  51          58
53  52          57
53  52          58
54  53          55
55  54          54
55  55          55
55  56          53
57  58          55
58  59          53
```

```
58  60              52
End data
Regression variables=Y X1 X2/     _____
  dependent=y/backward/           _____1_____
  residuals/                      _____
  Scatterplot=(*zresid,Y),        _____2_____
  (*zresid,X2),
  (*zresid,X1)/
```

1 - This is the subcommand for getting the backward elimination
    procedure. We could request the forward or stepwise procedures by
    changing the dependent subcommand to **dependent=
    y/forward/** and **dependent=y/stepwise/**, respectively.

2 - The scatterplot subcommand provides residual plots, which are used
    to test the assumptions of multiple regression. On the printout, the
    standardized residuals are given the name *ZRESID, and the
    predicted values are given the name *PRED.

Figure 4
Backward Elimination Two Predictors
Selected Printout from SPSSX

Multiple R	.85
R Squared	.73
Adjusted R Squared	.65
Standard Error	1.25

Analysis of Variance			
	Df	Sum of Squares	Mean Square
Regression (k)	2	29.14	14.57
Residual (n-k-1)	7	10.86	1.55
F=9.29			

Variable	B
X2	-.285714
X1	-.428571
Constant	92.285714
$Y' = -.4286X_1 - .2857X_2 + 92.29$	

Table 11

Graphical Checks for Violations of Regression Assumptions

Histogram of Standardized Residuals			
NExp N		(* = 1 Cases, . : = Normal Curve)	
0	.01	Out	
0	.02	3.00	
0	.04	2.67	
0	.09	2.33	
0	.18	2.00	
0	.33	1.67	
1	.55	1.33	:
1	.81	1.00	:
0	1.06	.67	.
3	1.25	.33	:**
1	1.32	.00	:
1	1.25	-.33	:
1	1.06	-.67	:
1	.81	-1.00	:
0	.55	-1.33	.
1	.33	-1.67	*
0	.18	-2.00	
0	.09	-2.33	
0	.04	-2.67	
0	.02	-3.00	
0	.01	Out	

This graph is a check for normality. The first and last out contain residuals more than 3.16 standard deviations from the mean. In practice, these outlier residuals would be examined in order to determine how they occurred. In large data sets, these outlier values may be the result of data entry errors. When observed and expected frequencies overlap, a colon is printed. It is not realistic to expect the residuals to be exactly normal.

The asterisks indicate a few cases that strayed from normality; however, overall the residuals appear to approach normality. Note: it is assumed that standardized residuals have equal variances; however, this has been shown not to be the case. The *SPSSX Advanced Statistics Guide* suggests that studentized residuals, in contrast to standardized residuals, more accurately reflect differences in true error variances and are recommended instead of standardized residuals. Studentized residuals can be obtained on SPSSX with the keyword ***SRESID**. The subcommand **residuals= outliers (resid, sresid, sdresid, mahal, cook, lever)/** produces outlier statistical information. See the *SPSSX Advanced Statistics Guide* (p. 61) for additional information on outlier statistics.

Test Anxiety: Applied Research

Table 12
Normal Probability (P-P) Plot
Standardized Residual

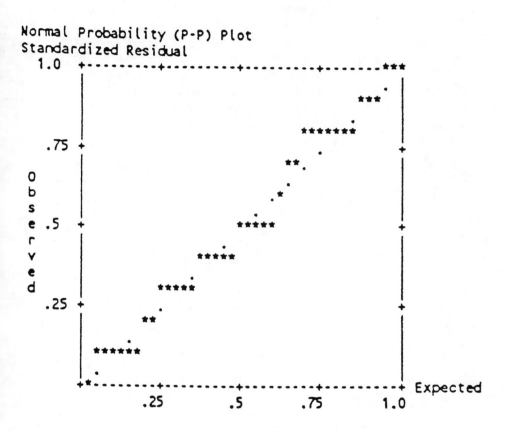

The normal probability plot is another check for normality. It
compares the residuals with expected values under the assumption of
normality. If the normal probability and residuals are identical, a straight

line results. Also, this plot suggests that the residuals appear close to
normality.

Table 13
Standardized Scatterplot

Across - Y   Down - *ZRESID

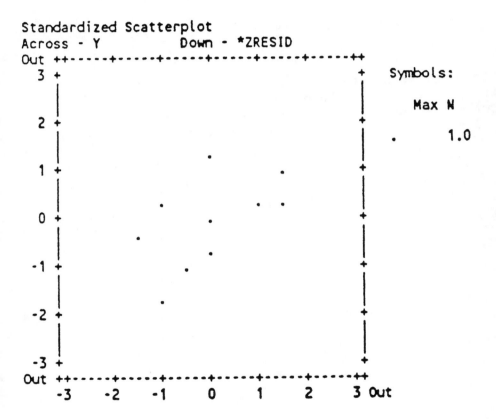

This is a plot of the dependent variable plotted against the
standardized residuals. Since there is a pattern between the residuals and
the dependent variable, this would normally suggest an assumption
violation. Actually, there is a .53 linear relationship between the
standardized residuals and the dependent variable. Since the residuals are

mathematically based partly on the dependent variables, this is to be expected. If this same scatterplot would have occurred with predictors X1 and X2, this would have indicated a violation of assumptions of regression.

Table 14
Standardized Scatterplot

Across - X1   Down - *ZRESID

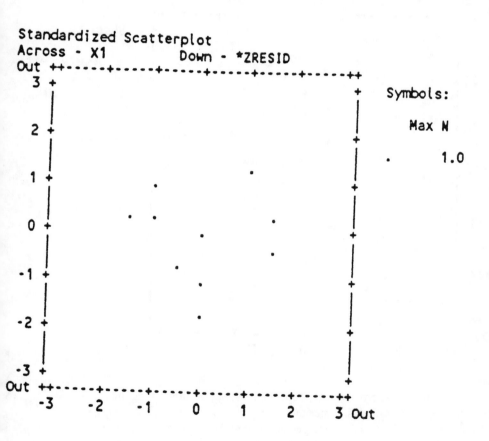

The residuals are plotted against the predictor X1. There is not an obvious pattern to the residuals. It appears that the assumptions are met, since the residuals randomly distributed about the horizontal straight line through 0. If assumptions are met, one will see a horizontal band of residuals randomly scattering about the horizontal line defined by 0. There should not be any systematic pattern or clustering of residuals.

Table 15
Standardized Scatterplot

Across - X2   Down - *ZRESID

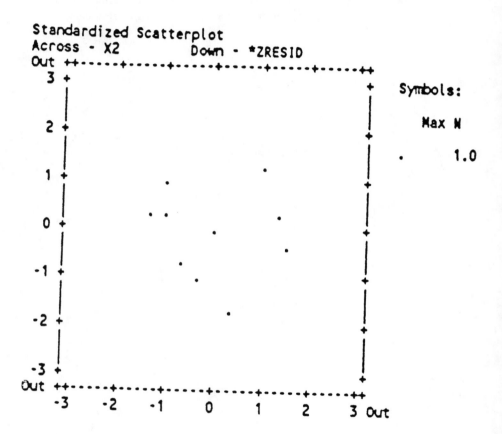

The residuals are plotted against the predictor X2. It appears that the assumptions are met, since the residuals randomly distributed about the horizontal straight line through 0. If assumptions are met, one will see a horizontal band of residuals not forming any systematic pattern.

7.16 MULTIPLE REGRESSION EXERCISES

1. Using SPSSX and SAS, run the data given in the regression example using the forward entry selection procedure, and write out the regression equation. Note the only changes in the control lines are the **dependent=y/forward/**. (Answer: The regression equation is: $Y = -.5667X_2 + 86.17$.)

2. Now perform the stepwise procedure on the same data. The change in the control lines is **dependent=y/stepwise/**. What is the standard error? Answer 1.18. What is the coefficient of determination? (Answer: .72.) What is the adjusted R squared due to shrinkage. Answer (.69). The reader should note that this adjusted R Squared is of limited utility, since it will not cross-validate. The following formula is by used to calculate the adjusted R-squared. It was developed by a statistician named **Wherry**, the formula is as follows:

$$R^2 = 1 - (n-1)/(n-k-1)(1-R^2)$$

Stevens (1986, p. 80) recommends calculating the adjusted R^2 using the following formula by statisticians **Herzberg** and **Stein**. This formula estimates the amount of shrinkage expected under cross-validation for multiple regression. The formula is:

$$R^2_g = 1 - (n-1)/(n-k-1) \ (n-2)/(n-k-2)(n+1)/n(1-R^2)$$

In each formula, n is the sample size and k is the number of predictors.

7.17 K GROUP MANOVA

The K group MANOVA or multivariate analysis of variance is a natural generalization of the K group ANOVA. One difference between the two is that with MANOVA subjects are measured on two or more dependent variables as opposed to one, which occurs with ANOVA. Moreover, MANOVA unlike ANOVA takes into account the correlation among variables. Since MANOVA can combine small differences among several dependent variables, it is more powerful than ANOVA. If one is interested in comparing two groups of subjects on five dependent measures of test anxiety; it would take five separate ANOVAs to analyze this data. With an alpha level of .05 times five separate ANOVA tests, the overall alpha for the set of tests is approximately .25. Thus, the use of multiple ANOVAs, like multiple t-tests, increase the chance of type I error. It is important to stress that dependent variables should only be combined together in MANOVA when there is a strong theoretical or empirical rationale.

7.18 ASSUMPTIONS OF MANOVA

The assumptions of MANOVA are generalizations of the univariate assumptions for the t-test for independent samples and the K group ANOVA. The assumptions are as follows:
1. The dependent variables are multivariate normal in each group.
2. Homogeneity of covariance matrices.
3. Independence of observations.

What happens when a given assumption is violated almost parallels what occurred at the univariate level. Graphical tests of scatter diagrams of pairs of variables are a partial check for multivariate normality. The control lines on SPSSX and SAS to perform these scatter diagrams are the same as the ones used to check assumption violations for regression.

If plots between all pairs of variables are approximately elliptical, the multivariate assumption is probably tenable. Like the univariate tests, MANOVA is robust to violations of the multivariate normality assumption. Thus, violation of this assumption has a minute effect on type I error. Also, violations of the homogeneity of covariance matrices is also similar to what occurred at the univariate level.

If the group sizes are approximately equal, the actual alpha level is very close to the nominal alpha level. If the largest group size is greater than 1.5 times the smaller group size, this indicates sharply unequal group sizes. When group sizes are sharply unequal and the largest variability is in the smallest group size, the test statistic is liberal, and if the larger variability is in the largest group size, the test statistic is conservative. Again, a similar finding occurred at the univariate level. On SPSSX and SAS, the **Box test**, which is the **multivariate generalization of the Bartlett univariate homogeneity of variance test** is used to test the assumption of homogeneity of covariance matrices, provided that the multivariate normality assumption is tenable because, like its univariate analogue, this test is sensitive to departure from multivariate normality.

Stevens (1986, p. 220; 1996) notes that when all group sizes are greater than twenty and the number of dependent variables are less than six and the number of groups is less than six, the Chi-Square approximation for the homogeneity of covariance test from the SPSSX printout should be used; otherwise, the F approximation from the SPSSX printout is more accurate for testing the homogeneity of covariance assumption.

7.19 SPSSX FOR K GROUP MANOVA

Suppose we had the following three group MANOVA situation, with subjects measured on three test anxiety variables. Below are the control lines and data for running this design. The design is first run as a MANOVA design, followed by the control lines for running it as a multivariate regression design. The reader should notice that both runs produce the same multivariate results. This indicates that MANOVA is a special case of multivariate regression.

```
Title `K group MANOVA'
Data list/TAI1 1-2 TAI2 4-5 TAI3 7-8 GPID 10
Begin data
52 51 58 1
53 52 57 1
53 52 58 1
54 53 55 2
55 54 54 2
55 55 55 2
55 56 53 3
57 58 55 3
58 59 53 3
58 60 52 3
End data
MANOVA TAI1 TAI2 TAI3 by GPID (1,3)/
 Print=cellinfo(means,cov,cor)homogeneity(Cochran,boxm)/[1]
```

[1]This subcommand is needed to get the Box test, which tests the assumption of homogeneity of covariance matrices.

SAS for K Group MANOVA

Data KMANOVA;
Input TAI1 1-2 TAI2 4-5 TAI3 7-8 GPID 10;
Cards;
Data Lines
Proc Print;
Proc GLM;
Class gpid;
Model TAI1 TAI2
TAI3=gpid/alpha=.05; 1
Means gpid/Tukey;

[1]Applies the Tukey procedure

SPSSX K Group MANOVA Run as
Multivariate Regression

Title `K group MANOVA run as multivariate regression'
Data list/TAI1 1-2 TAI2 4-5 TAI3 7-8 X1 10 X2 12
Begin data

52 51 58 1 0	*
53 52 57 1 0	*
53 52 58 1 0	*
54 53 55 0 1	**
55 54 54 0 1	**
55 55 55 0 1	**
55 56 53 0 0	***
57 58 55 0 0	***
58 59 53 0 0	***
58 60 52 0 0	***

End data
MANOVA TAI1 TAI2 TAI3 with X1 X2/

 *=the dummy coding of the predictors for subjects in group one.
 **=the dummy coding of the predictors for subjects in group two.
***=the dummy coding of predictors for subjects in group three.

The 0s and 1s are used to denote group membership. Since there are three groups, only k-1 = 2, two dummy variables are needed to denote group membership.

Table 16

Selected Output From MANOVA Run

Test Name Effect.GPID Multivariate Tests of Significance	Value	Approx F	Hypoth DF	Error DF	Sig of F
Pillais	1.51	6.20	6	12	.004*
Hottelings	11.60	7.73	6	8	.005*
Wilks	.04	7.13	6	10	.004*
Roys	.91				
*indicates the multivariate tests were significant					

Variable Effect.GPIU nivariate F-test with (2,7) D.F.	Hypoth SS	Error SS	Hypoth MS	Error MS	F	Sig of F
TAI1	32.67	7.33	16.33	1.05	15.60	.003**
TAI2	78.58	11.42	39.29	1.63	24.09	.001**
TAI3	33.92	6.08	16.96	.87	19.51	.001**
**indicates that the univariate tests were significant						

Post hoc procedures and planned comparisons can be performed with MANOVA. Tatsuoka (1988, p. 277) recommends following MANOVA with **discriminant analyses** which is a multivariate procedure used to determine a subject's group membership; however, Stevens (1986, p. 157) recommends following a significant k group MANOVA with all pairwise Hotelling's T-tests (for a two-group situation, Hotelling's T-tests and discriminant analysis produce equivalent results) to determine which pairs of variables differ significantly on a set of dependent variables. The Hotelling's T-test (multivariate MANOVA applied on two groups at a time) is followed by univariate t-tests each performed at the .05 alpha level, to determine which individual variables were contributing to the multivariate significance. In order to control type I error, the overall alpha level for the Hotelling's T-tests can be set at .15. For our example of 3 groups, there are 3 Hotelling Ts and each should be tested at the .15/3=.05 level of significance. This is a powerful procedure for controlling type I error, but it should be used cautiously when identifying individual variables. It is also possible to follow the Hotelling Ts with Tukey confidence interval, which were described in Chapter 6 for the k group independent ANOVA.

7.20 K GROUP MANOVA EXERCISES

1.   Run the 3 group MANOVA on SPSSX and SAS
     What is the p value for the Wilks's multivariate statistic? (Answer .004.) Were the univariate homogeneity of variance tests significant for any of the dependent variables? (Answer no.) As a post hoc test to MANOVA establish a Tukey confidence interval for groups 1 and 2 on the TAI1 variable.

$$q,\alpha = .05;3,7 = 4.165 \quad 4.165\sqrt{1.047/3} = 2.46$$

The mean for group 1 and 2 respectively on the TAI are 52.67 and 54.67. The difference between these means is 2.

$$2 \pm 2.46 = \quad .46\text{----------}4.46$$
$$\quad\quad\quad\quad\quad \text{lower} \quad\quad \text{upper}$$
$$\quad\quad\quad\quad\quad \text{limit} \quad\quad\; \text{limit}$$

2.   Run the MANOVA example as a multivariate regression problem. Compare multivariate tests statistics from each analysis.

7.21 FACTORIAL MULTIVARIATE ANALYSIS
OF VARIANCE

Factorial MANOVA is the multivariate generalization of the univariate factorial ANOVA. This statistic has the same assumptions as the k group MANOVA. In contrast to the univariate factorial design, with the multivariate factorial MANOVA, subjects are measured on two or more dependent variables simultaneously. Mentally visualize a 2 by 3 factorial MANOVA. Let us assume that men are in row one, and women are in row two. The men and women were simultaneously measured on two test anxiety instruments: the Test Anxiety Inventory (TAI) and the State Trait Anxiety Inventory (STAI). The columns represent three treatments for test anxiety: hypnosis, relaxation therapy, and cognitive-behavioral counseling. We are interested in knowing if there is a significant row by column interaction. Below are the data and control lines for running this design on SPSSX.

```
Title `Two-way MANOVA'
Data list/row 1 column 3 TAI1 5-6 STAI 8-9
Begin data
1 1 56 46
1 1 56 46
1 1 54 44
1 1 48 41
1 1 54 53
1 1 54 51
1 1 49 39
1 1 68 45
1 1 48 40
1 1 54 41
1 1 58 40
1 2 66 37
1 2 54 41
1 2 51 37
1 2 51 38
1 2 56 43
1 2 46 39
1 2 55 36
1 2 53 39
1 2 43 35
1 2 50 24
1 3 56 34
1 3 51 34
1 3 50 36
1 3 54 36
1 3 50 33
```

```
1 3 47 33
1 3 41 32
1 3 51 35
1 3 57 34
1 3 49 34
2 1 62 45
2 1 67 44
2 1 71 49
2 1 55 45
2 1 57 46
2 1 64 48
2 1 64 45
2 1 69 44
2 1 63 44
2 1 56 46
2 2 52 38
2 2 59 39
2 2 57 37
2 2 51 37
2 2 56 39
2 2 52 39
2 2 51 37
2 2 61 41
2 2 56 38
2 2 60 40
2 3 48 31
2 3 48 30
2 3 45 30
2 3 42 32
2 3 47 31
2 3 45 32
2 3 53 34
2 3 41 33
2 3 48 32
2 3 43 31
End data
MANOVA TAI1 STAI by row(1,2)column(1,3)/
 Print=cellinfo(means,cov,cor)/
 method=sstype(unique)/
```

design=row,column,row by column/

Table 17

Two-Way MANOVA

Selected Output from SPSSX Factorial MANOVA			
Effect. Row by Column Multivariate Tests of Significance			
Test Name	Value	Approx F	Sig of F
Pillais	.23	3.89	.006*
Hotellings	.32	4.16	.004*
Wilks	.75	4.03	.004*
Roys	.23		
*indicates a significant multivariate interaction effect.			

7.22 FACTORIAL MANOVA EXERCISES
1.   Run the 2 by 3 factorial MANOVA

a.   Is there a significant multivariate column effect?
(Answer: Yes, p=.000 for all multivariate tests.)

b.   What is the p value for the row effect? (Answer: .135.)

7.23 MULTIVARIATE ANALYSIS OF COVARIANCE:
THREE COVARIATES
THREE DEPENDENT VARIABLES

Multivariate Analysis of Covariance (MANCOVA) is the multivariate generalization of ANCOVA. The assumptions are the same as ANCOVA. With MANCOVA, like the other multivariate tests, subjects are measured on several dependent variables.

Suppose we are employing guided imagery to reduce both the worry and emotionality components of test anxiety; however, due to theory we hypothesize that since guided imagery is a cognitive therapy, it will have a greater impact on the worry than emotionality component in comparison to a Hawthorne control group. We are able to randomly assign two groups of subjects to a treatment group and a Hawthorne control group. Before treatment, we are able to obtain midterm average grade point averages for both groups. In addition, we are able to obtain pretests of worry and emotional measures of test anxiety. The dependent variables are final grade point averages, posttests worry, and emotionality measures of test anxiety. We have covariates for each group, a midterm average, and pretest worry and pretest emotionality test anxiety scores. To summarize, the covariates are midterm grade point averages, pretest worry test anxiety scores, and pretest emotionality test anxiety scores, while the dependent variables are final grade point averages, posttest measures of worry test anxiety, and posttest measures of emotionality test anxiety. The SPSSX control lines and data for this example are provided below.

Title `guided imagery for reducing worry and emotionality'
data list/gpid 1 midterm 3-4 final 6-7 prewor 9-10 postwor 12-13 preemot 15-16 postemot 18-19
Begin data
1 54 60 80 50 74 69
1 58 60 80 51 82 76
1 54 53 70 45 70 64
1 60 60 80 53 66 61
1 52 53 65 55 63 59
1 44 33 70 47 61 59
1 50 60 53 46 68 68
1 43 53 64 61 76 70
1 45 53 63 53 53 50
2 54 47 50 65 68 63
2 29 33 50 56 56 61
2 39 33 37 32 57 53
2 51 53 52 50 50 54
2 61 60 50 51 61 66
2 61 60 54 53 71 75
2 57 47 48 47 66 72
2 61 60 50 47 72 66
2 61 60 48 44 64 60
End data

MANOVA midterm prewor preemot final postwor postemot by gpid(1,2)/
  Analysis=final postwor postemot with midterm prewor preemot/
  Print=pmeans/
  Design/
  Analysis=final postwor postemot/
Design=midterm+prewor+preemot,GPID,midterm by GPID+prewor by
  GPID+preemot by GPID/
  Analysis=midterm prewor preemot/[1]

[1]This subcommand tests if the groups differ on the covariates and it
provides the Hotelling-Lawley Trace, which is called Hotellings' on the
SPSSX printout.

SAS MANCOVA

```
Title "MANCOVA";
Data MANCOVA;
Input gpid 1 midterm 3-4 final 6-7 prewor 9-10 postwor 12-13
preemot 15-16 postemot 18-19;
Cards;
Data Lines
Proc Print;
Proc Reg;
Model Final postwor postemot=midterm prewor preemot;
MTEST;
Proc GLM;
Classes gpid;
Model final postwar postemot=midterm gpid
midterm*gpid prewor gpid prewor*gpid
preemot gpid preemot*gpid;
MANOVA H=Midterm*gpid prewor*gpid preemot*gpid;
Proc GLM;
Model final postwor postemot=midterm gpid prewor gpid preemot
gpid;
MANOVA H=gpid;
Lmeans GPID/PDIFF;
```

Table 18

Selected Output from SPSSX for 3 Covariate 3 Dependent Variable MANCOVA			
Effect..Within Cells Regression Multivariate Tests of Significance			
Test Name	Value	Approx. F	Sig. of F
Pillais	1.49	4.94	.000*
Hotellings	5.74	7.44	.000*
Wilks	.07	6.91	.000*
Roys	.81		
*Indicates a significant relationship between the 3 covariates and 3 dependent variables. This is the within cells regression.			

7.24 FACTORIAL MANCOVA: ONE COVARIATE AND TWO DEPENDENT VARIABLES

Factorial MANCOVA is a combination of factorial MANOVA and the one-way MANCOVA. The control lines for running this analysis on SPSSX is basically an extension of previously given control lines in this chapter. Below are the control lines for running a one-covariate, two-dependent variable factorial MANCOVA.

```
Title 'Factorial MANCOVA'
Data List Free/row Column TAI STAI Covar
List
Begin Data
1   1   56      50      4
1   1   56      48      5
1   1   70      44      2
1   1   45      34      3
1   2   33      45      5
```

1	2	33	33	3
1	2	20	30	3
1	2	30	40	4
2	2	30	99	6
2	2	89	37	2
2	2	67	58	3
2	2	56	68	4
2	1	56	67	4
2	1	67	68	4
2	1	57	48	3
2	1	67	3	3

End data
MANOVA covar TAI STAI by row (1,2) column (1,2)/
 Method = SStype (unique)/
 analysis = TAI STAI with covar/
 Print = pmeans/
 Design/
 Analysis = TAI STAI/
 Design = covar, row, column, covar by row column/

7.25 ONE-WAY MANCOVA EXERCISES
1. Run the one-way MANCOVA exercise.
    Is the assumption of homogeneity of hyperplanes tenable? (Answer:
    Yes, Wilk's Lambda=.52, p=.076.)

7.26 POST HOC PROCEDURES FOR MANCOVA
Stevens (1986, p. 317) gives the multivariate analogue of the Bryant-Paulson procedure. For a randomized several covariate design, which is what occurred with the guided imagery example, the formula is:

$$\overline{Y}_i* - \overline{Y}_j*/\sqrt{MSW*[1 + 1/(J-1)TR(B_x W_x^{-1})/n}$$

For a nonrandomized several covariate design, the formula is:

$$\overline{Y}_i* - \overline{Y}_j*/\frac{\sqrt{MSW*2/n + d'W^{-1}d}}{2}$$

Where $\overline{Y}_i$ is the adjusted mean for group i, and $\overline{Y}_j*$ is the adjusted mean for group j.

MSW* is the error term for covariance

W_x is the within sum of the cross products matrix.

TR $(B_xW_x^{-1})$ is the **Hotelling-Lawley Trace**, which is given on the printout from MANOVA. It is obtained by the last analysis subcommand from the SPSSX control lines for MANCOVA. It tests if the groups differ on the set of covariates.

d' is a row vector or the difference between the ith and jth groups on the covariate.

Degress of freedom for the Bryant-Paulson procedure is N-J-C, where N is the sample size, J is the number of groups and C is the number of covariates. Critical values for the Bryant-Paulson procedure are found in Table E.

7.27 NESTED MANOVA

As stated in Chapter 4, factorial designs involve the complete crossing of all levels of one factor with all levels of another factor. Some researchers refer to these designs as incomplete designs, hierarchical designs, multilevel designs, and random-coefficient regression models. One major limitation of these designs is they do not allow a researcher to test interactional effects. Another difficulty with these designs can be determining the appropriate error term (Lindman, 1992).

Just as MANOVA is the multivariate generation of ANOVA, nested MANOVA is the multivariate generalization of univariate nested ANOVA designs. With nested MANOVA designs, participants are measured on several dependent variables. Suppose 48 classrooms of students were nested within two schools, and the classrooms of students were pretested on reading, language arts, and mathematics. This represents a nested design where classrooms are nested with schools. Suppose we had the following data where ROW represented the school factor with two levels and COLUMN represented the schools with 48 levels.

ROW	COLUMN	N	READ	LANG	MATH	TOTAL
1.00	1.00	15.00	532.07	534.67	497.73	521.60
1.00	1.00	13.00	564.31	549.92	523.85	546.08
1.00	1.00	16.00	535.75	540.25	498.69	524.88
1.00	1.00	21.00	543.00	535.67	488.95	522.57
1.00	2.00	15.00	541.53	542.20	504.60	529.33
1.00	2.00	13.00	550.85	552.00	497.08	533.23
1.00	2.00	15.00	534.40	539.00	496.67	523.27

ROW	COLUMN	N	READ	LANG	MATH	TOTAL
1.00	3.00	14.00	522.00	535.71	479.93	512.64
1.00	3.00	13.00	547.08	556.31	518.15	540.46
1.00..	3.00	14.00	536.29	545.36	506.21	529.29
1.00	3.00	13.00	541.00	558.31	520.62	540.00
1.00	4.00	15.00	550.33	560.93	525.93	545.73
1.00	4.00	14.00	544.00	557.14	507.93	536.29
1.00	4.00	14.00	542.71	559.79	532.36	544.93
1.00	5.00	22.00	541.59	556.32	501.77	533.23
1.00	6.00	13.00	529.46	540.54	494.77	521.62
1.00	6.00	13.00	520.46	510.23	483.31	504.69
1.00	7.00	17.00	539.25	536.00	508.82	528.13
1.00	7.00	18.00	527.83	538.39	498.83	521.78
1.00	7.00	16.00	529.44	526.69	484.94	513.69
1.00	7.00	18.00	528.11	547.33	501.56	525.61
1.00	8.00	6.00	540.00	529.00	496.00	521.67
1.00	8.00	14.00	525.71	531.64	476.93	511.50
1.00	8.00	7.00	527.57	504.00	498.14	510.14
1.00	9.00	11.00	535.00	527.00	494.82	519.50
1.00	9.00	10.00	552.30	547.20	508.60	536.10
1.00	9.00	11.00	529.73	535.00	472.09	512.36
1.00	9.00	14.00	533.00	529.93	479.79	514.14
1.00	10.00	8.00	539.63	506.75	495.75	514.00
1.00	10.00	14.00	517.14	512.36	490.00	506.50
1.00	10.00	15.00	530.00	515.73	507.00	517.47
1.00	11.00	10.00	529.50	524.80	477.90	510.80
1.00	11.00	10.00	526.50	517.60	480.90	508.40
1.00	11.00	11.00	530.73	524.73	512.09	522.45
1.00	12.00	13.00	544.23	532.46	489.31	522.08
1.00	12.00	13.00	525.00	525.18	473.85	508.55
1.00	13.00	15.00	551.67	545.47	526.13	541.07
1.00	13.00	11.00	504.55	514.45	482.00	502.20
1.00	13.00	13.00	549.85	534.08	501.00	528.38
1.00	13.00	11.00	519.36	518.82	486.45	508.18
1.00	13.00	12.00	529.33	512.17	479.00	506.83
1.00	14.00	13.00	512.85	499.00	465.08	492.31
1.00	14.00	13.00	525.08	521.69	482.00	510.58
1.00	14.00	13.00	523.38	520.46	478.38	507.38

ROW	COLUMN	N	READ	LANG	MATH	TOTAL
1.00	14.00	13.00	519.54	508.08	482.00	503.15
1.00	14.00	13.00	517.38	526.46	495.69	513.38
1.00	14.00	12.00	523.83	527.00	495.33	515.33
1.00	14.00	12.00	546.33	533.33	495.00	524.30
1.00	15.00	25.00	545.44	544.36	506.28	532.04
1.00	15.00	12.00	526.58	526.58	512.33	521.92
1.00	15.00	14.00	543.43	557.50	501.43	534.07
1.00	15.00	20.00	555.25	565.10	523.30	547.90
1.00	15.00	13.00	531.69	542.08	511.62	528.38
1.00	16.00	15.00	523.87	525.73	490.13	513.20
1.00	16.00	15.00	511.27	528.93	480.07	506.80
1.00	16.00	15.00	523.13	527.33	457.07	502.60
1.00	16.00	15.00	507.87	512.93	458.73	493.20
1.00	16.00	15.00	518.40	514.93	474.00	502.47
1.00	17.00	22.00	525.18	512.00	474.90	504.62
1.00	17.00	26.00	540.80	534.36	500.96	523.82
1.00	17.00	24.00	528.83	520.50	490.22	514.13
1.00	17.00	19.00	539.16	526.79	474.84	513.53
1.00	18.00	29.00	512.64	503.32	483.54	500.44
1.00	18.00	26.00	541.56	535.60	479.92	519.04
1.00	18.00	20.00	520.16	514.53	469.88	502.67
1.00	19.00	28.00	498.30	483.85	459.24	482.13
1.00	19.00	30.00	489.73	480.37	455.07	475.89
1.00	19.00	29.00	519.79	505.71	460.82	495.04
1.00	20.00	15.00	537.07	523.20	491.93	517.47
1.00	20.00	15.00	531.07	516.07	463.29	501.38
1.00	20.00	14.00	526.62	534.15	480.25	513.00
1.00	20.00	14.00	485.86	493.00	423.50	467.57
1.00	21.00	14.00	529.85	501.08	468.85	497.92
1.00	21.00	29.00	521.00	516.38	478.46	506.81
1.00	21.00	14.00	564.29	534.00	450.77	516.08
1.00	21.00	29.00	521.12	511.24	464.11	497.65
1.00	21.00	30.00	503.50	494.61	459.93	486.23
1.00	22.00	27.00	514.41	505.89	481.54	501.12
1.00	22.00	29.00	538.72	531.31	494.24	521.34
1.00	23.00	25.00	571.44	576.08	503.96	550.40
1.00	24.00	19.00	531.68	527.21	480.67	513.33

ROW	COLUMN	N	READ	LANG	MATH	TOTAL
1.00	25.00	10.00	523.33	518.11	499.33	510.25
1.00	25.00	14.00	538.23	542.23	500.15	530.58
1.00	25.00	13.00	561.92	558.33	513.58	545.36
1.00	26.00	8.00	555.50	533.38	531.75	540.25
1.00	27.00	16.00	523.00	494.63	445.94	487.88
1.00	27.00	13.00	525.31	492.62	494.00	504.15
1.00	27.00	15.00	494.73	474.73	469.13	479.53
1.00	27.00	14.00	535.77	530.38	513.71	527.23
1.00	28.00	14.00	549.29	547.71	514.36	537.07
1.00	28.00	13.00	546.54	540.15	519.15	535.31
1.00	28.00	13.00	545.31	524.69	516.46	528.85
1.00	28.00	13.00	535.85	516.85	478.15	510.38
1.00	29.00	12.00	551.50	563.50	510.50	541.92
1.00	30.00	12.00	527.67	552.75	529.42	536.58
1.00	30.00	15.00	548.80	554.60	509.15	539.46
1.00	30.00	15.00	539.87	535.20	513.80	529.60
1.00	30.00	15.00	546.40	543.80	522.33	537.53
1.00	30.00	156.00	550.00	544.27	512.67	535.60
2.00	32.00	21.00	537.81	542.10	501.62	527.24
2.00	33.00	21.00	535.10	534.05	493.67	520.95
2.00	33.00	18.00	571.89	563.22	510.11	548.39
2.00	33.00	16.00	555.56	571.25	516.56	547.94
2.00	34.00	21.00	353.71	539.10	493.00	522.67
2.00	34.00	23.00	532.74	536.00	495.30	521.35
2.00	35.00	23.00	538.61	536.00	493.61	522.70
2.00	35.00	28.00	558.86	558.75	519.57	545.75
2.00	36.00	24.00	539.08	520.21	489.46	516.25
2.00	36.00	24.00	513.17	489.33	455.04	485.83
2.00	36.00	24.00	517.13	523.83	467.25	503.70
2.00	37.00	23.00	555.73	552.14	501.96	536.09
2.00	37.00	21.00	550.40	559.40	510.75	542.95
2.00	37.00	20.00	542.00	518.74	495.50	519.16
2.00	38.00	6.00	529.83	545.33	488.17	521.17
2.00	38.00	18.00	543.88	534.56	493.35	523.87
2.00	38.00	19.00	555.88	550.24	510.78	541.25
2.00	38.00	8.00	548.25	559.63	501.25	536.38
2.00	38.00	9.00	557.33	548.89	485.00	530.22

ROW	COLUMN	N	READ	LANG	MATH	TOTAL
2.00	38.00	10.00	540.44	517.00	501.60	519.44
2.00	39.00	25.00	534.43	535.43	500.88	525.15
2.00	39.00	25.00	536.57	540.04	491.61	524.29
2.00	39.00	23.00	538.68	538.86	501.76	526.10
2.00	40.00	24.00	528.85	523.85	491.21	516.10
2.00	40.00	27.00	511.14	510.23	477.35	500.10
2.00	40.00	28.00	541.25	533.96	493.22	520.96
2.00	40.00	28.00	534.63	531.81	492.69	521.60
2.00	41.00	28.00	504.67	512.63	480.54	499.88
2.00	41.00	30.00	510.87	511.27	489.90	504.59
2.00	41.00	28.00	521.18	514.46	466.63	501.26
2.00	42.00	27.00	524.52	514.96	470.45	509.09
2.00	42.00	27.00	535.19	526.19	495.80	518.52
2.00	43.00	26.00	524.52	510.48	475.12	503.64
2.00	43.00	25.00	532.64	520.84	483.38	512.32
2.00	43.00	27.00	539.37	527.52	501.33	522.70
2.00	43.00	24.00	511.30	500.74	470.42	494.17
2.00	44.00	25.00	517.92	517.42	467.71	502.04
2.00	44.00	25.00	527.12	512.20	478.52	508.17
2.00	45.00	26.00	517.46	509.58	453.00	493.27
2.00	45.00	25.00	526.52	527.12	475.28	509.52
2.00	46.00	17.00	539.88	542.44	508.41	530.06
2.00	46.00	17.00	540.94	526.35	511.13	526.31
2.00	47.00	13.00	544.83	538.33	502.08	527.50
2.00	47.00	16.00	548.69	558.63	500.00	535.81
2.00	48.00	22.00	542.45	527.95	500.64	523.68

The SPSSX control lines for this run are the following:

SPSSX Nested MANOVA

Title "Nested MANOVA"
Data list free/row column N read lang math total
list
Data Lines
manova read lang math by row (1,2) column (1,48)/
  Design = row, column, column within row/

0means = table (row, column by row)/
print = cellinfo (Means, cov, cor) homogeneity (cochran, boxm)/

The following selected output are the multivariate test for the homogeneity assumption, which is tenable, the multivariate tests, and the univariate tests. Both the multivariate and univariate tests are statistically significant.

Homogeneity Tests

Multivariate test for Homogeneity of Dispersion matrices

Boxs M =   165.72284
F WITH (96,2240) DF =   1.07566,   P = .293 (Approx.)
Chi-Square with 96 DF =   110.36374,   P = .150 (Approx.)

Multivariate and Univariate Tests
Analysis of Variance - design 1
EFFECT .. COLUMN
Multivariate Tests of Significance (S=3, M=21, N=46½)

Test Name	Value	Approx. F	Hypoth. DF	Error DF	Sig. of F
Pillais	1.50238	2.11539	138.00	291.00	.000
Hotellings	3.82870	2.59870	138.00	281.00	.000
Wilks	.10372	2.33897	138.00	285.63	.000
Roys	.71126				

Effect .. Column
Univariate F-Tests with (46,97) D.F.

Variable	Hypoth. SS	Error SS	Hypoth MS	Error MS	F	Sig. of F
READ	18175.5635	15474.7496	395.12094	159.53350	2.47673	.000
LANG	37062.6478	16610.0302	805.70974	171.23742	4.70522	.000
MATH	34600.0923	19268.1857	752.17592	198.64109	3.78661	.000

7.28 SUMMARY

Multivariate analysis implies that subjects are measured on two or more dependent variables. It was stated that the one group repeated measures design is an extension of the t-test for correlated measures. In addition, it was demonstrated that an extension of the Tukey post hoc procedure can be applied to such a design. It was further illustrated that many multivariate tests have assumptions that parallel their univariate analogues.

Multiple regression is an extension of univariate regression; however, in contrast to the univariate case, multiple regression employs two or more predictors with subjects measured on a dependent variable. SPSSX was used to calculate regression equations. Through several examples, it was demonstrated that different regression approaches such as stepwise, forward entry, and back elimination can produce different results even with the same data. Multiple regression is a mathematical maximization procedure, in that SPSSX and SAS use various procedures to find the greatest correlation between a set of predictors and the dependent variable. Moreover, regression equations are linear combinations. The difficulty with multiple regression is that often regression equations are sample specific, implying they will not cross-validate on independent samples.

The k group MANOVA is the multivariate analogue of the k group ANOVA; however, with the multivariate case, subjects are measured on several dependent variables.　Similarly, factorial MANOVA is the multivariate generalization of the factorial ANOVA. With the factorial MANOVA, we are looking for a multivariate interaction of rows and columns. Likewise, MANCOVA which has the same assumptions as ANCOVA, involves measuring subjects on several dependent variables; however, any differences on the dependent variables are adjusted for by a covariate(s).

In summary, it was demonstrated that MANOVA like its univariate counterpart is a special case of multivariate regression. Through dummy coding, MANOVA can be run on SPSSX as a multivariate regression design. Finally, as with univariate tests, multivariate tests are followed by post hoc procedures. Similar to ANOVA, planned comparisons can be performed at the multivariate level.

7.29 CHOOSING A STATISTICAL PROCEDURE

From an applied standpoint, it can be difficult to select a statistical procedure. Before any statistics can be chosen, a proper research design must be constructed. If things become complicated, this may involve consulting with a research methodologist, or with someone who has done research in an area closely related to test anxiety. Once a proper research design is established, there are hundreds of statistical techniques that may be performed on the data, provided certain assumptions are met. Here a professional statistician may be useful. In this text, we have attempted to emphasize that when analyzing test anxiety data, one does not just simply perform some statistical analysis. First, one must look carefully at the assumptions of a certain statistical test. In addition, the research question one is attempting to answer also influences the statistics chosen.

In the central tendency and variability sections, we pointed out that the mean, standard deviation, and variance are the most commonly used descriptive statistics to describe test anxiety data. Later, we presented the assumptions of the t-test and indicated that there are two commonly used t-tests. If one has two independent groups and certain assumptions are met, one can analyze the groups using the t-test for independent samples. Similarly, if one has correlated groups, or a one-group pretest posttest design, the t-test for correlated measures can be used to analyze this type of data. If one is interested in the relationship between two variables, a correlation statistic can be performed.

Moreover, if one is interested in testing the effects of several treatments in reducing test anxiety, some form of the ANOVA must be employed. If there are three groups measured on one dependent variable, a one-way ANOVA may be applicable if certain assumptions are tenable. Suppose with the previously discussed design, a pretest of test anxiety is added; now, the ANCOVA is possible, again, if certain conditions are met. If one is interested in investigating effects of two or three independent variables on test anxiety, a factorial ANOVA may be appropriate. When one group of subjects are measured three or more times, one can analyze this data with a repeated measures ANOVA. When one is interested in making predictions, regression is a useful technique. Finally, when conducting test anxiety research within schools, one must take into account nested factors. There are univariate and multivariate nested designs.

With subjects measured on several dependent variables, multivariate tests come into play; and as with many of their univariate counterparts, there are specific assumptions for these tests. One could possibly summarize the use of various statistical tests by simply stating that the test chosen depends upon the research question and whether certain assumptions are tenable.

7.30 STATISTICAL APPLICATION EXERCISES

1. The following TAI scores represent sample data. What would be the best way to describe the population mean?
    Scores: 10 20 30 40 50 60 70 80 90
    (Answer the sample mean)

2. With the data from Exercise 1, assume one that we would like to know how much error exists in this data, or how far scores are from the mean. How could we answer this question?
    (Answer, the standard deviation or variance is a measure of precision or how much scores vary about the mean.)

3. Suppose the following situation existed and the assumptions of the t-test were tenable, how could the data be analyzed?

Experimental Group TAI scores	Control Group TAI score
60	90
50	70
30	20

    (Answer: t-test independent samples or F-test for one-way ANOVA.)

4. The data represent TAI scores from fraternal twins before and after a treatment for test anxiety. What would be the appropriate statistical analysis?

Before X	After
33	20
50	35
70	50

    (Answer: t-test repeated measures or repeated measures F-test.)

5. The following represent two random test anxiety variables. How could one test if there is a relationship between the two variables?

x	y
50	60
40	40
40	60
60	60
40	60

    (Answer: correlation analysis.)

6. Suppose with exercise 5 that an x score of 23 had occurred. How could one determine the corresponding y value?

(Answer: regression analysis.)

7. The following scores represent test anxiety scores of three groups of students from an examination. What would be the best way to determine if the groups differed on the dependent variable, or if the population means differed?

G1 G2   G3
61 62   63
61 62   63
40 59   39
37 58   58
47 48   48

(Answer: If certain assumptions are met, the F-test or one-way ANOVA.)

8. Suppose with exercise 7 that the null hypothesis is rejected. How can one determine if group one differed from group two?

(Answer: post hoc procedures such as the Tukey HSD.)

9. The following data represent an independent variable sex (males, females) combined factorially with three treatments (1, 2, and 3). The dependent variables are TAI scores. The first number on each line represent the row number and the second number the column number. The two digit numbers are the TAI scores.

1   1   50
1   1   60
1   2   70
1   2   60
1   3   50
1   3   68
2   1   70
2   1   68
2   2   56
2   2   44
2   3   67
2   3   46

How would you classify this design and what would be the appropriate statistical analysis?

(Answer: This is a 2 by 3 factorial ANOVA. The correct analysis is factorial ANOVA.)

10. The following test anxiety data is from three groups of subjects measured before and after a treatment.

Group1		Group2		Group3	
01 X	02	01 X	02	01 X	02
70	60	64	57	47	56
56	47	68	68	68	57
57	68	68	57	68	45

Provided that certain assumptions are met, how could you analyze these data?

(Answer: ANCOVA.)

11. Two groups of subjects are measured simultaneously on two test anxiety measures.

Group1		Group2	
46	47	48	72
45	57	58	58
78	72	34	65

How would you analyze this data?

(Answer: Hotelling's T test or K group MANOVA.)

12. Interpret the following: $F = (2,14) = 69.26$

(Answer: If one looks for the critical values for F in Table C, one would find critical value of F with 2,14 degrees of freedom equal to 6.51 at the .01 level. These results indicate statistical significance at the .01 level, or we could rewrite the results in journal form as $F(2,14) = 69.26, p<.01$.)

13. Interpret the following: $F = (2,14) = 2.12, p>.01$.

(Answer: This indicates that statistical significance was not reached at the .01 level.)

14. Interpret the following: Chi Square $(3) = 2.171, p>.05$.

(Answer: This indicates that the test statistic Chi Square is not significant at the .05 level.)

15. Interpret the following: $r = .91, N = 10$.

(Answer: Using table H and locating an r value with number of pairs minus two for degrees freedom (N-2 or 10-2 = 8), a critical value of $r = .765$ at the .01 level for a two-tailed test. This indicates statistical significance at the .01 level. The results can be rewritten as r(8), $p<.01$.)

16. Interpret the following: Suppose the Spearman rank-order correlation coefficient (rho) is determined to be -.70, with 9 pairs. What does this result mean?

(Answer: Using Table I for rho with 9 pairs, the critical value at the .05 level is .683 for a two-tailed test. This indicates that statistical significance was reached at this level. The results could be rewritten as rho(9) = -.70, p<.05.)

17. For exercise 16, how much variance is accounted for, or what is the coefficient of determination?
    (Answer: 49%.)

18. The data below represent the t scores from two test anxiety instruments. What is the relationship between the two variables?

x	y
51	51
52	54
53	52
54	56
55	53
56	55

    (Answer: r=.6(4), p>.05.)

19. Can a regression equation be applied to exercise 18?
    (Answer: no, since the correlation was not significant.)

20. Below are the t scores for 8 subjects on the TAI and STAI, two test anxiety instruments. If a score of 59 was obtain on the TAI, what would be the predicted value of STAI?

Subjects	TAI	STAI
1.	57	63
2.	56	59
3.	55	61
4.	54	57
5.	54	55
6.	53	57
7.	52	51
8.	51	53

    Answer: The regression equation is as follows:
    $y = -39.43 + 1.79X$
    Solving for X = 59 is
    $y = -39.43 + 1.79(59) = 66.18$.

21. Jane obtained a t score of 60 on the TAI. Assume that scores on the TAI are normally distributed with a mean of 50 and a standard deviation of 10. What is the probability of Jane getting a t score this large? Hint: One must use Table A for area under the normal curve.

(Answer: Probability can be found for normally distributed variables by finding the area beyond a certain z score, or the area in the smaller portion of the normal curve. A t score of 60 corresponds to a z score of 1, which cuts off 34.13% of the area on the right side of the normal curve. The entire right side of the normal curve represents 50% of the area, since this represents half of the normal curve. The area beyond this point can be found by subtracting .50-.3413 = .1587. This is a proportion or probability. Therefore, the probability of obtaining a t score of 60 on the TAI = .1587, or approximately a 16% chance.)

22. Suppose Jim obtained a raw score of 110 on a test that had a population mean of 80 and a population standard deviation of 16. Assume that the scores on the test are normally distributed. Five hundred ten students took this test. How many students in Jim's class scored above his raw score of 110?

(Answer: The first step is to find Jim's z scores, which is found by the following formula:

$z = \dfrac{x-\mu}{\sigma}$ μ is the population mean or 80
         σ is the population standard deviation or 16
         x = Jim's score of 110

by substitution, $z = \dfrac{110-80}{16} = 1.875$

The probability of getting a score this large (1.88 rounded) is .0304, which is the proportion of 510 students scoring this high. The final step for this solution is multiplying the proportion by the sample size. So, .0304(510)=15.504 or approximately 16 students.)

23. Describe the meaning of the following notation:

A X B X C(AB)

(This is a three-factor design with factor C nested within A by B. If one were to run this analysis on SPSSX, to indicate that C(AB), the SPSSX subcommand would be as follows:

C within A by B.)

References

Bock, R. D. (1975). *Multivariate statistical methods in behavioral research.* New York: McGraw-Hill.

Borg, W. R., & Gall, M. D. (1983). *Educational research: An introduction.* New York: Longman.

Finn, J. (1974). *A general model for multivariate analysis.* New York: Holt, Rinehart and Winston.

Greenhouse, S., & Geisser, J. (1959). On methods in the analysis of profile data. *Psychometrika, 24,* 95-112.

Huck, S., Cormier, W., & Bounds, W. (1974). *Reading statistics and research.* New York: Harper and Row.

Huynh, H., & Feldt, L. (1976). Estimation of the Box correction for degrees of freedom from sample data in the randomized block and split plot designs. *Journal of Educational Statistics, 1,* 69-82.

Johnson, N., & Wichern, D. (1982). *Applied multivariate statistical analysis.* Englewood Cliffs, NJ: Prentice-Hall.

Keppel, G. (1983). *Design and analysis: A researcher's handbook.* Englewood Cliffs, NJ: Prentice-Hall.

Kesselman, H., Rogan, J., Mendoza, J., & Breen, L. (1980). Testing the validity conditions of repeated measures F tests. *Psychological Bulletin, 87,* 479-481.

Lindman, H. R. (1992). *Analysis of variance in experimental design.* New York: Springer-Verlag.

Pedhazar, E. (1982). *Multiple regression in behavioral research.* New York: Holt, Rinehart and Winston.

Sapp, M. (1997). *Counseling and psychotherapy: Theories, associated research, and issues.* Lanham, MD: University Press of America.

SPSSX user's guide (2nd ed.). (1983). Chicago: SPSS, Inc.

SPSSX user's guide (3rd ed.). (1988). Chicago: SPSS, Inc.

Stevens, J. P. (1990). *Intermediate statistics: A modern approach.* Hillsdale, NJ: Lawrence Erlbaum Associates.

Stevens, J. P. (1986). *Applied multivariate statistics for the social sciences.* Hillsdale, NJ: Lawrence Erlbaum Associates.

Stevens, J. P. (1996). *Applied multivariate statistics for the social sciences* (3rd ed.). Hillsdale, NJ: Lawrence Erlbaum Associates.

Tatsuoka, M. M. (1988). *Multivariate analysis: Techniques for educational and psychological research* (2nd ed.). New York: Wiley.

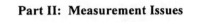
Part II: Measurement Issues

Chapter 8

CONTENTS

8.1 MEASUREMENT ISSUES

The measurement of test anxiety is an extremely complicated process. Currently, classical test theory, item response theory, and generalizability theory are the approaches that dominate measurement theory.

Classical theory is the model often taught in introductory psychological measurement courses. Psychologists have used this theory of measurement since the turn of the century. Often, it is used to find reliability measures such as test-retest, internal consistency, and so on. It is also referred to as the **true score theory**, and it has the following mathematical model:

$X = T + E$

X = a person's score or an observed score

T = a person's true score

E = the error score

Theoretically, reliability can be expressed as the ratio of true score variance divided by the observed score variance. If we symbolize reliability as r_{xx}, it can be expressed mathematically as

$$r_{xx} = \frac{S_t^2}{S_x^2} = \frac{\text{true score variance}}{\text{observed score variance}}$$

And if S_e denotes the standard error of measurement,

$$S_e = S_x\sqrt{1 - r_{xx}}$$

The standard error estimates intraindividual variability, and it provides a measure of variability of a person's score from repeated testings.

To summarize, classical theory states that a person's score is composed of two components: the person's true score and random error.

In contrast, item response theory (IRT) states that a person's score is the product of his or her ability and the easiness of a given item. IRT computes the odds that a participant will succeed on an item, denoted as O_{ni}.

$O_{ni} = Z_n E_i$

Z_n = the participant's ability

E_i = item easiness

According to IRT, the greater a participant's ability level the more likely he or she will answer a particular item correctly.

Generalizability (G) theory subsumes and extends classical test theory (Brennan, 1983). **G theory** can simultaneously estimate several sources of error variance and interactions among variance sources. Unlike classical test theory, which estimates one source of variance, G theory can estimate multiple sources of variance simultaneously. For example, test-retest reliability only estimates error due to time; internal consistency is based on error due to test items. The reader can consult Brennan, who shows how to perform generalizability studies using an ANOVA-type approach.

The study that follows describes the testing of the dimensionality of the worry component of the test anxiety inventory with economically and educationally at-risk high school students employing item response theory and principal components analysis.

8.2 TESTING THE DIMENSIONALITY OF THE WORRY COMPONENT OF THE TEST ANXIETY INVENTORY WITH ECONOMICALLY AND EDUCATIONALLY AT-RISK HIGH SCHOOL STUDENTS: EMPLOYING ITEM RESPONSE THEORY ANALYSIS AND PRINCIPAL COMPONENTS ANALYSIS

Item Response Theory

Hambleton and Swaminathan (1985, pp. 1-14) and Samejima (1969) compared and contrasted classical test theory models and neoclassical or modern test theory models (item response theory models). They found that each theory can produce a distinct form of item analysis. These researchers noted that classical test theory is based on "weak assumptions"; these are assumptions that can be "easily" met by most tests. Wright (1977a, 1977b), one of the earlier proponents and developers of IRT, distinguished between IRT and classical models by drawing the analogy between an individual approach to assessment versus a group method, with IRT being the individualistic model (Wright & Panchapakesan, 1969). The group assessment model (classical model) is based on standardization samples: the number of individuals who succeeded on an item and item difficulty, all of which are very dependent on the appropriateness of the standardization sample involved.

IRT, also called **latent trait theory**, makes no assumptions about the individuals involved. Instead, this simple model posits that a person's score is the project, in the arithmetic sense, of his or her ability and the easiness of an item. Essentially, the more capable a person, the greater his or her changes of succeeding on an item. Also, the easier an item, the greater the likelihood that an individual with a certain ability will solve that item (Fox & Jones, 1998).

greater the likelihood that an individual with a certain ability will solve that item (Fox & Jones, 1998).

IRT makes no assumptions about the abilities of the calibration sample. It allows the calibration of a test across an entire range of possibilities, even when everyone in the calibration sample gets the same score (Wright & Panchapakesan, 1969). This is possible because although everyone can theoretically get the same total score, they tend to differ on those items that they get correct. Once a pool of test items conforms to an item response analysis model, and has been calibrated, one can compute a calibration curve of estimated abilities for every possible score on any test or subtest (Wright & Panchapeksan, 1969) without the need for additional standardization samples.

IRT has two major statistical assumptions. First, it assumes unidimensionality. This assumption holds when a test measures only one underlying construct. The second assumption is local independence. It assumes that the error component of each item cannot be correlated across items. When a single score can be used to predict performance, and local independence holds, a test is said to be unidimensional (Allen & Yen, 1979, p. 57; Hambleton, 1983, p. 5).

In terms of item analysis models, IRT and classical theory have similar mathematical models. For example, classical test theory has the following model:

$$X = T + E$$

Where X = a person's score
T = the person's true score
E = the error.

The classical test theory model is often used to describe classical reliability theory. It states that a person's score (X) has two component parts: the person's true score (T) and some random error (E). A person's true score is unobservable; it is a theoretical construct, and it represents the part of a person's score not affected by error. This model is based upon three assumptions:
1. True and error scores are uncorrelated.
2. The mean of error scores in the population of examinees equals zero.
3. Error scores on parallel tests are not correlated.
IRT has the following model (Hambleton, 1983), p. 5):

$$\gamma_i = p_i\theta + \epsilon_i$$

Where γ_i = the latent response to item i

$p_i\theta$ = the correlation between γ_i and θ. This is the regression coefficient of γ_i on θ.

θ is a person's ability level or odds of success on an item; theoretically, it can range $\pm \infty$; however, in practice the value seldom exceeds ± 4.0.

ϵ_i = an error component with a mean of zero and a standard deviation $\sigma(\epsilon_i)$.

One can see that the classical test theory model and IRT model have some similarities. For example, both models are mathematical functions with error components. In addition, $p_i\theta$, which is analogous to a person's true score under the classical model, is unobservable. For example, one can also view θ as a person's underlying ability or latent trait measured by items on a test. When we present an item to a person, for example the ith item, a response γ_i is elicited; this response can have the same values as θ. When an item is a perfect indicator of a trait, γ_i and θ are equal. For practical purposes, γ_i has an error component because it is not a perfect indicator of a trait. We see a similar occurrence with the classical model where a person's true score has to be adjusted with an error component (Hambleton, 1983, p. 4). In summary, IRT models have two assumptions: 1) a single ability underlies test performance—called unidimensionality of the test and 2) the relationship between item performance and ability can be represented by one, two, or three parameter logistic function.

The Rasch or 1-parameter logistic model, the simplest IRT model, is the one employed in this study. It is based upon an objective method of transforming data into measurements. There are two conditions for this process. First, the calibration of the measuring instrument must be independent of the items used for calibration. Second, the measurement of objects must be independent of the instrument (Fox & Jones, 1998).

The Rasch model is based on object-free instrument calibration and instrument-free calibration, which allows generalization beyond the particular instrument (i.e., set of items) used. The Rasch model simply states that when a person encounters a test item his or her outcome is governed by the product of his or her ability and the easiness of the item (proportion of correct responses). For example, the odds of success O_{ni} are:

$O_{ni} = Z_n E_i$

Z_n = ability of subject

E_i = item easiness or proportion of correct responses

Specifically, the higher the person's ability level the more likely he or she is to answer a particular item correctly. Likewise, the easier a particular item the greater the likelihood that any person will get it correct.

In terms of independence for obtaining odds of success, the Rasch model states (Waller, 1973, 1976):

$O_{AB} = O_A \, O_B$

O_{AB} = Odds of obtaining AB

Odds denotes the ratio of success to failure during probability calculations. The Rasch model states that the parameters O_A and O_B (odds of obtaining AB) are independent.

Also, under the Rasch model:

P_{ij} = Person "i" on the "j_{th}" item.

$P_{ij} = \dfrac{Z_i \, E_j}{1+Z_i \, E_j}$, which implies that P_{ij} = Pr (Person "i" gets the "j_{th}" item correct given his or her ability).

This equation indicates that the probability that a person will get an item correct with easiness E_j is the product $Z_n E_j$ divided by one plus the product $Z_n E_j$.

With the Rasch model, we estimate Z_i. For example if:

$$r_{ij} = \begin{cases} 1 \text{ means person i is correct on item i} \\ 0 \text{ means person j is wrong on item j} \end{cases}$$

$P_{ij} = \text{Pr} \, (r_{ij} = 1)$

Pr is the probability of obtaining a given response vector.

Therefore, if the person's response vector V_i is:

$V_i = \{r_{ij}\} = \{1110001000\}$ 	Remember that 1's mean an item is correct and 0's an item is incorrect.

We want a Z_i that maximizes the probability of obtaining the correct data.

The principle of maximum likelihood estimation states that one should use an estimate of the parameter (i.e., ability) value that maximizes the probability or likelihood of getting the data obtained, V_i.

So, Pr (V_i) = Pr $(r_{ii}=1 \; r_{i2}=1 \; r_{13}=1 \; r_{14}=0 \; r_{15}=0 \; r_{16}=0 \; r_{17}=1 \; r_{18}=0 \; r_{19}=0)$

Let $Q_{ij} = 1 - P_{ij}$

Q_{ij} is the probability of not obtaining a given response vector.
Only if we assume local independence will

$$\Pr\,(\underline{V})= \quad P_{jj}{}^{r_{ij}}\, Q_{ij}{}^{1-r_{ij}}, \text{ which is the likelihood function.}$$

Substituting for $P_{ij} = \dfrac{Z_i\, E_j}{1 + Z_i\, E_j}$

And $Q_{ij} = 1 - P_{ij}$

$$PR(V) = \prod_{J\,=\,1}^{n} \left(\frac{Z_i\, E_j}{1 + Z_i\, E_j} \right)^{r_{ij}} \left(1 - \frac{Z_i\, E_j}{1 + Z_i\, E_j} \right)^{1-r_{ij}}$$

If we let a person's ability parameter $\theta_i, = \log Z_i$.

Then, $\theta_i, = \log eZ_i$, where e is a constant that equals 2.7183, and $\log eZ_i$ is read logarithm to the base e of Z_i or logarithm of Z_i to the base of e. Well, $\log eZ_i = Z_i = e$.
A person's difficulty parameter
$\partial = \log eE_j = \partial = e^{Ei}$

$$P_{ij} = \frac{e^{\theta i}\, e^{\partial j}}{1 + e^{\theta i}\, e^{\partial j}}$$

$$= \frac{e^{\theta i\, \partial j}}{1 + e^{\theta i\, \partial j}}$$

Logs are used to transform the scale so the center is around zero.

The derivative $\dfrac{dP}{d\theta} = P_{ij}\, Q_{ij}.$

This implies that there is a maximum likelihood that is unique.
Summarizing, IRT can be employed to test the unidimensionality of a scale or test. If unidimensionality holds, students' ability level can be obtained and is independent of the instrument used. Essentially, IRT is a method of item analyses or scaling that is not based on group norms.

The Dimensionality of the Worry Component of the TAI

Traditionally, test anxiety, as measured by the Test Anxiety Inventory (TAI), is composed of two components: worry and emotionality (Liebert & Morris, 1967; Morris & Liebert, 1970; Morris & Perez, 1972; Sapp, 1993, 1996b; Spielberger, 1980). Worry is the cognitive concern about performance whereas emotionality is the physiological reaction to anxiety (Sapp, 1994a, 1994b, 1996b).

Sarason (1972, 1980) pointed out that cognitive overload during a test situation or learning situation can result in impaired learning and performance. Essentially, test anxiety makes demands on the attention by dividing attention into task-relevant and task-irrelevant cognitions and behaviors. Benjamin, McKeachie, and Lin (1987) characterized these cognitive models of test anxiety along the lines of a computer model. They viewed a student's capacity to store information as analogous to a computer's capacity to store data; hence, their model is called an information processing view of test anxiety.

Doctor and Altman (1969) factor analyzed Liebert and Morris' Test Anxiety Questionnaire (TAQ), a precursor to the TAI, and found that worry is more complex than Spielberger had conceptualized it. They did find that worry appears to be a trait factor whereas emotionality corresponds to a state factor; however, they further differentiated worry into cognitive perceptual features that result in a cognitive perceptual distortion of unpleasantness and self-evaluation. In addition, Finger and Galassi (1977) found that treatments designed to reduce worry also reduced emotionality. Their research suggests that worry and emotionality interact in some complex fashion. There is also research by Richardson, O'Neil, Whitmore, and Judd (1977) that failed to confirm the factor structure of the Liebert-Morris Scale using confirmatory factor analysis. Specifically, they did not find worry and emotionality emerging as factor structures.

Salamé (1984) conducted factor analysis and path analysis on the worry and emotionality components of test anxiety and found that neither worry nor emotionality were unidimensional. Salamé's factor analysis revealed four factors for the worry component, each of which had high internal consistency. The factors composing worry were:

(1) lack of confidence in ability to succeed,
(2) fear of failure and its consequences to academic career,
(3) expressing fearful anticipations of failure and worry about the consequences of failure, and

(4) fear of social devaluations.

Salamé's (1984) path analysis showed that "fear of social devaluation" appears to be a direct or indirect precursor to the other four factors. Path analysis also indicated that doubts about one's competence, lack of ability to succeed, and fear of failure serve as intervening variables between precursors of test anxiety and subsequent test anxiety reactions.

Salamé's (1984) factor analysis of the emotionality component revealed two factors: "apprehension" and "other anxiety reactions." The apprehension factor consisted of items that measure one's concern about exams without references to failure relating to one's ability or the degree of preparation for an exam. This factor appears to be a pure concern variable.   The second factor, other anxiety reaction, included psychophysiological reactions, restlessness, rapid heartbeat, jitteryness, and situation and personality interferences.

Hagtvet (1984), Hagtvet and Johnsen (1992), and Schwarzer, Van der Ploeg and Spielberger (1982, 1989) also questioned the assumed unitary structure of the worry and emotionality components of test anxiety. Worry and emotionality are seen as determined by fear of failure. Actually, test anxiety as contextualized by Hagtvet is a fear of failure construct. This is in direct opposition to Sarason's (1980) theory; Sarason (1984) reported that individuals scoring high on the test anxiety rarely experienced fear of failure. Also, Sarason (1984) suggests that test anxiety scales may measure cognitive components of test anxiety in contrast to affective ones. Finally, Hagtvet (1984) suggests that fear of failure, worry, and emotionality are three different constructs; however, fear of failure can produce worry and emotionality response; hence they can serve as test anxiety measures.

The purpose of this study is to apply the Rasch model of item analysis to worry test anxiety measures obtained from economically and educationally at-risk high school students.

Method

Participants

One hundred and one high school students were identified as being both educationally and economically disadvantaged. Students were attending an Educational Opportunity Program (EOP) at a northeastern university. This is a program designed to provide academic assistance for educationally and economically disadvantaged high school students. During the summer of 1993, students were enrolled in a five-week developmental summer program. Forty percent of the students were African American, 32% were Latino, 17% were Asian American, and 11% did not identify their racial heritage. Forty-eight percent of the students were male, and 52% were female. Students were high school seniors, ranging between 17 and 19 years of age. Many of the students were from a large metropolitan urban area located within a large northeastern state. The average family income of participating students was below $17,000.

The computer program used for the item response analysis (IRT) was an augmented version of LOGOG (Kolakowski & Bock, 1973). IRT assumes a one-dimensional underlying trait (Samejima, 1969). This program estimates ability and difficulty parameters through a quasi-marginal maximum likelihood procedure that continues through an iterative process (Newton-Raphson) until a convergent criterion is obtained. Specifically, the estimation procedure is as follows: first, ability and difficulty parameters are estimated together, then difficulty parameters are estimated singly, next ability and difficulty parameters are estimated again, and finally the ability and difficulty parameters are estimated with estimations of ability held constant. LOGOG rank orders participants and distributes them into 10 score groups or fractiles (Waller, 1989). The Rasch model assumes a unidimensional underlying trait. Chi-square goodness-of-fit statistics allow one to determine if items deviate from unidimensionality. LOGOG calculates a goodness-of-fit chi-square for each item. Items with the best fit have the smallest chi-square values.

A chi-square (χ^2) goodness-of-fit test statistic (Kolakowski & Bock, 1973) is used to test the unitary dimensionality of the worry scale. Significant χ^2 tests for any items of the worry scale suggests that it is not contributing to unidimensionality. Also, if the overall χ^2 test is significant, this suggests that unidimensionality is not tenable for the entire instrument. We wanted to determine if the worry subscale of the TAI consisted of more than one component; therefore, in addition to the Rasch analysis, we performed principle components analysis on the worry scale using the SPSSX computer program (1988).

Independent Variables
Students were given diagnostic tests to assess writing, mathematical, and reading ability. Each test was given under standardized conditions; proctors read the instructions for each test aloud, while students read them silently.

Essays constituted the writing test. Students were required to respond to one of two possible passages on two controversial contemporary issues: drug legislation or women in combat. Students chose one of the passages and constructed an essay. One hour and fifteen minutes was the alotted time students had to complete their responses.

Department of English faculty and graduate assistants from the English Department and the university's learning skills center rated essays.

Raters looked for the following:

Ability to identify an issue and develop an argument,

- Capacity to proceed in a logical and orderly manner,
- Skills to specify general and abstract points,
- The ability to address intended audience with appropriate tone and sense of purpose,
- Ability to write clearly and economically,
- Ability to express oneself in a natural voice,
- Using grammar correctly, and
- Spelling and punctuating correctly.

The above criteria were rated on a scale of 1 to 6 by one rater. The rating was used to place students in English courses. In summary, the writing test was a diagnostic and placement tool used to assess the writing skill level of all entering first time college students at this university.

The Department of Mathematical Sciences faculty constructed the mathematics tests. Primarily, this test was used to place students into the appropriate math courses. The math test was multiple choice, with five options for each question, and comprised of 43 total questions divided into three clusters of increasing difficulty. Scoring in the highest cluster suggested readiness for a basic calculus course, scoring within the second cluster indicated placement for a pre-calculus class, and scoring within the third cluster indicated placement in beginning or intermediate algebra. These tests were administered to all students during a 2½ day summer orientation.

Dependent Variable

The worry subscale of the Test Anxiety Inventory (TAI) was used as a measure of test anxiety. The worry subscale consists of eight items designed to measure the worry component of test anxiety. Since copyright permission could not be obtained, the eight items of the TAI worry subscale were paraphrased to give readers a feel for the actual items.

TAI 3   –   Thoughts about my grade interferes with my course work on tests.

TAI 4   –   Important exams cause me to freeze.

TAI 5   –   Exams cause me to question if I will get through school.

TAI 6   –   Working hard on a test causes me to get confused.

TAI 7   –   Thoughts of performing poorly on tests interfere with my concentration.

TAI 14 –   I defeat myself when working on important exams.

TAI 17 –   I think about failing when taking exams.

TAI 20 –   I forget facts I really know during exams.

Sapp (1993, 1996b) reported validity coefficients of the worry scale of .79 for males and .70 for females. Reliability coefficients for a six month period was .66. The worry raw scores, using a table of norms, were converted into t-scores which have a mean of 50 and a standard deviation of 10.

Research Design

Students were pretested on the worry subscale of the TAI and randomly assigned to one of three battery of tests designed to measure writing, mathematics, and reading ability. The three test sequences students were assigned to were: (1) writing, mathematics, and reading; (2) mathematics, writing, and reading; (3) reading, writing, and mathematics. After taking the test battery, students were posttested on the TAI worry test anxiety. Posttest worry scores were used for the IRT and principal components analysis.

Results

The results of the item response analysis attempted to fit the eight items of the worry scale to a unidimensional model using the LOGOG. It is assumed that each item contributes to unidimensionality; therefore, if one item deviates from unidimensionality the scale is probably not unidimensional. LOGOG suggests that the eight items of the worry test of the TAI are not measuring a unidimensional construct, $\chi^2 = 211.5538$ (100), p<.001. The results of each item from the worry scale is found in Table 1. Coefficient alpha for the worry scale was .824, p<.01.

The correlation matrix for inter-item correlations for worry is found in Table 2. Results of the principal components analysis performed on the worry inter-item correlation matrix is found in Table 3. Stevens (1992 pp. 374-407) recommends using principal components analysis to determine if data from a correlation matrix measure several constructs or principal components. Using the SPSSX (1988) varimax rotation procedure, two factors emerge, accounting for 64.8 of the variance on worry test anxiety. This program employs eigenvalues greater than one as the criteria for determining the number of components to retain.

Items 3, 4, 6, 7, 14, and 17 load highly on factor 1, while items 5 and 20 load highly on factor 2. Factor 1, having an eigenvalue of 3.81, accounts for 47.6 of the variance on worry, and factor 2 with an eigenvalue of 1.37, accounts for 17.2 of the variance on worry. All loadings on both factors are significant, using the double standard error of a correlation .256(2)=.512, at the .01 level of significance.

All six items on factor 1 have significant loadings. For example, item 3 has a loading of .80, item 4 has a loading of .62, and item 6 has a loading of .81, while the loadings for items 7, 14, and 17 have the following respective loadings, .72, .81, and .80. Also, factor 2 has significant loadings for items 5 and 20 which are .86 and .88, respectively. Loadings for both factors are significant. On factor 1, significant loadings range from .62 to .81, while factor 2 has significant loadings ranging between .86 and .88. In terms of overall test anxiety, as measured by worry, there are pretest-posttest changes t(100) = 3.11, p < .01. The mean and standard deviation for pretest worry scores are 65.16 and 23.30, respectively. The mean posttest scores for worry are 61.09, and the standard deviation is 23.20.

Discussion

The results of IRT and principal components analysis suggest that worry is not a unitary construct. Specifically, for the IRT analysis, chi-square values for all items, except two (TAI 4 and TAI 17), did not contribute to an unidimensional model. In addition, the adjusted total model fit statistic, expressed as a chi-square statistic, was also significant, indicating that worry is not a one-dimensional construct. More correctly, it indicates that the worry subscale of the TAI does not measure a unitary construct.

In addition, principal components analysis of the worry scale substantiated the results of IRT analyses. Varimax rotation extracted two factors accounting for 64.8 of the total variance on worry. Specifically, factor 1, with an eigenvalue of 3.81, accounted for 47.6 of the variance on worry. Moreover, factor 2, having an eigenvalue of 1.37, accounted for 17.2 of the variance on worry.

Six variables had large loadings on factor 1, while 2 variables had large loadings on factor 2. The principal components analysis supports Sarason's (1980) (Sapp, Durand, & Farrell, 1995; Sapp, Farrell, & Durand, 1995) conclusion that the worry component of test anxiety consists of more than one factor or component. We named factor 1 worry and factor 2 test-irrelevant thinking, corresponding to Sarason's conceptualization. These results support the theories of Sapp (1993, 1996a, 1996b), Tobias (1985), Salamé (1984), Hagtvet (1984), Finger and Galassi (1977), and Richardson et al. (1977). Our results did not support the unidimensional theory of worry test anxiety as proposed by Liebert and Morris (1967). Conceptualizing worry test anxiety as a unitary construct may have heuristic value, but worry test anxiety is more complex than just one factor or component.

In terms of recommendations for administrators, counseling psychologists, counselors, and personnel workers, this study shows that educationally and economically disadvantaged high school students do report substantially higher levels of worry, as measured by the worry scale of the TAI, in actual testing situations, compared to the normative sample. We found that after testing, students reported lower levels of worry than on pretest measures. This relationship between increased worry scores and a testing situation suggests that tests serve as a stimulus for worry test anxiety. Statistical analyses substantiated this notion. *The practical significance of these results is that testing situations can be modified to reduce test anxiety.*

Since worry test anxiety is primarily a cognitive construct, we believe that cognitive-behavioral interventions may be helpful (Sapp, 1994a, 1994b, 1996a, 1996b, 1997; Sapp & Farrell, 1994). Specifically, a combination of relaxation procedures and study skills training could be useful (Sapp, 1993, pp. 233-262). In addition, supportive counseling provided before taking an examination has been shown to reduce test anxiety. Here, counselors could work with groups of students and allow them to express their fear of taking tests. Sapp (1993, 1996b) reports success with this form of counseling with students who are not economically and educationally disadvantaged. It is conceivable that such a strategy would allay worry test anxiety with this population. In summary, a combination of supportive counseling, study skills training, and relaxation procedures would be part of a package to allay worry test anxiety with economically and educationally at-risk high school students (Sapp, 1994; Sapp & Farrell, 1994).

There are limitations in this study. First, these results only apply to academically and economically disadvantaged high school students. Moreover, the sample size was only 101 subjects, which could have produced unreliable results with the principal components analysis and IRT analysis; however, Lord (1983, pp. 51-61) has justified using sample sizes of approximately 100 with the Rasch IRT model.

In addition, Stevens (1992) pointed out that reliable principal components analyses will yield accurate results when $Q/P < .30$, where P is the number of variables and Q is the number of factors. In the current study, $Q/P = 2/8 = .25$, which is less than .30. These results are accurate when compared to Kaiser's rule of using eigenvalues greater than one as the true number of factors to retain (Kaiser, 1960).

Finally, research is needed to investigate which types of treatments affect the components of test anxiety with educationally and economically disadvantaged high school students.   This study suggests that theoretically, worry is the most important variable to reduce with these students. We recommend applying cognitive-behavioral techniques with educationally and economically disadvantaged high school students who have heightened levels of test anxiety (Farrell, Sapp, Johnson, & Pollard, 1994; Sapp, 1994, 1996a; Sapp & Farrell, 1994). With these students, we believe that worry and emotionality overlap; if this is the case, treatments that reduce worry will also reduce emotionality.

Table 1
Chi-Square Tests of Unidimensionality

	Chi-Square	Probability	Iterations
TAI 3	38.9526(26)	.04600*	4
TAI 4	23.6137(26)	.59804	3
TAI 5	90.9371(26)	.00000*	3
TAI 6	57.7772(26)	.00015*	4
TAI 7	36.3204(26)	.04940*	4
TAI 14	83.0142(26)	.00015*	4
TAI 17	29.2313(26)	.12510	4
TAI 20	80.1856(26)	.00000*	2
Total Model Fit	440.0320(208)	.00000*	
Adjusted Total	211.5538(100)	.00000*	

*Indicates statistically significant lack of unidimensional model fit at the .05 level.

Table 2

Inter-Item Correlation Matrix for Worry

	TAI 3	TAI 4	TAI 5	TAI 6	TAI 7	TAI 14	TAI 17	TAI 20
TAI 3	1.00							
TAI 4	.51	1.00						
TAI 5	-.23	-.15	1.00					
TAI 6	.57	.42	-.22	1.00				
TAI 7	.49	.30	-.33	.53	1.00			
TAI 14	.47	.47	-.14	.60	.55	1.00		
TAI 17	.80	.31	-.23	.60	.59	.51	1.00	
TAI 20	-.28	-.18	.56	-.18	-.18	-.06	-.27	1.00

The following are the SPSSX control lines for a principal component analysis of this correlation matrix:

Title: "Principal Components for Worry"
Data list free/ TAI3 TAI4 TAI5 TAI6 TAI7 TAI17 TAI20
begin data
Note: Insert Correlation Matrix
End data
Factor Variables TAI2 to TAI20/
        Rotation = Norotation/
        Plot = Eigen/
        Format = Sort blank (.25)/

Table 3
Varimax Rotation for Worry

	Factor 1	Factor 2
TAI 6	.81*	
TAI 14	.81*	
TAI 17	.80*	
TAI 3	.80*	
TAI 7	.72*	
TAI 4	.62*	
TAI 20		.88*
TAI 5		.86*

Factor	Eigenvalue	Percent of Variance Accounted For
1	3.81	47.6
2	1.37	17.2
		64.8 = Total Variance Accounted For

Significant loadings at α =.01 for a two-tailed test were found by doubling the standard error for a correlation with an N = 100 which has a critical value of .256. The resulting value is .256(2) = .512.

References

Brennan, R. L. (1983). *Elements of generalizability theory*. Iowa City, IA: American Testing Program.

Allen, M. J., & Yen, W. M. (1979). *Introduction to measurement theory*. Belmont, CA: Wadsworth, Inc.

Benjamin, M., McKeachie, W. J., & Lin, Y. (1987). Two types of test anxious students: Support for an information processing mode. *Journal of Educational Psychology, 79*(2), 131-136.

Doctor, R., & Altman, F. (1969). Worry and emotionality as components of test anxiety: Replications and further data. *Psychological Reports, 24*, 563-568.

Farrell, W., Sapp, M., Johnson, J., & Pollard, D. (1994). Assessing college aspirations among at-risk high school students: A principal component analysis. *The High School Journal, 77*(4), 294-303.

Finger, R., & Galassi, J. P. (1977). Effects of modifying cognitive versus emotionality responses in the treatment of test anxiety. *Journal of Consulting and Clinical Psychology, 45*, 280-287.

Hagtvet, K. A. (1984). Fear of failure, worry and emotionality: Their suggestive causal relationships to mathematical performance and state anxiety. In H. M. Van Der Ploeg, R. Schwarzer, & C. D. Spielberger (Eds.), *Advances in test anxiety research* (Vol. 3) (pp. 211-224). Lisse/Hillsdale, NJ: Swets and Zeitlinger/Erlbaum.

Hambleton, R. K. (1983). *Applications of item response theory*. Vancouver, B.C.: Educational Research Institute of British Columbia.

Hambleton, R. K., & Swaminathan, H. (1985). *The response theory: Principles and applications*. Dordrecht, The Netherlands: Kluwer-Nijhoff Publishing.

Kaiser, H. F. (1960). The application of electronic computers to factor analysis. *Educational and Psychological Measurement, 20*, 141-151.

Fox, C. M., & Jones, J. A. (1998). Uses of Rasch modeling in counseling psychology research. *Journal of Counseling Psychology, 45*(1), 30-45.

Kolakowski, D., & Bock, R. D. (1973). A Fortran IV program for maximum likelihood item analyses and test scoring: Logistic Model for multiple item responses. *Statistical Laboratory Research Memorandum* No. 13, Department of Education, University of Chicago.

Liebert, R., & Morris, L. W. (1967). Cognitive and emotional components of test anxiety: A distinction and some initial data. *Psychological Reports, 20*, 975-978.

Lord, F. M. (1983). Small N justifies Rasch model. In D. Weis (Ed.), *New horizons in testing: Latent trait theory and computerized adaptive testing* (pp. 51-61). New York: Academic Press.

Morris, L. W., & Liebert, R. M. (1970). Relationship of cognitive and emotional components of test anxiety to physiological arousal and academic performance. *Journal of Consulting and Clinical Psychology, 35*, 332-337.

Morris, L. W., & Perez, T. L. (1972). Effects of test-interruption on emotional arousal and performance. *Psychological Reports, 31*, 559-564.

Richardson, F. C., O'Neil, H. F., Whitmore, J., & Judd, W. A. (1977). Factor analysis of the Test Anxiety Scale and evidence concerning components of test anxiety. *Journal of Consulting and Clinical Psychology, 45*, 704-705.

Salamé, R. F. (1984). Test anxiety: Its determinants, manifestations and consequences. In H. M. Van Der Ploeg, R. Schwarzer, & C. D. Spielberger (Eds.), *Advances in test anxiety research* (Vol. 3) (pp. 83-121). Lisse/Hillsdale, NJ: Swets and Zeitlinger/Erlbaum.

Samejima, F. (1969). Estimation of latent ability using a response pattern of graded scores. *Psychometrika Monograph Supplement No. 17*.

Sapp, M. (1993). *Test anxiety: Applied research, assessment, and treatment intervention*. Lanham, MD: University Press of America.

Sapp, M. (1994a). The effects of guided imagery in reducing the worry and emotionality components of test anxiety. *Journal of Mental Imagery, 18*(3 & 4), 165-180.

Sapp, M. (1994b). Cognitive-behavioral counseling: Applications for African American middle school students who are academically at risk. *Journal of Instructional Psychology, 77*(4), 294-303.

Sapp, M. (1996a). Irrational beliefs that can lead to academic failure for African American middle school students who are academically at risk. *Journal of Rational-Emotive and Cognitive-Behavior Therapy, 14*(2), 123-134.

Sapp, M. (1996b). Three treatments for reducing the worry and emotionality components of test anxiety with undergraduate and graduate college students: Cognitive-behavior hypnosis, relaxation therapy, and supportive counseling. *Journal of College Student Development, 37*(1), 79-87.

Sapp, M. (1997). *Counseling and psychotherapy: Theories, associated research, and issues.* Lanham, MD: University Press of America.

Sapp, M., Durand, H., & Farrell, W. (1995). Measures of actual test anxiety in educationally and economically disadvantaged college students. *College Student Journal, 29*(1), 65-72.

Sapp, M., & Farrell, W. (1994). Cognitive-behavioral interventions: Applications for academically at-risk and special education students. *Preventing School Failure, 38*(2), 19-24.

Sapp, M., Farrell, W., & Durand, H. (1995). The effects of mathematics, reading, and writing tests in producing worry and emotionality test anxiety with economically and educationally disadvantaged colldge students. *College Student Journal, 29*(1), 165-180.

Sarason, I. G. (1972). Experimental approaches to test anxiety: Attention and uses of information. In C. D. Spielberger (Ed.), *Anxiety: Current trends in theory and research* (Vol. 1) (pp. 383-400). New York: Academic Press.

Sarason, I. G. (1980). *Test anxiety: Theory, research and applications.* Hillsdale, NJ: Lawrence Erlbaum.

Sarason, I. G. (1984). Stress, anxiety and worry, and interference: Reactions to tests. *Journal of Personality and Social Psychology, 46,* 929-938.

Schwarzer, R., Van der Ploeg, H. M., & Spielberger, C. D. (1982). *Advances in test anxiety research* (Vol. 1) (pp. 1-3). Lisse/Hillsdale, NJ: Swets and Zeitlinger/Erlbaum.

Schwarzer, R., Van der Ploeg, H. M., & Spielberger, C. D. (1989). *Advances in test anxiety research* (Vol. 6) (pp. V-VI). Lisse/Hillsdale, NJ: Swets and Zeitlinger/Erlbaum.

Spielberger, C. D. (1980). *Test Anxiety Inventory.* Palo Alto, CA: Consulting Psychologists Press.

SPSSX User's guide (3rd ed.). (1988). Chicago: SPSS, Inc.

Stevens, J. P. (1992). *Applied multivariate statistics for the social sciences.* Hillsdale, NJ: Lawrence Erlbaum Associates.

Tobias, S. (1985). Test anxiety: Interference, defective skills and cognitive capacity. *Educational Psychologist, 20*(3), 135-142.

Waller, M. I. (1973). *Removing the effects of random guessing from latent trait ability estimates.* Unpublished doctoral dissertation. University of Chicago.

Waller, M. I. (1976). *Estimating parameters in the Rasch Model: Removing the effects of random guessing* (Research Bulletin RB-76-8). Princeton, NJ: Educational Testing Service.

Waller, M. I. (1989). Modeling Guessing Behavior: A Comparison of Two IRT Models. *Applied Psychological Measurement, 13*(3), pp. 233-243.

Wright, B., & Panchapakesan, N. (1969). A procedure for sample-free item analysis. *Educational and Psychological Measurement, 29*, 23-48.

Wright, B. D. (1977a). Solving measurement problems with the Rasch model. *Journal of Educational Measurement, 14*, 97-116.

Wright, B. D. (1977b). Misunderstanding the Rasch model. *Journal of Educational Measurement, 14*, 219-225.

Chapter 9

CONTENTS

9.1 OVERVIEW OF STRUCTURAL EQUATION MODELS

Exploratory factor analysis, confirmatory factor analysis, multiple regression, canonical correlation, path analysis, MANOVA, and ANOVA are all special cases of structural equation models (SEM). Hoyle (1995) refers to SEMs as LISREL models, analysis of covariance structures, classical simultaneous equation models, latent-variable analysis, linear structural relationships, and analysis of moment structures. Exploratory factor analysis and confirmatory factor analysis do not make predictor-criterion distinctions; in contrast multiple regression, canonical correlation, and path analysis do make predictor-criterion distinctions (Dunn, Everitt, & Pickles, 1993; Pedhazur & Schmelkin, 1991; Schumacker & Lomax, 1996).

All of these statistical procedures are based on a covariance or correlation matrix. **Covariance** is the sum of the cross-products $\Sigma(X-\bar{x})$ $(Y-\bar{y})$ divided by the number of pairs. Thus, the covariance of (X,Y) is $\Sigma(X-\bar{x})(Y-\bar{y})/n$. This is analogous to the population variance formula, which is $\Sigma(X-\bar{x})(X-\bar{x})/n$. And the correlation is the covariance divided by the product of the population standard deviation of X and Y or:

$$r = \frac{\Sigma(X-\bar{X})(Y-\bar{Y})/n}{\sigma_x \sigma_y}$$

the **simplest structural equation** model is the **basic regression model**:

$$Y' = bX + a$$

This model can be depicted as:

$$X \rightarrow Y \leftarrow e$$

Straight lines indicate a **causal relationship** between X and Y, or, simply, X causes changes on Y. Often, these diagrams are referred to as **path diagrams**. The "e" is the random error on Y. As you remember, X is referred to as an **independent variable**, and Y is the **dependent variable**. We assume that causes precede effects. See Bollen (1989) for a discussion of the criteria for causal inferences; however, the reader should note that the issue of causality is not a statistical one, but an issue that involves logic and research methodology. Some researchers argue that three conditions are necessary, but not sufficient, to imply causality.

First, X must precede Y. **Second**, X and Y must covary. **Third**, no rival hypothesis can account as well for the covariance of X and Y.

Obviously, with nonexperimental research, the conclusions one can reach are not as strong as one's obtained from true experimental research. Structural equation modeling is a **theory-testing procedure** (Stevens, 1996), and it has to be based on strong theoretical and empirical foundations. *Structural equation models cannot control for threats to internal validity, and they estimate the magnitude of causal effect if X were truly a cause of Y (McClendon, 1994).* In contrast, true experimental designs allow a research to state that X caused Y within a certain probability level. The notion of causality is a methodological issue, not a statistical matter

The model X $\rightarrow$ Y is called a **direct effect**. When a model is mediated by an intervening variable, it is referred to as an indirect effect. The following depicts an **indirect effect model**:

$X_1 \rightarrow X_2 \rightarrow Y$

X_1 causes a change on X_2, and X_2 causes a change on Y; however, X_1 has an indirect effect on Y because X_2 mediates the relationship between X_1 and Y.

Formally, **path analysis** is a special case of a structural equation model in which the correlations among variables are expressed as graphs (Tabachnick & Fidell, 1996). These variables are observed. In contrast, with confirmatory factor analysis, latent or unobserved variables are analyzed. For example, Sapp, Farrell, and Durand (1995) tested the relationship among self-esteem, academic self-concept, grades, and reading scores with at-risk African American middle school students. The following path model was obtained.

$$.66^* \quad \text{Grades}$$

Self-esteem $\rightarrow$ Academic self-concept
$$.64^*$$

$$.60^* \quad \text{Reading Scores}$$

$^*p < .05$

The **path coefficients** are .64, .66, and .60. These coefficients are standardized regression coefficients or beta weights. The direct effect of self-esteem on academic self-concept is .64 and the direct effect of academic self-concept on grades is .66, and the direct effect of academic self-concept on reading scores is .60. Indirect effects can be found by multiplying the path coefficients. For example, the indirect effects of self-esteem on grades is .64 (.66), or .42, and the indirect effect of self-esteem on reading scores is .64 (.60), or .38. Finally, the total effect is the sum of the direct effects plus the indirect effects.

There are certain primary symbols that are used in path analysis. Rectangular or square boxes signify observed or manifest variables. These are the dependent variables. A circle or ellipse signifies a factor, unobserved, or latent variable. A straight line → signifies that one variable caused another. Finally, a curved, two-headed symbol signifies the correlation between two variables, or factors, as in this case.

Similarly to the simple regression equation, $Y = B_1X_1 + e_1$, an equation can be written that expresses the relationships of observed variables, factors, and measurement errors. For a predictor denoted as X_j, this equation would be:

$$X_j = \lambda_{21}\xi + \delta_2$$

The symbol "λ" (lambda) indicates a factor loading, or the path from a factor to an observed variable. And "ξ" (Ksi) corresponds to a latent factor or variable. The symbol "δ" (delta) is the measurement error. Two other common symbols are $\theta\delta$ (theta delta), which are the covariances among measurement errors. Finally, the symbol "ϕ" (phi) is the correlations or covariances among factors.

As previously stated, structural equation modeling (SEM) tests the relationship between a sample covariance or correlation matrix denoted by S and a population covariance or correlation matrix denoted by Σ. The matrices for the equality of Σ is the following:

$$\Sigma = \Lambda\phi\Lambda' + \theta\delta.$$

This equality shows that the covariance matrix can be broken down into the confirmatory factor analytic matrices

Λ, ϕ, and $\theta\delta$.

As described by Jöreskog and Sörbon (1993), the following two equations express the measurement models for y and x:

$$y = \Lambda_y \eta + \varepsilon$$

$$x = \Lambda_x \xi + \delta$$

y   is a vector of indicators of latent endogenous (variables within the system) variables.

Λ_y (Lambda Y) is a matrix of coefficients or loadings on y.

η (eta) are the latent variables.

ε (epsilon) is a vector of errors.

x   is a vector of latent exogenous (variables outside the system) variables.

Λ_x (Lambda X) is a matrix of coefficients or loadings of X on the exogenous (variables outside of the system) latent variables.

ξ (xi) is latent exogenous variables.

ζs   (zeta) are residuals or errors.

δ (Delta) is a vector of errors of measurement of X.

β (Beta) is a matrix of regression coefficients among the dependent variables.

Γ (capital gamma) is a matrix of regression coefficients among dependent variables and independent variables.

Finally, the structural model equation is as follows:

$$\begin{vmatrix} \eta_1 \\ \eta_1 \end{vmatrix} = \begin{vmatrix} 0 & 0 \\ \beta_{21} & 0 \end{vmatrix} \begin{vmatrix} \eta_1 \\ \eta_1 \end{vmatrix} + \begin{vmatrix} \gamma_{11} & 0 \\ \gamma_{21} & \gamma_{22} \end{vmatrix} \begin{vmatrix} \xi_1 \\ \xi_2 \end{vmatrix} + \begin{vmatrix} \zeta_1 \\ \zeta_2 \end{vmatrix}$$

η	β	η	Γ	ξ	ζ
(eta)	(beta)		(capital gamma)	(ksi or xi)	(zeta)

9.2 BASIC ELEMENTS OF THE EQS
CONTROL LANGUAGE

EQS input files must be saved as a DOS text file. The EQS program can be started by typing EQS at the MS-DOS prompt and hitting the return key. EQS will give you a prompt asking for the name of the input file and the name of the output file. EQS is an iterative program, and it monitors the number of iterations needed for a run. Once the program is complete, the following statement appears on the screen: *EQS is done.*

Program Input
/TITLE
The title paragraph provides a title for the program.
/SPECIFICATIONS
The specification paragraph gives information about the number of cases, the number of variables, and the method of estimation.
/Labels
The labels paragraph gives the variables names.
/Equations
The characters "V" and "F" refer to measured variables and latent variables, respectively.

The character "E" is the residual (error) of an observed variable. And the character "D" is the residual (error) or disturbance of a latent variable.

Observed variables such as V1, V2... are regressed or loaded on factors (F1, F2...).

The symbol "*", which occurs before a factor, tells EQS that the regression coefficient or loading is a free parameter to be estimated at some starting value.
/Variances
This keyword provides the variances of the independent variables.
/Covariances specifies the covariation among independent variables.
/Matrix
The matrix paragraph is needed for a covariance matrix or correlation matrix.
/Standard Deviations
This paragraph allows the standard deviations of the variables to be entered.

9.3 EQS PATH ANALYSIS
The following are the control lines for running a path analysis on EQS:
/Title path analysis Data from Schumacker and Lomax (1996)
/Specifications
Cases=100; Variables=4; ME=ML;
/Labels

V1=Y; V2=X1; V3=X2; V4=X3;
/Equations
V4=1*V2 + 1*V3 + 1*E4;
V1=1*V2 + 1*V3 + 1*V4 + 1*E1;
/Variances
V2, V3=1*;
E4, E1=1;
/Covariances
V2, V3=1*;
/Matrix
1.000
.507 1.000
.480 .224 1.000
.275 .062 .577 1.000
/End

9.4 SELECTED OUTPUT FROM EQS PATH ANALYSIS
GOODNESS OF FIT SUMMARY

INDEPENDENCE MODEL CHI-SQUARE = 96.369 ON 6 DEGREES
OF FREEDOM

INDEPENDENCE AIC =	84.36935	INDEPENDENCE CAIC =	62.73833
MODEL AIC =	4.00000	MODEL CAIC =	11.21034

CHI-SQUARE = 0.000 BASED ON =2 DEGREES OF FREEDOM
NONPOSITIVE DEGREES OF FREEDOM.   PROBABILITY
COMPUTATIONS ARE UNDEFINED.
BENTLER-BONETT NORMED FIT INDEX = 1.000
NON-NORMED FIT INDEX WILL NOT BE COMPUTED BECAUSE THE
DEGREES OF FREEDOM IS ZERO.

The chi-square statistic did not support the hypothesized model
because a nonsignificant chi-square is needed to support a model. Path
coefficients are obtained from this program under the heading titled
"Measurement Equations with Standard Errors and Test Statistics."

9.5 EQS CONFIRMATORY FACTOR ANALYSIS
The following are the EQS control lines for a confirmatory factor
analysis using data from Dunn, Everitt, and Pickles (1993).

```
/title
Data from Dunn, Everitt, and Pickles (1993)
/specification
cases=15;
variables=4;
Method=ML;
Matrix=correlation;
Analysis=Covariance;
/Labels
V1=one;
V2=two;
V3=Three;
V4=Four;
F1=factor;
/equations
V1=1F1+E1;
V2=1*F1+E2;
V3=1*F1+E3;
V4=1*F1+E4;
/Variances
F1=3.0*;
E1 To E4=.1*;
/Matrix
1.000
.9802 1.000
.9811 .9553 1.000
.9899 .9807 .9684 1.000
/Standard Deviations
1.9692 1.4563 1.6294 1.787
/end
```

9.6 SELECTED OUTPUT FROM CONFIRMATORY FACTOR ANALYSIS

GOODNESS OF FIT SUMMARY

INDEPENDENCE MODEL CHI-SQUARE = 148.520 ON 6 DEGREES OF FREEDOM

INDEPENDENCE AIC =	136.52009	INDEPENDENCE CAIC =	126.27179
MODEL AIC =	-1.65251	MODEL CAIC =	-5.06861

CHI-SQUARE = 2.347 BASED ON =2 DEGREES OF FREEDOM
PROBABILITY VALUE FOR THE CHI-SQUARE STATISTIC IS 0.30921
THE NORMAL THEORY RLS CHI-SQUARE FOR THIS ML SOLUTION IS
2.535.

BENTLER-BONETT NORMED FIT INDEX	=	0.984
BENTLER-BONETT NONNORMED FIT INDEX	=	0.993
COMPARATIVE FIT INDEX (CFI)	=	0.998

Note: That is, model was supported, since the p-value for the Chi-Square
statistic is .30921. This indicated that there was a good model fit.
Moreover, the FIT INDICES are well beyond .90, which indicates a good
fit.

Measurement Equations with Standard Errors and Test Statistics

| ONE | =V1 = | 1.000 F1 | + 1.000 | E1 |

TWO =V2 =   .727*F1   + 1.000   E2
                .039
                18.710

THREE =V3 =   .813*F1   + 1.000   E3
                 .044
                 18.398

FOUR =V4 =   .906*F1   + 1.000   E4
                .035
                26.233

Note that V2 =   .727*F1 + 1.000 E2 is a measurement equation.
                 .039
                 18.710
The .727 is the factor loading, .039 is the standard error, and 18.710 is the
t value.

STANDARDIZED SOLUTION:

ONE   =V1=   .999 F1   + .048   E1

TWO   =V2=   .982*F1   + .190   E2

THREE =V3=   .981*F1   + .193   E3

FOUR   =V4=   .991*F1   + .132   E4

9.7 CONFIRMATORY FACTOR
ANALYSIS EXERCISE

Run the following confirmatory factor analysis on EQS:
/Title
  Confirmatory Factor Analysis;
/Specifications
Cases=205; Vars=15; ME=ML; MA=Cov;
/Equations

```
V1=1.000*F3+E1;
V2=1.000*F1+E2;
V3=1.000*F4+E3;
V4=1.000*F2+E4;
V5=1.000*F3+F5;
V6=1.000*F3+E6;
V7=1.000*F2+E7;
V8=1.000*F2+E8;
V9=1.000*F3+E9;
V10=1.000*F3+E10;
V11=1.000*F1+E11;
V12=1.000*F1+E12;
V13=1.000*F2+E13;
V14=1.000*F1+E14;
V15=1.000*F1+E15;
/Variances
E1 TO E15=.500*;
F1 TO F2=.3*;
F2 TO F3=.3*;
F3 TO F4=.3*;
F1,F4=.3*;
/Matrix
1
.332   1
.265   .266   1
.096   .126   .339   1
.007  -.002   .136   .366   1
.171   .107   .293   .431   .522   1
.094  -.008   .520   .186   .226   .406   1
.321   .062   .500   .373   .164   .236   .286   1
.222   .089   .265   .387   .181   .171   .094   .610   1
.126   .079   .156   .284   .262   .199   .048   .122   .034   1
.369   .221   .213   .308   .355   .531   .176   .138   .116   .642   1
.266   .267   .155   .199   .269   .369   .132   .386   .325   .122   .260   1
.189   .179   .104   .233   .249   .276   .019   .295   .368   .051   .114   .586   1
.253   .228   .329   .359   .413   .418   .228   .000   .001   .000   .000   .000   .000   1
.447   .319   .297   .449   .452   .520   .099   .000   .000   .000   .000   .000   .000   .000   1
```

/STANDARD DEVIATIONS
.25   .54   .54   .50   .28   .44   .66   .42   .25   .53   .48   .41   .40   .41   .58
/LMTEST;/WTEST;
/END

9.8 IDENTIFICATION

Identification determines if unique values can be estimated for the parameters of a model. The number of unique values within a covariance matrix is equal to:

p* =   the number of unique values
p   =   the number of observed values

Therefore, $p^* = p(p+1)/2$.

Bollen (1989) recommends at least **three variables** per factor for a model to be identified. And usually a minimum sample size of 200 is needed to have reliable results in maximum likelihood confirmatory factor analysis (Stevens, 1996). Models with more unique values than unknown parameters are called **identified** or **overidentified**, and they can be solved uniquely.

In contrast, models with more unknown parameters than unique values are **unidentified** or **underidentified**, and they cannot be solved uniquely. Finally, models with just as many unique values as unknown parameters are called **just identified**, and they can be solved uniquely, but they cannot be tested statistically.

9.9 MODEL MODIFICATION

The **Lagrange Multiplier (LMTEST)** and the **WALD (WTEST)** tests determine if parameters can be dropped from a model without significantly affecting the overall fit. These tests identify sources of misfit and should only be used with new samples to respecify models. This suggests that the results of SEMs tend not to **crossvalidate**. There is a tendency for researchers to perform post hoc model modifications on a given sample and to assume that these modifications will apply to separate, independent samples. Hutchinson (1998) found that with severe model misspecifications, post hoc model modifications tended to be unstable unless $N \geq 1,200$. Her study found that post hoc model modifications are not completely stable, even with extremely large sample sizes. In summary, it is not recommended that researchers use specification indices such as the LMTEST and Wald tests to perform post hoc model modification because model modification should be performed on separate, independent samples, not the original sample.

9.10 SUMMARY

Exploratory factor analysis, confirmatory factor analysis, multiple regression, canonical analysis, MANOVA, ANOVA, and path analysis are special cases of SEM. They are all based on correlation matrices, and they have an assumption of normality, specifically multivariate normality, when participants are measured on two or more dependent variables.

Five steps characterize SEMs. **First**, a model has to be specified. This is usually based on theoretical and empirical information. **Second**, identification, can unique bits of information be found for the parameters that are estimated in the theoretical model? **Third**, use an estimation procedure such as least square or maximum likelihood, and so on. **Fourth**, determine if the fit indices suggest that the sample data fit a theoretical model. **Fifth**, if there is a poor fit between the sample data, the researcher can modify the paths in the model with an independent sample of data.

Even though SEMs are useful for theory testing, they must have a strong theoretical and strong empirical base. Finally, SEMs cannot overcome poor reliability and validity. They only allow one to test a theory and to produce a parsimonious description of data.

References

Bollen, K. A. (1989). *Structural equations with latent variables*. New York: Wiley.

Dunn, G., Everitt, B., & Pickles, A. (1993). *Modeling covariances and latent variables using EQS*. London: Chapman and Hall.

Hoyle, R. H. (Ed.). (1995). *Structural equation modeling*. Newbury park, CA: SAGE.

Hutchinson, S. R. (1998). The stability of post hoc model modifications in confirmatory factor analysis models. *The Journal of Experimental Education, 66*(4), 361-380.

Jöreskog, K. G., & Sörbom, D. (1993). *LISREL 8 user's reference guide*. Chicago: Scientific Software.

McClendon, M. J. (1994). *Multiple regression and causal analysis*. Itasca, IL: F. E. Peacock.

Pedhazur, E. J., & Schmelkin, L. (1991). *Measurement, design, and analysis: An integrated approach*. Hillsdale, NJ: Erlbaum.

Sapp, M., Farrell, W., & Durand, H. (1995). Cognitive-behavioral therapy: Applications for African American middle school at-risk students. *Journal of Educational Psychology, 22*(2), 169-177.

Schumacker, R. E., & Lomax, R. C. (1996). *A beginner's guide to structural equation modeling.* Hillsdale, NJ: Erlbaum.

Stevens, J. P. (1996). *Applied multivariate statistics for the social sciences* (3rd ed.) Hillsdale, NJ: Erlbaum.

Tabacknick, B. G., & Fidell, L. S. (1996). *Using multivariate statistics* (3rd ed.). New York: HarperCollins.

Part III: Assessment

Chapter 10

CONTENTS

10.1 CONSTRUCTS OF TEST ANXIETY

Mandler and Sarason (1952) theorized that test anxiety was a **single latent or underlying trait**, and they developed the Test Anxiety Scale to measure this construct. Spielberger (1980) ' questioned the **unidimensionality** of test anxiety and theorized and substantiated through principal components analysis that test anxiety is composed of **two factors**, namely **worry** and **emotionality test anxiety** from the Test Anxiety Inventory (TAI). Worry and emotionality are defined n the section on components of test anxiety. In 1984 Sarason conceptualized test anxiety as being composed of **four latent factors, traits**, or **dimensions**. He developed the **Reactions to Tests (RTT)** to measure his hypothesized four constructs of test anxiety. Sarason retained Spielberger's worry dimension, and he reconceptualized emotionality as existing of two distinct dimensions, **"person's bodily arousal and tension."** Finally, Sarason's fourth dimension of test anxiety was test-irrelevant thinking.

Recently Spielberger and Vagg (1995) presented a **transactional process model** for test anxiety. This is a comprehensive theory of test anxiety that specifies the interpersonal perceptions and cognitions, informational processing, retrieval mechanisms that mediate the effects of worry and emotionality on performance. In addition, Spielberger and Vagg identify the important correlates of test anxiety such as study habits, study skills, test-taking skills, test-wiseness, and task-irrelevant thoughts. This model is a situation-specific process in which test anxiety is a trait that is evoked by state anxiety and worry and emotionality during examinations.

For example, a test-anxious student enters an examination with the perceptions that a testing situation is threatening. The state anxiety leads to self-defeating cognitions, emotional reactions, and test-irrelevant thoughts. In contrast, students with good test-taking skills tend to perceive examinations as less threatening than students who lack test-wiseness; therefore, there will be a decrease in state anxiety, a decrease in worry cognitions, and there will be a reappraisal of the test situation as less threatening. In summary, this model views the interaction of the components of test anxiety as a **dynamic** and **continuous process**. That is, the test situation affects the person, and the person affects the testing situation. Moreover, some individuals have a vulnerability to trait anxiety and respond differently to threatening perceptions, and some individuals cope better with anxiety than other individuals.

10.2 DEFINING TEST ANXIETY

Test anxiety is a special case of **general anxiety** consisting of **phenomenological, physiological**, and **behavioral responses** related to fear of failure (Sieber, cited in Sarason, 1980). It is the harsh emotions that have physiological and behavioral concomitants that one experiences in evaluative situations. When test anxiety occurs many cognitive and attentional processes interfere with effective task performance (Dusek, 1980).   Measures of test anxiety are negatively correlated with achievement and intelligence measures; nevertheless, other variables such as study skills and motivation are also related to achievement. Therefore, achievement measures are influenced by many variables, not just test anxiety.

10.3 PARENT-CHILD INTERACTIONS AND THE DEVELOPMENT OF TEST ANXIETY

Research suggests that test anxiety is formulated during preschool and the early school years (Dusek, 1980, p. 88). Sarason (1960) viewed test anxiety as a personality characteristic that develops during the time children interact with their parents. He suggested that test anxiety results when a child's performance does not correspond with a parent's **unrealistic expectations**. Parents' negative communication patterns are a major contributor for the development of test anxiety in children. For example, many times parents communicate what Goulding (1987, p. 288) called **injunctions** or **negative messages** that children internalize. Injunctions do not have to be direct, since children are capable of inferring these messages from parents' nonverbal mannerisms. Criticism, particularly parents' negative judgment of a child's performance, is experienced by the child as hostility and guilt. Often these feelings of hostility, guilt, and resentment children experience are not acknowledged and they accumulate as emotional debris, resulting in what Polster and Polster (1973) called **unfinished business**. Unfinished business are unexpressed feelings associated with a child's failure at a task. These feelings can take the form of anxiety, guilt, grief, pain, and so on.

The literature suggests that nonfacilitative parent-child interactions are associated with the development of test anxiety. Even though literature investigating the etiology of test anxiety is sparse, parental child rearing techniques are related to its development in children (Dusek, 1980, p. 106). For example, failure of a parent to provide emotional support to a child while in a problem solving situation and the failure to reinforce an internal locus of evaluation can result in lower achievement scores and a child who is not task-oriented. If this cycle continues, as a child gets older, there is a greater reliance on external evaluation of one's performance. This leads to greater levels of anxiety and stress. Similarly, Dusek (1980) suggests that high test anxious children spend more time attending to task irrelevant material, in contrast to low test anxious children who have a greater sense of self-evaluation and are highly task-oriented (Anderson & Sauser, 1995; Anton & Lillibridge, 1995; Zeidner, 1998).

In conclusion, more research is needed into the etiology of test anxiety. Similarly, additional research is needed investigating the effects of parental influences and child-parental interactions and their possible long term effects. Also, research investigating the components of test anxiety is nonexistent for children. Additional research is needed that clearly demonstrates the mechanisms under which test anxiety is acquired. Finally, Sapp (1996a) suggested that there are developmental aspects of test anxiety.

10.4 MEASURING TEST ANXIETY IN CHILDREN

The most widely used self-report questionnaire used to measure test anxiety is the Test Anxiety Scale for Children (TASC). The TASC, developed by S. B. Sarason, Davidson, Lighthall, Waite, and Ruebush (1960) and by I. G. Sarason and Ganzer (1962), is a **multidimensional group administered paper and pencil test**. It is comprised of 30 items, to which the child replies with "yes" or "no" by circling the appropriate response on an answer sheet as the questions are read by an examiner. The TASC is reported to have adequate reliability and validity (Hill, 1972; Ruebush, 1963; I. G. Sarason & Ganzer, 1962). S. B. Sarason, Davidson, Lighthall, Waite, and Ruebush (1960) have developed two scales to deal with the problem of children's defensiveness in not admitting anxiety. First, there is the **Lie Scale for Children (LSC)** which is composed of 11 items that ask questions in which nearly all children will report yes. For example: Have you ever feared being hurt, or do you every worry? The score on the LSC is the number of times the child reports no.

Second, there is the **Defensiveness Scale for Children (DSC)** which is comprised of 27 items that measure a child's willingness to admit to a variety of emotions (S. B. Sarason, 1966; S. B. Sarason, Hill, & Zimbardo, 1964). For example, do you you ever feel like hurting someone? It is assumed that most children experience these emotions. The score for DSC is the summation of no responses. In summary, the LSC and DSC are highly correlated and are usually given simultaneously. The child's total defensive score is the summation of no responses from the combined items of the DSC (27) and LSC (11) which totals to 38 possible no responses.

There is another instrument used to measure test anxiety in children, the **TASC-R$_x$,** a revised version of the TASC, in which items are presented in a positively worded format. For example, "When taking tests, do you feel relaxed?" Feld and Lewis (1969) revised the TASC into this positive wording. Employing factor analysis, a statistical technique that empirically determines the number of dimensions that account for the most variance on an instrument, Feld and Lewis (1969) found that four major factors accounted for the most variance on the TASC-R$_x$. These factors were the following: (1) worry about tests, (2) physiological reactions to evaluative pressure, (3) negative self-evaluation, and (4) worry about school while at home. Hill and Wigfield (1984) concluded that both the TASC and TASC-R$_x$ have been found to be reliable and valid measures of test anxiety in children.

Test anxiety measures obtained in children are **negatively correlated** with achievement. This negative correlation increases throughout the elementary school period. Specifically, Hill and Wigfield (1984) described a 5-year longitudinal study of about 700 elementary school children from middle and working class backgrounds. Statistical analyses indicated a negative correlation between test anxiety (TASC) and achievement test scores which steadily increased across the elementary school period. During first grade, the correlation between test anxiety and achievement was small. In third grade, the correlation between the two measures was about -.25, p<.05. By the fifth and sixth grades, the correlation between test anxiety and achievement reached -.45, being significant beyond the .05 level. In addition, test anxiety scores correlated negatively with IQ test scores, grades, and failure to be promoted to the next grade.

This study reported that the relationship between test anxiety and achievement was also strong among junior high and high school students, with a correlation reading -.60 by the eleventh grade. In sum, Hill and Wigfield (1984) reported a strong negative correlation between test anxiety and performance in black, white, and Hispanic late-elementary and middle school students. Moreover, negative success-failure attributions also correlated inversely with achievement test performance, especially for black students. In conclusion, test anxiety and other forms of negative affect were major difficulties for children from a broad spectrum of ethnic backgrounds. This occurred for boys and girls and for middle and working class children.

10.5 THE SCHOOL ENVIRONMENT, MOTIVATION, LEARNED HELPLESSNESS, AND TEST ANXIETY

Phillips, Pitcher, Worsham, and Miller (1980) argued that test anxiety is related to the school environment. These researchers proposed for an **ecological perspective** in viewing test anxiety. They noted that many test anxiety studies have been conducted in laboratory settings. They underscored that many results and principles found in laboratory studies have not been shown to apply to the classroom; therefore, they endorsed an ecological validity viewpoint of test anxiety.

Phillips et al. (1980) recommended changing the school environment to minimize the development of test anxiety and for ameliorating its debilitating effects. One point they make is that it is important to decrease the external nature of evaluation in the schools and to increase intrinsic interest in school achievement. They recommend teaching students to cope with the possible debilitating effects of test anxiety. For example, they suggest increasing students' self-concept and students' tolerance for stress and anxiety. Phillips et al. (1980) recommend a fundamental change in school organization, curricular structure, instructional procedures, and educational philosophy. It should be noted that **self-concept** is a student's cognitive view of himself or herself, whereas **self-esteem** is a student's feelings. Smith, Sapp, Farrell, and Johnson (1998) found that academic self-concept is consistently related to achievement; however, self esteem is not consistently correlated with achievement.

Motivational theory suggests that one's motivational orientation will interact with test anxiety. In addition, one's motivational orientation can sensitize one to feedback, which in turn may influence self-confidence and test anxiety. Weiner (1990) noted that formerly the motivational theory literature was focused primarily on the study of achievement strivings. Pintrich and DeGroot (1990) combined achievement motivation with the study of cognitive variables, such as one's cognitions about the causes of one's failure. Butler (1987, 1988) described the motivational relationship between test anxiety and feedback, suggesting that motivation and test anxiety are associated with individual differences in responding to testing situations. In summary, Thorkildsen and Nicholls (1991) utilized developmental theory to describe motivational orientations of test anxiety, while Zimmerman and Martinez-Pons (1990) investigated the relationship among motivational orientation, feedback conditions, and self-efficacy as predictors of changes in test anxiety.

By viewing test anxiety as a motivational construct, the concept **learned helplessness**, defined as the perception of independence between one's responses and the occurrences or termination of aversive stimuli, summarizes Phillips et al.'s (1980) conception of test anxiety. This conception suggests that high test anxious children have a stronger motive to avoid criticism than to attain praise; however, both motives are stronger in high test anxious than low test anxious children. Similarly, low test anxious students are more concerned about succeeding and obtaining approval. In contrast, high test anxious children are more concerned with avoiding failure and disapproval. Since anxious children are sensitive to avoiding failure and disapproval, it seems likely that many fall within Rotter's (1966) **external locus of control** and Seligman's (Overmier & Seligman, 1967) **learned helplessness dimensions**.

10.6 SELF-EFFICACY AND TEST ANXIETY

Bandura (1982), a social learning theorist, assumes that test anxiety develops within a **social context**. Part of the social mechanism that contributes to test anxiety is **modeling** or **observational learning** during early childhood. Bandura suggests that test anxiety can develop through vicarious reinforcement or learning by observing the behavior of others. Recently, Bandura (1983) has expanded his theory to include a wider range of cognitive factors. His theory can best be described as a **social-cognitive theory**. Sophisticated readers are aware that social learning theory is subsumed under behaviorism. See Sapp (1997) for a thorough discussion of this topic. Currently, Bandura employs **reciprocal determinism** as a process through which test anxiety develops. With reciprocal determinism, Bandura postulates that **personal, behavioral**, and **situational factors** are constantly interacting to determine what one feels, thinks, and does. Essentially, reciprocal determinism assumes that the person, situation, and behavior mutually interact to influence each other. This model adds a social flavor to how test anxiety develops and possibly adds to the **ecological view** of test anxiety.

The **self**, according to Bandura (1986), is a cognitive process concerned with thinking, evaluation, and perception. Being consistent with reciprocal determinism, the self has at least two aspects: **self-reinforcement and self-efficacy**. For adults and older children, self-reinforcement is at least as important as reinforcement occurring from others in social situations. **Self-reinforcement** are the rewards and punishments administered by an individual for reaching, exceeding, or failing at one's expectations or standards. The degree that one meets his or her standards determines self-efficacy, which refers to one's sense of self-esteem and self-worth. Self-efficacy is a person's perception that he or she can successfully perform behaviors necessary to produce a desired outcome. Similarly, self-efficacy involves feelings of adequacy and efficiency in adapting to life events. Self-efficacy is also one's ability to regulate life events.

Test-anxious individuals usually have low levels of self-efficacy. The test-anxious person feels helpless and unable to influence testing events (Schunk, 1991). As a result, he or she, on a cognitive level, believes that any efforts to succeed on any tests are futile. When obstacles occur during a test, individuals with debilitating test anxiety are likely to quickly capitulate if initial attempts to overcome these obstacles are ineffective.

In contrast to individuals with low self-efficacy, individuals with high self-efficacy are better able to cope with obstacles during a testing situation. They are more likely to keep attempting to overcome an obstacle during a test. The higher level of self-efficacy gives low test-anxious individuals greater confidence in their abilities and this results in sustained effort and constant work to overcome obstacles which leads to better performance on tests than their high test-anxious, low self-efficacious counterparts. By persevering with difficult tasks during a test, individuals with high self-efficacy often perform at a high level.

It is clear that repeated failure on tests lower one's sense of efficacy. In contrast, observing others who are similar to oneself perform successfully on tests can strengthen self-efficacy (Woolfolk & Hoy, 1990). During early childhood, test-anxious children can be helped through **verbal persuasion** from parents, teachers, and friends. This is, telling a child he or she possesses the abilities to achieve on tests. It is important that verbal persuasion occur in a realistic context; otherwise, it is pointless, for example, telling a child experiencing moderate mental retardation that he or she has the testing skills to become an attorney is nonsensical.

Bandura (1986) describes self-efficacy as a process that can vary over the life span. In addition, Bandura discusses four specific ways self-efficacy can be enhanced for test-anxious persons. **First**, a person must be exposed to successful testing experiences by establishing testing situations through which one can reach realistic goals; thus, increasing one's sense of achievement. **Second**, exposing an individual to appropriate models who can successfully perform during testing situations. This enhances one's vicarious success through testing experiences. **Third**, by providing verbal persuasion and encouragement concerning test taking can also enhance self-efficacy, if it occurs in a realistic context. **Fourth**, the last method to increase a test-anxious person's self-efficacy is by strengthening physiological arousal. Physiological arousal, in this instance, is not synonymous with visceral tension. **Physiological arousal** corresponds to one's physical strength and stamina, which can be increased through diet and exercise.

Finally, Bandura (1986) has successfully applied techniques of enhancing self-efficacy with a variety of conditions, such as mathematics test anxiety, phobias, smoking cessation, and physical pain. Recently, Dykeman (1992), using an experimental design demonstrated that students with high self-efficacy showed a reduction in test anxiety, while low self-efficacy students showed an increase in test anxiety. Finally, Dykeman reported statistical significance supporting Bandura's theoretical position at the .05 level of significance.

10.7 MEASURING TEST-WISENESS
A construct related to test anxiety is test-wiseness. Benson, Urman, and Hocevar (1986) defined **test-wiseness** as a construct, related to intelligence, that permits a test-taker to utilize the characteristics and forms of tests and/or test-taking situation to receive a high score. Test-wiseness is cognitive ability that is independent of examinees' knowledge of material being tested. Sarnacki (1979) developed a taxonomy of test-wiseness which included the following four elements: **(1) test-using strategy, (2) error-avoidance strategy, (3) guessing strategy, (4) deductive reasoning strategy, (5) intent consideration strategy and cue-using strategy**. The taxonomy can be summarized as: being able to work as rapidly as possible with reasonable accuracy, paying close attention to directions, guessing when there is not a severe penalty for guessing, making use of relevant content information in other test items and options, answering items as the test constructor intended, recognizing

and making use of any consistent idiosyncracies of the test that distinguish the correct answer from incorrect options (Anderson & Sauser, 1995).

Gibb (1964) was the first to measure test-wiseness for high school students. He constructed a 70-item multiple choice scale that included 10 items for each of the following types of cues:

1. stem-option similarities
2. absurd relationships
3. specific determiners
4. precise options
5. long length options
6. grammatical clues
7. item giveaways

Gibb found that Kuder-Richardson-20 reliability measures were .72 for untrained subjects and .90 for subjects receiving training in the 7 test-wiseness skills. Since test-wiseness is a distinct construct, it correlates only .49 with intelligence. Test-wiseness also positively correlates up to .46 with knowledge of grammar, vocabulary, and sentence structure. Similarly, test-wiseness correlates with achievement measures from .63 to .70. Limited research suggests that test-wiseness correlates with test anxiety. Sarnacki (1979) recommends test-wiseness instructions as early as elementary school but not later than middle or junior high school. Samson (1985) argues that early instruction in test-wiseness may begin to narrow the gap among tested achievement levels of various ethnic groups.

Specifically, Hembree (1988), using meta-analytic findings, found that African American students in grades 2–4 had significantly higher test anxiety scores than their White counterparts. At the high school and college level, Hembree (1988) did not find significant differences between African American and White students. Additional research is needed to determine more exactly the nature of ethnic differences in test anxiety.

10.8 THE COMPONENTS OF TEST ANXIETY

Theoretically, Wine (1980) describes test anxiety as a **cognitive-attentional construct**. Wine notes that students high in test anxiety tend to perform poorer than their low test anxiety counterparts. The differences between the performance of the two groups tends to exacerbate for students high in test anxiety if a task is difficult or complex.

Furthermore, Wine proposed that the component common to general self-report measures of test anxiety is actually **evaluation anxiety**. Individuals high in evaluation anxiety tend to react to evaluation cues with a habitual set of **overlearned irrational** and **debilitating cognitions**. These cognitions tend to be constant within the individual. Similarly, these debilitating cognitions serve as a signal for heightened emotional responses. In contrast, individuals low in evaluation anxiety tend to react to performance evaluation with task focused cognitions or cognitions conducive to understanding the situation. Finally, individuals with high levels of evaluation anxiety tend to report negative self-descriptions of themselves on paper-and-pencil personality measures.

There is a significant negative correlation between self-reported self-esteem measures and test anxiety (Many & Many, 1975). Nicholls (1976) examined the Test Anxiety Scale for children and concluded that negative self-evaluations were the major component of this scale. High test anxious individuals are preoccupied with negative self-evaluations during task performance.

However, unlike low test anxious persons, high test anxious individuals are not helped by not receiving feedback during task performance. Meunier and Rule (1967) found that under no feedback trials high test anxious individuals reported low confidence levels. Similarly, under negative feedback trials, test anxious individuals also reported low confidence levels. During a testing situation high test anxious students tended to divide attention between task cues and internally focused self-defacing dialogue and autonomic reactivity, while the attention of the low test anxious person tends to focus primarily on task cues. This supports Wine's (1980) cognitive-attentional view of test anxiety.

A series of studies (Anderson & Sauser, 1995; Liebert & Morris, 1967; Morris & Liebert, 1969, 1970; Morris & Perez, 1972; Spielberger & Vagg, 1995; Zeidner, 1998) suggested that test anxiety is composed of two major components: worry, a cognitive concern over performance, and emotionality, the autonomic reactivity aspect of anxiety. S. B. Sarason (1966) reported that children experiencing self-reported test anxiety seldom experience painful emotional anxiety reactions. In sum, cognitive and corresponding physiological reactivity are the major components of test anxiety.

Taking a **cognitive-behavioral view** of test anxiety, Sapp (1994a, 1994b, 1996a, 1996b) conceptualized **worry** as the **cognitive component** of test anxiety and **emotionality** as the **behavioral response**. Sapp viewed the **thoughts** and **feelings** that result from test anxiety as **behaviors**. Hence, the cognitions and emotions that one has toward examinations is partly due to reinforcement contingencies, and they are the byproducts of one's experience; therefore, theoretically, cognitive-behavioral strategies would be logical treatments.

Worry cognitions scores are fairly **constant across time**, but **emotionality scores** tend to **peak** immediately before a test and **decrease** rapidly after a testing situation. Worry scores can be reduced by constructive performance feedback, while emotionality scores cannot theoretically be reduced by performance feedback. Similarly, worry scores are negatively correlated with actual performance, while emotionality scores are not significantly correlated with test performance.

Emotionality also has a **diffused transient quality** which is confined to the testing situation. Worry, on the other hand, is a stable personality disposition that interferes with cognitive performance and triggers autonomic reactivity and maintains test anxiety (Kim & Rocklin, 1994; Kleign, Van der Ploeg, & Topman, 1994; Kurosawa & Harackiewicz, 1995).

Sieber (1969) stated that test anxiety is associated with a **faulty short-term memory.** Cognitive interference or negative self-preoccupation results in difficulty with the short-term memory. Sarason (1972) found that instructions directed away from worry cognitions, which are task-oriented and provide information about problem-solving strategies, are helpful for test anxious students' cognitive functioning.

Sarason (1972, 1973, 1975) found that exposing test anxious students to task-oriented instructions with cognitive structuring cues was beneficial for performance. Furthermore, models demonstrating overt cognitive strategies for handling test anxiety were therapeutic for test anxious students (Sarason & Ganzer, 1973; Spence, Duric, & Roeder, 1996; Wells & Matthews, 1994).

A theory related to Wine's cognitive-attentional construct of test anxiety is the **task utilization perspective.** Easterbrook (1959), in a classic review of the literature on **cue utilization,** presented empirical evidence that there is a relationship between test anxiety and cue utilization.

Easterbrook indicated that heightened emotionality was consistently related to a narrowing of range for task cues utilized during task performance. West, Lee, and Anderson (1969) and Geen (1976) reported results supporting the cue utilization hypothesis. They concluded that highly test anxious subjects were less likely than low test anxious subjects to utilize relevant and irrelevant task cues during performance. One can surmise that during evaluative situations, the highly test anxious student's attention is partitioned among task cues, self-deprecatory cognitions, and emotionality, while the low test anxious student's attention is more focused on task cues. In addition, the highly test anxious person often misinterprets informational cues and experiences attentional obstructions. Moreover, Wine (1980) suggested that test anxiety results in students directing attention internally rather than toward a task. Also, in contrast to the low test anxious student, the highly test anxious student attends to fewer task cues. This theory that anxiety reduces the range of cue utilization cannot account for all findings in the literature.

For example, Geen (1980) found that anxiety was related to a broadened range of perceptual and visual stimuli. In an attempt to link the cue utilization hypothesis to individual differences of test anxiety, Geen proposed a **cognitive labeling paradigm**. He proposed that the way information is utilized by a person accounts for test anxiety. This involves a process of interpretation and appraisal. To illustrate, if a student interprets a high level of emotionality as worry, there is a high probability of a debilitating effect on performance; whereas, if the state of emotionality is not labeled worry, there is a possibility of enhancement in performance (Calvo, Eysenck, Ramos, & Jimenz, 1994; Carver, 1996).

In summary, worry is the major component occurring during test anxiety unless an individual attends to emotional arousal. This is in essence the **direction-of-attention hypothesis**, which states that test anxiety is the result of the misdirection of attention and debilitating cognitions that stimulate physiological reactivity (Sarason, 1984; Zeidner, 1994, 1995a, 1995b, 1995c, 1996).

During the last four decades, theories of test anxiety have moved from **drive-oriented** (Mandler & Sarason, 1952) to cognitive attentional (Wine, 1971). Recently, Paulman and Kennelly (1984) emphasized a skills deficit model. The **skills deficit construct** holds that a deficit in adequate study skills and test taking skills and not anxiety is central to the impaired performance of test anxious students. This is in essence an ineffective test taking formulation of test anxiety. There is support for this theory in that study skills and test taking skills of high test anxious students are usually poor (Culler & Holahan, 1980); however, anxiety reduction techniques seldom impact performance on cognitive tasks, classroom examinations, or grades (Allen, Elias, & Zlotlow, 1980). **A point to be remembered is that study skills training alone neither decreases test anxiety nor improves academic achievement.** Also, the transactional models of test anxiety (see Spielberger & Vagg, 1995; Zeidner, 1996) support this position.

Tobias (1985) explains the poor test performance of high anxious students by combining three models—**cognitive interference, cognitive capacity**, and **study skills deficit models**. He assumes that these models are not mutually exclusive and they are viewed as interactive.

The **cognitive interference** model states that test anxiety interferes with students' ability to recall prior learning during an examination. Tobias suggested that a limited cognitive processing capacity exists that cannot account for the effects of both test anxiety and study skills. He asserts that students have a finite capacity for processing information at any point in time. The cognitive representation of test anxiety absorbs some of students' processing capacity, resulting in a diminished portion for task solution. When task demands exceed processing capabilities, interference in learning or performance occurs. As Sarason (1972, 1980) noted, the cognitive representation of test anxiety makes additional demands on cognitive processing by dividing the attention of test anxious students into task-relevant and task-irrelevant behaviors. Moreover, Benjamin, McKeachie, and Lin (1987) offered additional support for this **informational processing view** of test anxiety.

Tobias hypothesized that **study skills training** can enable students to organize tasks so that they require less cognitive attention than those needed by students with poor study habits. Good study skills enable students to reduce the cognitive demands of a task, and they can improve performance by permitting tasks to fit into the available processing capacity. Paulman and Kennelly (1984) provided support for this **cognitive capacity model**. Their findings suggested that as processing demands increase, test anxiety becomes more devastating due to task demands absorbed by test anxiety which exceeds available processing capacity (Vagg & Papsdorf, 1995; Wessel & Mersch, 1994).

Culler and Holahan (1980) provided support for the study skills deficit model of test anxiety. They found that study skills was a good predictor of grade point averages. Similarly, Culler and Holahan found that students with low anxiety had better study skills than students with high anxiety. Moreover, Culler and Holahan contradicted the common scenario of a highly anxious student who knows the subject matter but freezes on the examination. Their findings indicate that highly test anxious students reported spending more time studying than their less test anxious counterparts; however, as an examination approaches, high test anxious students report concentration difficulties and actually study less during the final stages of study (Most & Zeidner, 1995; Parker, Vagg, & Papsdorf, 1995; Schwarzer & Schwarzer, 1996; Seipp & Schwarzer, 1996)..

Culler and Holahan also reported that study time was significantly related to grade point averages for highly test anxious students, but not for those with low test anxiety. This suggests that highly test anxious students compensate for poor study skills by studying longer but not effectively. Paulman and Kennelly (1984) found that test anxiety and test taking skills affected students performance in evaluative situations.

Bruch (1981) presented evidence that high and low test anxious students differed in their knowledge of test taking strategies, even when scholastic aptitude measures were held constant through analysis of covariance. Moreover, test taking strategies were significantly related to differences in achievement between high and low test anxious students.

Bruch, Juster, and Kaflowitz (1983) found test taking ability significantly affected performance on simulated essay and multiple choice tests but to a lesser extent on mathematics examinations. These researchers presented results at variance with Sarason (1972, 1980). They did not find a relationship between test performance and students' levels of anxiety, nor a relationship between test performance and the types of self-statements students reported during examinations. Sarason (1972, 1980) reported greater cognitive interference for highly test-anxious students due to negative self-cognitions (Carver & Scheirer, 1994; Endler, Kantor, & Parker, 1994; Eysenck, 1997; Fletscher & Spielberger, 1995; Gonzalez, 1995).

To summarize, Tobias (1985), using an **informational processing** theory, integrates a **cognitive interference, study skills deficit**, and a **cognitive capacity model** to explain test anxiety. He suggests that test anxiety debilitates performance by reducing cognitive capacity available for task solution. Likewise, study or test taking skills facilitate learning and test performance by reducing the cognitive capacity of different task demands.

10.9 RECOMMENDATIONS FOR PARENTS

During the elementary school years, it is important for parents to form a **positive relationship** with their children. This is extremely pertinent for fostering successful academic performance and a minimal level of test anxiety, especially for preschool or elementary children.

What are some characteristics of a positive relationship between a parent and child? Earlier the topic of injunctions was discussed, which are messages communicated to a child by parents. These messages, communicated by parents to children, are unnecessarily critical. Furthermore, these messages suggest to a child behaviors that are perceived as required in order to obtain recognition.

An example of a message that can occur at an overt or covert level is "don't succeed." This message is communicated when a child is relentlessly criticized and therefore stops trying to succeed on tasks. The child concludes that he or she cannot perform any act correctly. Also, permitting a child to have some individuality is important for constructive self-esteem development. To illustrate, if the injunction "don't be you" is communicated to a child, the result can be low self-esteem and poor academic performance. Through this type of injunction, a parent is only reinforcing behavior that supports an external locus of evaluation. In essence, this teaches a child to measure his or her worth with material gains and external reinforcers.

Exactly what can a parent do to help a child develop healthy self-esteem, self-concept, and increase the probability of academic success and minimal test anxiety? **First**, it is important for a parent to adopt consciously a philosophy that is nurturing and will propel a child towards self-actualization. **Second**, parents must demonstrate genuineness with children. In addition to being authentic, this is just simply communicating to children that even parents are fallible and are bound to make mistakes. It is important to communicate to children that to err is normal. **Third**, acceptance of a child as an individual and demonstrating caring is another contributing factor for positive self-esteem and academic success. **Fourth**, it is important for parents to reflect and discuss a child's feelings. On a daily basis it is important to ask a child how he or she feels about certain life events. This is especially important when a child has been involved in an intense situation.

In summary, if parents practice the philosophy just discussed, the probability for constructive growth of a child's self-esteem and successful academic performance can be greatly enhanced. (For a series of studies that explore the psychoeducational factors that correlate with achievement, see Farrell, Sapp, Johnson, & Pollard, 1994; Sapp, 1984, 1985, 1996; Sapp, Durand, & Farrell, 1995; Sapp & Farrell, 1994; Sapp, Farrell, & Durand, 1995; Smith, Sapp, Farrell, & Johnson, 1998.)

10.10 TEST ANXIETY AND PERFORMANCE

In a classic study, Yerkes and Dodson (1908) demonstrated that **moderate levels of anxiety** can lead to **optimal performance** on certain tasks; nevertheless, performance can deteriorate when anxiety is too high or low. Heightened levels of test anxiety can improve performance on **simple tasks**; in contrast, as tasks increase in complexity, **heightened** levels of test anxiety can serve as a **distraction** from the task at hand. These behaviors include but are not limited to being overly concerned about the passage of time, constant compulsive rechecking of answers which results in incomplete tests. Similarly, the test anxious person is distracted by negative self-evaluative cognitions, such as "I can't remember the answers. I am going to fail this exam." Likewise, physiological arousal such as somatic sensations, perspiration, abdominal pangs, muscle rigidity, and nervousness are also irrelevant task distractions. In summary, this theory predicts a curvilinear relationship between test anxiety and performance.

In contrast to the **Yerkes and Dodson principle**, Rocklin and Thompson (1985) discussed a **monotonic relationship** between test anxiety and performance. **Monotonic** denotes a sequence that is constantly increasing or decreasing. In essence, this is a one-directional linear as opposed to a curvilinear relationship. Similarly, Rocklin and Thompson (1985) discussed an **interaction** between test anxiety and item difficulty. These researchers hypothesized that difficult tests would raise examinees' anxiety more than easier tests. This is particularly the case for extremely anxious students who may be unable to do well on any test. Generally, for extremely difficult examinations, the relationship between anxiety and performance is **monotonically negative**; in contrast, to easy examinations, where the relationship is **monotonically positive**.

Using an experimental design Rocklin and Thompson (1985) investigated the interactive effects of test anxiety, test difficulty, and feedback. Results indicated that examinees' performance was affected in complex ways by the examinees' anxiety level. The least anxious examinees in the study performed best on extremely difficult tests, and moderately anxious examinees performed optimally on easy examinations, whereas the most anxious examinees did poorly on both difficult and easy examinations. Finally, examinees who were given an easy examination and immediate feedback improved on examination performance.

Recently, Matthews (1992) and Zeidner (1998) have criticized the hypothesized notion of a **curvilinear relationship** between performance and test anxiety. They argued that the Yerkes Dodson principle does not describe the nature of the test-anxiety–performance relationship. They do not see any reason why arousal, task difficulty, and performance level should be related. Even though there are few studies within this area, Eysenck (1982), Mandler and Sarason (1952), and Rocklin and Thompson (1985) found a curvilinear relationship between test anxiety and performance. It is doubtful that the 1950s arousal theory of test anxiety is correct, but test anxiety and performance appear to be more complex than a simple univariate linear relationship. It is recommended that a **meta-analysis** be performed in this area, along with graphs and **trend analyses**, in order to summarize what is known about the relationship between test anxiety and performance (Anderson & Sauser, 1998).

In summary, if one were to graph the relationship between practice and several learning trials, the relationship is curvilinear exactly as predicted by the Yerkes Dodson principle; however, this relationship is also consistently positive in that an increase in performance tends to correspond with an increase in practice, suggesting support for Rocklin and Thompson's monotonic relationship between anxiety and performance.

10.11 TEST ANXIETY MEASURES FOR ADOLESCENTS AND ADULTS

There are many available measures of test anxiety on the market. See Anderson and Sauser (1998) for an extensive annotated list of objective self-report measures of test anxiety and related measures. Each measure is guided by a particular theory. The following eight measures of test anxiety will be discussed: 1. *State Anxiety Inventory* developed by Spielberger, Gorsuch, and Lushene (1970), published by Consulting Psychologists Press. 2. *Test Anxiety Questionnaire* found in Mandler and Sarason (1952). A study of anxiety and learning, *Journal of Abnormal and Social Psychology, 47*, 166-173. 3. *Test Anxiety Scale* in Sarason (Ed.) (1980). *Test Anxiety: Theory, research, and applications.* Hillsdale, NJ: Lawrence Erlbaum. 4. *Liebert-Morris Emotionality and Worry Scales* found in Liebert and Morris (1967), Cognitive and emotional components of test anxiety: A distinction and some initial data. *Psychological Reports, 20*, 975-978. 5. *Test Anxiety Inventory* developed by Spielberger (1977), published by Consulting Psychologists Press. 6. *Achievement Anxiety Scale* developed by Alpert and Haber (1960). Anxiety in academic achievement situations. *Journal of Abnormal and Social Psychology, 61*, 207-215. 7. *Suinn Test Anxiety Behavior Scale* developed by Suinn (1969). The STABS, a measure of test anxiety for behavior therapy: Normative data. *Behaviour Research and Therapy, 7*, 335-339. 8. *Mathematic Anxiety Scale* found in Sarason (Ed.) (1980). Test Anxiety: Theory, research, and applications. Hillsdale, NJ: Lawrence Erlbaum. Four test anxiety instruments are provided in this text. In Table 1 is the *Test Anxiety Scale*, Table 2 the *Mathematics Anxiety Scale*, Table 3 the *Achievement Anxiety Scale*, and Table 4 the *Suinn Test Anxiety Behavior Scale*.

1. State Anxiety Inventory

State Anxiety Inventory describes test anxiety as an emotional reaction that varies from situation to situation (Hodapp, Glanzmann, & Laux, 1995). Actually, the State Anxiety Inventory (A-State) is part of a larger inventory called the State-Trait Anxiety Inventory (STAI). This inventory has good validity and reliability. It was developed by Spielberger and his colleagues, Gorsuch, Lushene, Vagg, and Jacobs. Spielberger (1983) reported validity measures from .75 to .85 and test-retest reliability measures from .73 to .86. The test-retest reliability measures for A-State is supposed to vary over time; since this is the case, it does have a low test-retest reliability measure of .16 to .54.

2. Test Anxiety Questionnaire

The **Test Anxiety Questionnaire (TAQ)** was developed by Mandler and Sarason (1952). The TAQ has two components: one measures task relevant responses and the other measures task-irrelevant responses. This is a 37-item questionnaire designed to measure a person's tendency to perform in ways that interfere with task completion. Split-half reliability measures of the TAQ are approximately .99 and test-retest measures are approximately .82. Mandler and Sarason (1952) did report that individuals with high TAQ scores actually performed poorer on cognitive tasks than individuals with low measures (Spielberger & Vagg, 1995).

3. Test Anxiety Scale

The **Test Anxiety Scale (TAS)** is a **trait measure** of test anxiety and an improvement over the TAQ, which has been criticized for being primarily a measure of state and not trait anxiety. Hence, the TAS is a shift in focus for test anxiety from the situation to the person. Therefore, the TAS is designed to determine which individuals are most likely to be test anxious. Sarason (1958, 1975) presents convincing evidence that the TAS does differentiate between persons with high and low levels of test anxiety. Kaplan and Saccuzzo (1982, pp. 423-425) reported that it is among the most extensively researched test anxiety instruments in the literature, and it has been confirmed as a valid measure of test anxiety. Similarly, Kaplan and Saccuzzo (1982, pp. 423-425) concluded that poor performance on tests results from a combination of two factors: being test anxious and a situation that evoke anxiety. The TAS is provided in table 1 and the keyed answers are in parentheses. The greater of true responses an individual reports, the greater the level of test anxiety.

4. Liebert-Morris Emotionality and Worry Scales

The **Liebert-Morris Emotionality** and **Worry Scales** were developed by Liebert and Morris (1967) who proposed that test anxiety had two components—worry and emotionality. **Worry** is the cognitive concern about failing and the self-defeating beliefs associated with failure. **Emotionality** is the physiological reaction to a testing situation. Features of emotionality include sensations of tension, nervousness, heart pounding, and so on. These are, in a sense, behavioral responses to worry.

Theoretically, with test anxious individuals, worry is a relatively constant component, whereas emotionality varies depending on the evaluative situation. For example, for test anxious individuals it increases as the date for an evaluative situation increases, peaks immediately before an evaluative situation, and decreases rapidly once the situation is completed. Doctor and Altman (1969) made a greater differentiation of the worry component of test anxiety by suggesting that there are trait-like factors of worry which decreases after an evaluative situation. In addition, there is a cognitive perceptual feature of worry which includes a perceived unpleasantness of an evaluative situation. By performing factor analysis on the TAQ, Liebert and Morris concluded that test anxiety is multidimensional as opposed to unidimensional construct. The Liebert and Morris theory has not been totally substantiated. For example, Finger and Galassi (1977) conducted a study using two treatments to reduce the worry and emotionality components of test anxiety. One treatment was designed to treat the worry component, while the other was expected to treat emotionality. Contrary to theory, the treatment that reduced emotionality also reduced worry. This study suggested that it is possible that worry and emotionality operate together as a single process during test anxiety. Finally, Richardson, O'Neil, Whitmore, and Judd (1977) made an attempt to perform a confirmatory factor analysis on the Liebert-Morris Scales and contrary to Liebert and Morris, they did not support the theory that worry and emotionality are distinct factors.

5. Test Anxiety Inventory

The **Test Anxiety Inventory (TAI)** was created in the midst of the controversy with the Liebert-Morris Scales as a separate test anxiety scale. It was developed by Spielberger and his colleagues, Anton and Bedell (1976). Previously, it was suggested that Spielberger proposed a state-trait anxiety theory of anxiety. Within this schema of the state-trait theory, worry is analogous to trait anxiety; whereas emotionality corresponds to state anxiety. This understanding clarifies how the A-state of the STAI can be used as a test anxiety measure. The TAI suggests that individuals high in the worry trait are also affected by emotionality in that an evaluative situation interacts with the tendency to worry; hence, producing greater measures of emotionality during a stressful situation. Unlike traditional test anxiety measures, the TAI suggests that worry is not the most important component to interfere with test performance. It is the combination of high worry and emotionality scores that affect test performance.

The TAI consists of 20 items which describe reactions before, during, and after examinations. Respondents indicate how they generally feel by stating how frequently they experience each reaction which is on a Likert scale (almost never, sometimes, often, almost always).

Anastasi (1988) described the TAI as primarily a trait measure scale restricted to a specified class of situations centering around examinations. The TAI has total score of test anxiety proneness and subscores that measure the two major components of test anxiety identified through factor analysis, worry and emotionality.

Normative data are available for total TAI scores and the subscores. Spielberger (1980) reported validity coefficients of .82 for male and .83 for females. Reliability coefficients were reported at .80 for 3 weeks and .81 for 1 month intervals. Using tables of norms, raw scores from the TAI are converted into standardized t-scores with a mean of 50 and standard deviation of 10. There are significant negative correlations among grades and the TAI. They have a lower range of -.18 and an upper range of -.31. In summary, the TAI has good psychometric properties.

6. Achievement Anxiety Scale

Alpert and Haber (1960) also constructed an instrument designed to measure two components of test anxiety called the **Achievement Anxiety Scale (AAS)**. The AAS is found in Table 3.

Alpert and Haber (1960) theorized that there are components of test anxiety. One of these components actually facilitates performance. For example, the anxiety that motivates one to study would be considered facilitative or beneficial. This corresponds to the Yerkes and Dodson's principles which suggested that a moderate level of anxiety is necessary for optimal performance. The AAS is a 19-item scale that measures two components of test anxiety: facilitative anxiety and debilitating anxiety. The **facilitating scale** is made up of nine items, while the debilitating scale consists of ten items. Facilitating anxiety motivates one to perform. It is considered helpful, while debilitating anxiety measures the extent in which anxiety interferes with performance.

The **debilitating anxiety** is similar to the anxiety that other test anxiety scales measure; however, the novel scale is the facilitating scale. The AAS has excellent validity and reliability. Using an objective dependent measure such as grades, the facilitating scale correlates .37 with grade point averages; in contrast, the debilitating scale correlates -.35 with grades. Similarly, McCordick, Kaplan, Smith, and Finn (1981) demonstrated that the AAS predicts grade point averages nearly as well as the Scholastic Aptitude Test.

In terms of reliability, Alpert and Haber (1960) reported test-retest reliabilities over a 10-week period to be .83 for the facilitating scale and .87 for the debilitating scale. Evidence suggests that the two scales measure opposite components, since they are negatively correlated, $r = -.37$.

The debilitating scale correlates .64 with the TAS. Additional support that the facilitating scale measures a component which is the opposite of traditional test anxiety measures, lies in the fact that the correlation between this scale and the TAS is significantly negative $r = -.40$ (Kaplan & Saccuzzo, 1982, p. 430). The AAS is scored on a five-point scale. Alpert and Haber reported an average mean and standard deviation from four samples on the debilitating scale to be a mean=26.33 and a standard deviation of 5.33.

7. Suinn Test Anxiety Scale

The **Suinn Test Anxiety Behavior Scale (STABS)** is designed for behaviorally oriented therapists (Suinn, 1969); hence, it is a behaviorally anchored scale. Many of the test anxiety instruments previously discussed place a greater emphasis on cognition than behavior. The STABS was designed to evaluate behavior therapy treatments for test anxiety research. It has three important characteristics. First, it can serve as a diagnostic tool for test anxiety. In addition, it can facilitate the development of a test anxiety hierarchy that can be used during behavioral treatments. Second, Suinn reported normative data for the STABS. Third, Suinn reports the changes that can be expected in test anxiety scores without treatment.

The STABS has good reliability and validity. For example, test-retest reliability over a 6-week period was .74 and .78 over a 4-week period. In terms of validity the STABS correlated .59 with the TAS which is significant beyond the .001 level. Similarly, the STABS correlates between -.24 and -.28 with errors on course examinations and final course grades, respectively. In summary, the STABS differs from other test anxiety instruments in that it is designed for behaviorally oriented therapists.

10. Mathematics Anxiety Scale

The **Mathematics Anxiety Scale (MARS)** measures mathematics anxiety (Sarason, 1980, pp. 274-278). Brush (1976) reported a strong relationship between the STABS and the MARS $r = .65$, $p < .001$. The MARS is a 40-item instrument with a five-point scale designed to measure mathematics anxiety. Suinn, Edie, Nicoletti, and Spinelli (1972) and Richardson and Suinn (1972) presented psychometric data on the MARS. In addition, Richardson and Suinn (1972) reported an internal consistency reliability coefficient of .93. Test-retest reliability measures for the MARS were reported between .78 and .85. The validity coefficients for the MARS range from .35 and .64. The MARS is presented in Table 2.

Mathematics anxiety is a **specific form** of test anxiety. Richardson and Woolfolk (1980) concluded that the cognitive and emotional dynamics of mathematics anxiety parallel that of general test anxiety. Mathematics anxiety is also a response to mathematical content and the connotative interpretations that are attributed to mathematics in our society. For example, mathematical sciences are considered to be for the highly intelligent, the analytically meticulous, and are considered an arcane domain. Likewise, the early teaching of mathematics is often presented as monotonous, mechanical, and devoid of common sense, thus reinforcing the stereotype held by society.

11. Reactions to Tests

Sarason presented a **four-dimensional** or **factor theory** of test anxiety. Two of the dimensions—worry and emotionality—correspond to Spielberger's (1980) two-dimensional model. Sarason added two new dimensions—bodily symptoms and test irrelevant thinking. The Reactions to Tests (RTT) is a 40-item self-report questionnaire that measures Sarason's four dimensions of test anxiety.

10.12 THE DEVELOPMENT OF MATHEMATICAL TEST ANXIETY

Bashman (1984) and Mitchell and Collins (1991) pointed out that mathematics test anxiety is rampant. If one were to look clearly at the teaching of mathematics, it is apparent that it is taught mainly through a memorization approach. However, simple rote memorization discourages the higher level metacognitive processes that are imperative for learning advanced levels of mathematics. Often the notion that one experiences mathematical test anxiety is socially acceptable, this encourages the trend towards mathematical test anxiety in our society.

It appears that mathematics test anxiety evolves along a **social-cognitive-developmental perspective**. This partially substantiates the notion that if one experiences mathematical test anxiety, it is socially acceptable. Developmentally, from a social and cognitive perspective, how could mathematical test anxiety develop? As a child progresses through stages of development, he or she acquires cognitions about his or her social world. This includes the ability of role taking, and being able to imagine oneself in another's place. As a child continues to develop, he or she interprets the cognitions, actions, and emotions of others. Eventually, a child links cognitive and social behaviors that reinforce the interpretation that mathematics is dull, boring, and only for geniuses. Once a child accepts these cognitive and social schemes, he or she will consistently avoid as much as possible mathematics which, in turn, results in deficient mathematical skills.

10.13 TEST ANXIETY IN THE ACADEMICALLY AT-RISK

Sapp and Farrell (1994) state that "at-risk" is a relatively new term in education. In March, 1980 the term was introduced as a descriptor in the Thesaurus of ERIC Descriptors. Prior to 1980, the term was occasionally indexed under the term "educationally disadvantage." This terms was introduced as a descriptor in July, 1966. **At-risk students**, as defined by the Thesaurus of ERIC Descriptors, are students with normal intelligence whose academic background or prior performance may cause them to be perceived as candidates for future academic failure or early withdrawal from school. Similarly, educationally disadvantaged are individuals or groups whose schooling is judged to be qualitatively or quantitatively inferior as compared with what is considered necessary for achievement in a particular society. In summary, the term at-risk is a new descriptor in the educational and psychological literature.

In the 1990s the term "at risk" has received a great deal of attention. For example, Loughrey and Harris (1990) discussed issues related to at-risk students. Moreover, they defined at-risk by the following criteria: a student who is a dropout, a pupil who is a parent, a pupil who has been adjudicated delinquent, a student who is one or more years behind his/her age or grade level group in the number of credits attained, and a student who is one or more years behind his/her age or grade level group in mathematics or reading skill levels. Similarly, Michael (1990) discussed how the at-risk phenomenon continues to baffle educators and counselors in terms of possible treatment interventions. The current at-risk literature indicates that at-risk students are not restricted to urban schools. Reglin (1990) describes how the at-risk dilemma impacts rural schools. He reported that increasing the length of the school day in a rural public school system resulted in an increase in drop-out rate among rural at-risk students. In summary, the term at risk has become an issue of greater importance during the 1990s.

In the educational literature, many characteristics are used to denote at-risk. Sapp (1994a, 1996a). Howard and Anderson (1978), Lloyd (1978), and Kelley, Veldman, and McGuire (1964) used the following factors to describe at-risk students: **(1) students who do not receive a high school diploma, (2) students who graduate with inadequate competencies; and (3) students who do not become successfully employed. In practical terms, students who are at-risk are those who are unlikely to graduate from high school.** Schreiber (1968) reported that high risk factors for at-risk students include low achievement, retention in grade, behavior problems, poor attendance, low socio-economic status, and attendance at schools with large numbers of poor students. Slavin, Karweit, and Madden (1989, pp. 3–17) concluded that these factors are associated with dropping out of school. Based on similar factors, Howard and Anderson (1978) demonstrated that one can reliably predict which students will drop out and which will complete school by the third grade.

As one would expect, Sapp (1992) reported that academically at-risk middle school students did have significantly high levels of test anxiety. Similarly, he described empirically based psychoeducational variables important for improving their academic achievement. Earlier, Shavelson and Bolus (1982) and Slavin (1987) suggested that academic self-concept and self-esteem were correlated with achievement. Sapp, Farrell, and Durand (1995) statistically explored the relationship among self-esteem, academic self-concept, grades, and reading scores with at-risk African American middle school students. Employing a randomized pretest/posttest design, they found significant changes on grade point averages, number of days absent, and number of days tardy after students received cognitive-behavioral therapy. A path analysis suggested that academic self-concept was the mediating variable between cognitive-behavioral therapy and academic achievement.

Sapp (1990a) assessed empirically the academic performance, academic self-concept, and self-esteem of at-risk junior high school students. Sapp using a correlational design tested three levels of hypotheses stated before conducting his study.

The **first level of hypotheses** involved multivariate regression. This hypothesis stated that using academic self-concept and self-esteem as predictors and standardized reading, arithmetic, and spelling scores as dependent variables, there would be a significant relationship between the predictors and dependent variables.

The **second level of hypotheses** involved a forced multiple regression procedure. This hypothesis stated that academic self-concept would be a more significant predictor of achievement than self-esteem when forced into a regression equation.

The **third level of hypotheses** involved two univariate hypotheses which stated that there would be a significant relationship among grades and academic self-concept, and there would be a significant relationship among grades and standardized reading, mathematics, and spelling scores. Statistical evidence supported all three levels of hypotheses.

After extensive statistical analyses, Sapp concluded that **academic self-concept was a significant predictor of achievement**. Similarly, Sapp's results from multivariate and multiple regression supported his univariate hypotheses. **He suggests that increasing at-risk students' academic self-concept should correspondingly increase academic achievement.** Moreover, Sapp recommends cognitive-behavioral counseling as a means of helping at-risk students identify negative cognitions and to replace them with positive self-statements. Furthermore, he recommends that at-risk students learn to monitor their cognitive processes, which can help break the cycles of cognitive distortion. Finally, Sapp recommends providing at-risk students with extensive academic remediation coupled with cognitive-behavioral counseling, which can improve ego-strength and academic skills.

10.14 SUMMARY
There are as many definitions of test anxiety as theories attempting to define it. Research suggests that the parent-child interaction is related to the development of test anxiety in children. The **TASC** is a **multidimensional group administered paper and pencil test** used to assess test anxiety in children. Test wiseness, a term related to test anxiety, is a subject's ability to employ characteristics of a test to receive a high score. McPhail (1981) suggested two reasons for teaching test wiseness. First, to improve the validity of test results and second to promote equal educational opportunity for minority students who tend to experience higher levels of test anxiety than majority students.

Cognitive theories have had the most dominant impact on test anxiety research. The major components of test anxiety, worry and emotionality, can be explained by many cognitive theories such as the **cognitive-attentional construct, informational processing theory, direction of attention hypothesis, cognitive interference model, study skills deficits models, cognitive capacity model**, and the **cue utilization hypothesis**.

In terms of test anxiety and performance, there are many factors that account for this relationship. For example, time pressures, examinees' anxiety levels, methods of feedback, and difficulty levels of examinations are related to examination performance. Similarly, motivational variables and the classroom environment are also associated with examination performance.

Eight commonly used measures of test anxiety were discussed in this chapter along with references whereby they can be obtained. Mathematical anxiety is possibly the most common form of test anxiety found in the American society. Finally, the topic of test anxiety in the academically at-risk was treated in some detail, and the psychoeducational educational variables that are important for predicting and improving their academic success were also described.

Table 1

Test Anxiety Scale

(Keyed answers are in parentheses)

(T)   1. While taking an important exam, I find myself thinking of how much brighter the other students are than I am. T or F

(T)   2. If I were to take an intelligence test, I would worry a great deal before taking it. T or F

(F)   3. If I knew I was going to take an intelligence test, I would feel confident and relaxed. T or F

(T)   4. While taking an important examination, I perspire a great deal.

(T)   5. During course examinations, I find myself thinking of things unrelated to the actual course material. T or F

(T)   6. I get to feel very panicky when I have to take a surprise exam.

(T)   7. During a test, I find myself thinking of the consequences of failing. T or F

(T)   8. After important tests, I am frequently so tense that my stomach gets upset. T or F

(T)   9. I freeze up on things like intelligence tests and final exams.

(T) 10. Getting good grades on one test doesn't seem to increase my confidence on the second. T or F

(T) 11. I sometimes feel my heart beating very fast during important exams. T or F

(T) 12. After taking a test, I always feel I could have done better than I actually did. T or F

(T) 13. I usually get depressed after taking a test. T or F

(T) 14. I have an uneasy, upset feeling before taking a final examination. T or F

(F) 15. When taking a test, my emotional feelings do not interfere with my performance. T or F

(T)   16. During a course examination, I frequently get so nervous that I forget facts I really know. T or F

(T)   17. I seem to defeat myself while working on important tests. T or F

(T)   18. The harder I work at taking a test or studying for one, the more confused I get. T or F

(T)   19. As soon as an exam is over, I try to stop worrying about it, but I just can't. T or F

(T)   20. During exams, I sometimes wonder if I'll ever get through college. T or F

(T)   21. I would rather write a paper than take an examination for my grade in a course. T or F

(T)   22. I wish examinations did not bother me so much. T or F

(T)   23. I think I could do much better on test if I could take them alone and not feel pressured by time limits. T or F

(T)   24. Thinking about the grade I may get in a course interferes with my studying and my performance on tests. T or F

(T)   25. If examinations could be done away with, I think I would actually learn more. T or F

(F)   26. On exams I take the attitude, "If I don't know it now, there's no point worrying about it." T or F

(F)   27. I really don't see why some people get so upset about tests. T or F

(T)   28. Thoughts of doing poorly interfere with my performance on tests. T or F

(F)   29. I don't study any harder for final exams than for the rest of my course work. T or F

(F)   30. Even when I'm well prepared for a test, I feel very anxious about it. T or F

(T)   31. I don't enjoy eating before an important test. T or F

(T)   32. Before an important examination, I find my hands or arms trembling. T or F

(F)   33. I seldom feel the need for "cramming" before an exam. T or F

(T)   34. The university should recognize that some students are more nervous than others about tests and that this affects their performance. T or F

(T)   35. It seems to me that examination periods should not be made such intense situations. T or F

(T) 36. I start feeling very uneasy just before getting a test paper back. T or F
(T) 37. I dread courses where the professor has the habits of giving "pop" quizzes. T or F

Scoring: Add the number of (T) responses; this represents the TAS score.

Table 2
Mathematic Anxiety Scale

	Not at All	A Little	A Fair Amount	Much	Very Much
Score Value	1	2	3	4	5

1. Thinking about an upcoming math test one day before.
    1   2   3   4   5
2. Picking up a math textbook to begin a difficult reading assignment.
    1   2   3   4   5
3. Opening a math or stat book and seeing a page full of problems.
    1   2   3   4   5
4. Studying for a math test.
    1   2   3   4   5
5. Thinking about an upcoming math test one week before.
    1   2   3   4   5
6. Taking an examination (quiz) in a math course.
    1   2   3   4   5
7. Listening to a lecture in a math class.
    1   2   3   4   5
8. Starting a new chapter in a math book.
    1   2   3   4   5
9. Signing up for a math course.
    1   2   3   4   5

10. Picking up the math textbook to begin working on a homework assignment.

           1   2   3   4   5

11. Thinking about an upcoming math test one hour before.

           1   2   3   4   5

12. Realizing that you have to take a certain number of math classes to fulfill the requirements in your major.

           1   2   3   4   5

13. Not knowing the formula needed to solve a particular problem.

           1   2   3   4   5

14. Taking the math section of a college entrance exam.

           1   2   3   4   5

15. Being given a homework assignment of many difficult math problems which is due the next class meeting.

           1   2   3   4   5

16. Being given a "pop" quiz in a math class.

           1   2   3   4   5

17. Listening to another student explain a math formula.

           1   2   3   4   5

18. Working on an abstract mathematical problem, such as: "If x=outstanding bills, and v=total income, calculate how much you have left for recreational expenditures."

           1   2   3   4   5

19. Getting ready to study for a math test.

           1   2   3   4   5

20. Hearing a friend try to teach you a math procedure and finding that you cannot understand what he is telling you.

           1   2   3   4   5

21. Walking on campus and thinking about a math course.

           1   2   3   4   5

22. Taking an examination (final) in a math course.

           1   2   3   4   5

23. Reading a formula in chemistry.

           1   2   3   4   5

24. Watching a teacher work an algebraic equation on the blackboard.

           1   2   3   4   5

25. Looking through the pages of a math text.

           1   2   3   4   5

26. Solving a square root problem.

    1   2   3   4   5

27. Walking into a math class.

    1   2   3   4   5

28. Having to use the tables in the back of a math book.

    1   2   3   4   5

29. Walking to a math class.

    1   2   3   4   5

30. Talking to someone in your class who does well about a problem
    and not being able to understand what he is explaining.

    1   2   3   4   5

31. Thinking about an upcoming math test 5 minutes before.

    1   2   3   4   5

32. Being asked to explain how you arrive at a particular solution for a
    problem.

    1   2   3   4   5

33. Receiving your final math grade in the mail.

    1   2   3   4   5

34. Reading and interpreting graphs or charts.

    1   2   3   4   5

35. Tallying up the results of a survey or poll.

    1   2   3   4   5

36. Doing a word problem in algebra.

    1   2   3   4   5

37. Sitting in a math class and waiting for the instructor to arrive.

    1   2   3   4   5

38. Being called upon to recite in a math class when you are prepared.

    1   2   3   4   5

39. Buying a math textbook.

    1   2   3   4   5

40. Asking your math instructor to help you with a problem that you
    don't understand.

    1   2   3   4   5

Reproduced from Sarason, I. G. (1980). *Test Anxiety: Theory, research and application.* Permission granted by Lawrence Erlbaum Associates, Inc.

Scoring: Add the values obtained for each item. For example, a response of 1 corresponds to "not at all" and 2 to a little anxiety, and so on.

Table 3
Achievement Anxiety Scale

	Not at All	A Little	A Fair Amount	Much	Very Much
Score Value	1	2	3	4	5

Facilitating Anxiety Scale

1. I work most effectively under pressure, as when the task is very important.

    1   2   3   4   5

2. While I may (or may not) be nervous before taking an exam, once I start, I seem to forget to be nervous. I always forget—I am always nervous during an exam.

    1   2   3   4   5

3. Nervousness while taking a test helps me do better. It never helps—It often helps.

    1   2   3   4   5

4. When I start a test, nothing is able to distract me. This is always true for me—This is not true for me.

    1   2   3   4   5

5. In courses in which the total grade is based mainly on one exam, I seem to do better than other people.

    1   2   3   4   5

6. I look forward to exams.

    1   2   3   4   5

7. Although "cramming" under pre-examination tension is not effective for most people, I find that if the need arises, I can learn material immediately before an exam, even under considerable pressure, and successfully retain it to use the exam. I am always able to use the "crammed" material successfully.

    1   2   3   4   5

8. I enjoy taking a difficult exam more than an easy one.

    1   2   3   4   5

9. The more important the exam or test, the better I seem to do. This is true for me—This is not true for me.

    1   2   3   4   5

Debilitating Anxiety Scale

1. Nervousness while taking an exam or test hinders me from doing well.

    1   2   3   4   5

2. In a course where I have been doing poorly, my fear of a bad grade cuts down my efficiency.

    1   2   3   4   5

3. When I am poorly prepared for an exam or test, I get upset and do less well than even my restricted knowledge should allow. This never happens to me—This practically always happens to me.

    1   2   3   4   5

4. The more important the examination, the less well I seem to do.

    1   2   3   4   5

5. During exams or tests, I block on questions to which I know the answers, even though I might remember them as soon as the exam is over. This always happens to me—I never block on questions to which I know the answers.

    1   2   3   4   5

6. I find that my mind goes blank at the beginning of an exam, and it takes me a few minutes before I can function. I almost always blank out at first—I never blank out at first.

    1   2   3   4   5

7. I am so tired from worrying about an exam, that I find I almost don't care how well I do by the time I start the test. I never feel this way—I almost always feel this way.

    1   2   3   4   5

8. Time pressure on an exam causes me to do worse than the rest of the group under similar conditions. Time pressure always seems to make me do worse on an exam than others—Time pressure never seems to make me do worse on an exam than others.

    1   2   3   4   5

9. I find myself reading exam questions without understanding them, and I must go back over them so that they will make sense.

    1   2   3   4   5

10. When I don't do well on a difficult item at the beginning of an exam, it tends to upset me so that I block on even easy questions later on. This never happens to me—This almost always happens to me.

      1   2   3   4   5

Reproduced from Albert, R., & Haber, R. N. (1960). Anxiety in academic achievement situations. *Journal of Abnormal and Social Psychology 61*, 207-215. Permission granted by the American Psychological Association.

Scoring: Add the values obtained for each scale.

Table 4
Suinn Test Anxiety Scale

	Not at All	A Little	A Fair Amount	Much	Very Much
Score Value	1	2	3	4	5

1. Going into regularly scheduled class period in which the professor asks the students to participate.

    1   2   3   4   5

2. Re-reading the answers I gave on the test before turning it in.

    1   2   3   4   5

3. Sitting down to study before a regularly scheduled class.

    1   2   3   4   5

4. Turning my completed test paper in.

    1   2   3   4   5

5. Hearing the announcement of a coming test.

    1   2   3   4   5

6. Having a test returned.

    1   2   3   4   5

7. Reading the first question on a final exam.

    1   2   3   4   5

8. Studying for a class in which I am scared of the professor.

    1   2   3   4   5

9. Being in class waiting for my corrected test to be returned.

    1   2   3   4   5

10. Seeing a test question and not being sure of the answer.

        1   2   3   4   5

11. Studying for a test the night before.

        1   2   3   4   5

12. Waiting to enter the room where a test is to be given.

        1   2   3   4   5

13. Waiting for a test to be handed out.

        1   2   3   4   5

14. Being called on to answer a question in class by a professor who scares me.

        1   2   3   4   5

15. Waiting for the day my corrected test will be returned.

        1   2   3   4   5

16. Discussing with the instructor an answer I believed to be right but which was marked wrong.

        1   2   3   4   5

17. Seeing my standing on the exam relative to other people's standing.

18. Waiting to see my letter grade on the test.

        1   2   3   4   5

19. Studying for a quiz.

        1   2   3   4   5

20. Studying for a midterm.

        1   2   3   4   5

21. Studying for a final.

        1   2   3   4   5

22. Discussing my approaching test with friends a few weeks before the test is due.

        1   2   3   4   5

23. After the test, listening to the answers which my friends selected.

        1   2   3   4   5

24. Looking at the clock to see how much time remains during an exam.

        1   2   3   4   5

25. Seeing the number of questions that need to be answered on the test.

        1   2   3   4   5

26. On an essay exam, seeing a question I cannot answer.

        1   2   3   4   5

27. On a multiple choice test, seeing a question I cannot answer.

        1   2   3   4   5

28. Being asked by someone if I am ready for a forthcoming exam.
         1   2   3   4   5
29. Being the first to finish an exam and turn it in.
         1   2   3   4   5
30. Being asked by a friend concerning my standing in a class.
         1   2   3   4   5
31. Being asked by a friend concerning results of a test on which I did
     poorly.
         1   2   3   4   5
32. Discovering I need an A or B on the next exam in order to pass the
     course.
         1   2   3   4   5
33. Discovering I need an A or B on the final exam to maintain the
     grade point average necessary to remain in school.
         1   2   3   4   5
34. Thinking about "warning slips" from the Dean's office.
         1   2   3   4   5
35. Reading a "warning slip" from the Dean's office.
         1   2   3   4   5
36. Remembering my past reactions while preparing for another test.
         1   2   3   4   5
37. Seeking out the teaching assistant or instructor for advice or help.
         1   2   3   4   5
38. Being told to see the instructor concerning some aspect of my class
     work.
         1   2   3   4   5
39. Asking for a make-up exam after missing the scheduled exam.
         1   2   3   4   5
40. Discussing the course content with the fellow students just before
     entering the classroom the day of the exam.
         1   2   3   4   5
41. Being the last one to finish an exam and turn it in.
         1   2   3   4   5
42. Reviewing study materials the night before an exam.
         1   2   3   4   5
43. On the first day of the course, hearing the instructor announce the
     dates of the midterm and final examination.
         1   2   3   4   5

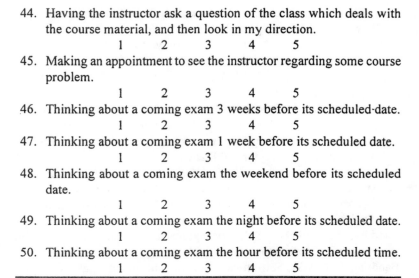

44. Having the instructor ask a question of the class which deals with the course material, and then look in my direction.
    1   2   3   4   5
45. Making an appointment to see the instructor regarding some course problem.
    1   2   3   4   5
46. Thinking about a coming exam 3 weeks before its scheduled·date.
    1   2   3   4   5
47. Thinking about a coming exam 1 week before its scheduled date.
    1   2   3   4   5
48. Thinking about a coming exam the weekend before its scheduled date.
    1   2   3   4   5
49. Thinking about a coming exam the night before its scheduled date.
    1   2   3   4   5
50. Thinking about a coming exam the hour before its scheduled time.
    1   2   3   4   5

Reproduced from Suinn, R. M. (1969). The STABS, a measure of test anxiety for behavior therapy: Normative data. *Behavior Research and Therapy, 7*, 335-339. Permission granted by Pergamon Press, Inc.

Scoring: Add the values obtained for each item.

A 10-point decline in before and after measures indicates a significant reduction of test anxiety. A reduction of about ten points is expected without treatment intervention. Suinn reported a mean pretest of 122.00 and a standard deviation of 30.46 and a posttest mean of 114.22 and a standard deviation of 32.56 for a state university of Colorado sample.

For a state university of Hawaii sample, he reported a pretest mean of 145.76 and a standard deviation of 34.93 and a posttest mean of 135.42 and a standard deviation of 32.67. Suinn provides normative data and percentile ranks.

References
Allen, G. J., Elias, M. J., & Zlotlow, S. F. (1980). Behavioral interventions for alleviating test anxiety: A methodological overview of current therapeutic practices. In I. G. Sarason (Ed.), *Test anxiety:*

Theory research and applications (pp. 155-185). Hillsdale, NJ: Lawrence Erlbaum.

Alpert, R., & Haber, R. N. (1960). Anxiety in academic achievement situations. *Journal of Abnormal and Social Psychology, 61*, 207-215.

Anastasi, A. (1988). *Psychological testing* (6th ed.). New York: Macmillan.

Anderson, S. B., & Sauser, W. I., Jr. (1995). Measurement of test anxiety: An overview. In C. D. Spielberger & P. R. Vagg (Eds.), *Test anxiety: Theory, assessment, and treatment* (pp. 15–34). Washington, DC: Taylor and Francis.

Anton, W. D., & Lillibridge, E. M. (1995). Cast studies of test-anxious students. In C. D. Spielberger & P. R. Vagg (Eds.), *Test anxiety: Theory, assessment, and treatment* (pp. 61–78). Washington, DC: Taylor and Francis.

Bandura, A. (1982). Self-efficacy mechanism in human agency. *American Psychologist, 37*, 122-147.

Bandura, A. (1983). Self-efficacy determinants of anticipated fears and calamities. *Journal of Personality and Social Psychology, 45*, 464-469.

Bandura, A. (1986). *Social foundations of thought and action: A social cognitive theory.* Englewood Cliffs, NJ: Prentice-Hall.

Bashman, R. (1984). *Indirect suggestion versus cognitive therapy in the treatment of mathematics test anxiety: A comparative treatment outcome study.* Unpublished doctoral dissertation, University of Washington, Seattle, WA.

Benjamin, M., McKeachie, W. J., & Lin, Y. (1987). Two types of test-anxious students: Support for an information processing mode. *Journal of Educational Psychology, 79*(2), 131-136.

Benson, J., Urman, H., & Hocevar, D. (1986). Effects of test-wiseness training and ethnicity on achievement of third and fifth grade students. *Measurement and Evaluation in Counseling and Development, 18*(4), 154-162.

Bruch, M. A. (1981). Relationship of test-taking strategies to test anxiety and performance: Towards a task analysis of examination behavior. *Cognitive Therapy and Research, 5*, 41-56.

Bruch, M. A., Juster, H., & Kaflowitz, N. (1983). Relationships of cognitive components of test anxiety to test performance: Implications for assessment and treatment. *Journal of Counseling Psychology, 30*, 527-536.

Butler, R. (1987). Task-involving and ego-involving properties of evaluation: The effects of different feedback conditions on motivational perceptions, interest and performance. *Journal of Educational Psychology, 79*, 474-482.

Butler, R. (1988). Enhancing and undermining intrinsic motivation: The effects of task-involving evaluations on interest and performance. *British Journal of Educational Psychology, 58*, 1-14.

Calvo, M. G., Eysenck, M. W., Ramos, P. M., & Jimenz, A. (1994). Compensatory reading strategies in test anxiety. *Anxiety, Stress, and Coping, 7*, 97-117.

Carver, C. S. (1996). Cognitive interference and the structure of behavior. In I. G. Sarason, G. R. Pierce, & B. R. Sarason (Eds.), *Cognitive interference: Theories, methods, and findings* (pp. 25-45). Mahway, NJ: Erlbaum.

Carver, C. S., & Scheirer, M. F. (1994). Situational coping and coping dispositions in a stressful transaction. *Journal of Personality and Social Psychology, 66*, 184-195.

Culler, R. E., & Holahan, C. J. (1980). Test anxiety and academic performance: The effects of study-related behaviors. *Journal of Educational Psychology, 72*, 16-20.

Doctor, R., & Altman, F. (1969). Worry and emotionality as components of test anxiety: Replication and further data. *Psychological Reports, 24*, 563-568.

Dusek, J. B. (1980). The development of test anxiety in children. In I. G. Sarason (Ed.), *Test anxiety: Theory, research and applications* (pp. 87-110). Hillsdale, NJ: Lawrence Erlbaum.

Dykeman, B. F. (1992). *The effects of motivational orientation, feedback condition, and self-efficacy on test anxiety.* Unpublished doctoral dissertation, University of Wisconsin-Milwaukee, Milwaukee, Wisconsin.

Easterbrook, J. A. (1959). The effect of emotion on cue utilization and the organization of behavior. *Psychological Review, 66*, 183-201.

Endler, N. S., Kantor, L., & Parker, J. D. A. (1994). State-trait coping, state-trait anxiety, and academic performance. *Personality and Individual Differences, 16*, 663-670.

Eysenck, M. W. (1982). *Attention and arousal: Cognition and performance.* Berlin: Springer-Verlag.

Eysenck, M. W. (1997). *Anxiety and cognition.* Hove, East Sussex: Psychology Press.

Farrell, W., Sapp, M., Johnson, J., & Pollard, D. (1994). Assessing college aspirations among at-risk high school students: A principal component analysis. *The High School Journal, 77*(4), 294–303.

Feld, S. C., & Lewis, J. (1969). The assessment of achievement anxieties in children. In C. P. Smith (Ed.), *Achievement-related motives in children* (pp. 1-50). New York: Sage.

Finger, R., & Galassi, J. P. (1977). Effects of modifying cognitive versus emotionality responses in the treatment of test anxiety. *Journal of Consulting and Clinical Psychology, 45,* 280-287.

Fletcher, T. M., & Spielberger, C. D. (1995). Comparison of cognitive therapy and rational emotive therapy in the treatment of test anxiety. In C. D. Spielberger & P. R. Vagg (Eds.), *Test anxiety: Theory, assessment, and treatment* (pp. 153–169). Washington, DC: Taylor and Francis.

Geen, R. G. (1976). Test anxiety, observation, and range of cue utilization. *British Journal of Social and Clinical Psychology, 15,* 253-259.

Geen, R. G. (1980). Test anxiety and cue utilization. In I. C. Sarason (Ed.), *Test anxiety: Theory, Research and Applications* (pp. 43-54). Hillsdale, NJ: Lawrence Erlbaum.

Gibb, B. G. (1964). *Test-wiseness as a secondary cue response.* Unpublished doctoral dissertation, Stanford University.

Gonzalez, H. P. (1995). Systematic desensitization, study skills counseling, anxiety-coping training in the treatment of test anxiety. In C. D. Spielberger & P. R. Vagg (Eds.), *Test anxiety: Theory, assessment, and treatment* (pp.1171-132). Washington, DC: Taylor and Francis.

Goulding, R. L. (1987). Group therapy: Mainline or sideline? In J. K. Zeig (Ed.), *The evolution of psychotherapy* (pp. 300-311). New York: Brunner/Mazel.

Hembree, R. (1988). Correlates, causes, effects, and treatments for test anxiety. *Review of Educational Research, 58*(1), 47-77.

Hill, K. T. (1972). Anxiety in the evaluative context. In W. Hartup (Ed.), *The young child (Vol. 2).* Washington, DC: National Association for the Education of Young Children.

Hill, K. T., & Wigfield, A. (1984). Test anxiety: A major educational problem and what can be done about it. *The Elementary School Journal, 85*(6), 105-126.

Hodapp, V., Glanzmann, P. R., & Laux, L. (1995). Theory and measurement of test anxiety as a situational trait. In C. D. Spielberger & P. R. Vagg (Eds.), *Test anxiety: Theory, assessment, and treatment* (pp. 47–58). Washington, DC: Taylor and Francis.

Howard, M. A. P., & Anderson, R. J. (1978). Early identification of potential school dropouts: A literature review. *Child Welfare, 52,* 221-231.

Kaplan, R. M., & Saccuzzo, D. P. (1982). *Psychological testing: principles, applications and issues.* Pacific Grove, CA: Brooks/Cole.

Kelly, F. J., Veldman, D. J., & McGuire, C. (1964). Multiple discriminant prediction of delinquency and school dropouts. *Educational and Psychological Measurement, 24,* 535-544.

Kim, S. H., & Rocklin, T. (1994). The temporal patterns of worry and emotionality and their differential effects on test performance. *Anxiety, Stress, and Coping: An International Journal, 7,* 117–130.

Kleign, W. C., Van der Ploeg, H., & Topman, R. M. (1994). Cognition, study habits, test anxiety, and academic performance. *Psychological Reports, 75,* 1219-1226.

Kurosawa, K., & Harackiewicz, J. M. (1995). Test anxiety, self-awareness, and cognitive interference: A process analysis. *Journal of Personality, 63,* 931–951.

Liebert, R., & Morris, L. W. (1967). Cognitive and emotional components of test anxiety: A distinction and some initial data. *Psychological Reports, 20,* 975-978.

Lloyd, D. P. (1978). Predictions of school failure from third-grade data. *Educational and Psychological Measurement, 38,* 1193-1200.

Loughrey, M. E., Harris, M. B. (1990). A descriptive study of at-risk high school students. *The High School Journal, 73*(4), 187-193.

Mandler, M. J., & Sarason, S. B. (1952). A study of anxiety and learning. *Journal of Abnormal and Social Psychology, 47,* 166-173.

Many, M. A., & Many, W. A. (1975). The relationship between self-esteem and anxiety in grades four through eight. *Educational and Psychological Measurement, 35,* 1017-1021.

Matthews, G. (1992). Mood. In A. P. Smith & D. M. Jones (Eds.), *Handbook of human performance* (pp. 161–193). London: Academic Press.

McCordick, S., Kaplan, R. M., Smith, S., & Finn, M. B. (1981). Variations in cognitive behavior modification for test anxiety. *Psychotherapy: Theory, Research and Practice, 18,* 170-178.

McPhail, I. P. (1981). Why teach test wiseness? *Journal of Reading,* *25*(1), 32-38.

Meunier, C., & Rule, R. G. (1967). Anxiety, confidence and conformity. *Journal of Personality, 35,* 498-504.

Michael, W. (1990). Participants' views of a drop-out prevention program: Louisiana Statute youth opportunities unlimited. *The High School Journal, 73*(4), 200-212.

Mitchell, C., & Collins, L. (1991). *Math anxiety.* Dubuque, IA: Kendall/Hunt Publishing Company.

Morris, L. W., & Liebert, R. M. (1969). Effects of anxiety on timed and untimed intelligence tests. *Journal of Consulting and Clinical psychology, 33,* 240-244.

Morris, L. W., & Liebert, R. M. (1970). Relationship of cognitive and emotional components of test anxiety to physiological arousal and academic performance. *Journal of Consulting and Clinical Psychology, 35,* 332-337.

Morris, L. W., & Perez, T. L. (1972). Effects or tests-interruption on emotional arousal and performance. *Psychological Reports, 31,* 559-564.

Most, R. B., & Zeidner, M. (1995). Constructing personality and intelligence instruments: Methods and issues. In D. H. Saklofske & M. Zeidner (Eds.), *International handbook of personality and intelligence* (pp. 475–503). New York: Plenum Press.

Nicholls, J. G. (1976). When a scale measures more than it denotes: The case of the Test Anxiety Scale for Children. *Journal of Consulting and Clinical Psychology, 44,* 976-985.

Overmier, J. B., & Seligman, M. E. P. (1967). Effects of inescapable shock on subsequent escape and avoidance responding. *Journal of Comparative and Physiological Psychology, 63,* 28-33.

Parker, J. C., IV, Vagg, P. R., & Papsdorf, J. D. (1995). Systematic desensitization, cognitive coping and biofeedback in reduction of test anxiety. In C. D. Spielberger & P. R. Vagg (Eds.), *Test anxiety: Theory, assessment, and treatment* (pp. 171–182). Washington, DC: Taylor and Francis.

Paulman, R. C., & Kennelly, K. J. (1984). Test anxiety and ineffective test taking: Different names same construct? *Journal of Educational Psychology, 76*(2), 279-288.

Phillips, B. N., Pitcher, G. D., Worsham, M. E, & Miller, S. C. (1980). Test anxiety and the school environment. In I. G. Sarason (Ed.), *Test anxiety: Theory, research and applications* (pp. 327-346). Hillsdale, NJ: Lawrence Erlbaum.

Pintrich, P. R., & De Groot, E. V. (1990). Motivational and self-regulated learning components of classroom academic performance. *Journal of Educational Psychology, 85*(1), 33-40.

Polster, E., & Polster, M. (1973). *Gestalt therapy integrated: Contours of theory and practice.* New York: Brunner/Mazel.

Reglin, C. L. (1990). Rural high school dropouts grade the rural public school system. *The High School Journal, 73*(4), 312-217.

Richardson, F. C., O'Neil, H. F., Whitmore, J., & Judd, W. A. (1977). Factor analysis of the test anxiety scale and evidence concerning components of test anxiety. *Journal of Consulting and Clinical Psychology, 45*, 704-705.

Richardson, F. C., & Suinn, R. M. (1972). The mathematics anxiety rating scale: Psychometric data. *Journal of Counseling Psychology, 19*, 551-554.

Richardson, F. C., & Woolfolk, R. C. (1980). Mathematics anxiety. In I. G. Sarason (Ed.), *Test anxiety: Theory, research and applications* (pp. 271-288). Hillsdale, NJ: Lawrence Erlbaum.

Rocklin, T., & Thompson, J. M. (1985). Interactive effects of test anxiety, test difficulty, and feedback. *Journal of Educational Psychology, 77*(3), 368-372.

Rotter, J. B. (1966). Generalized expectancies for internal versus external control of reinforcement. *Psychological monographs, 80*, 1-28.

Ruebush, B. K. (1963). Anxiety. In H. W. Stevenson, J. Kagan, & C. Spiker (Eds.), *NSSE sixty-second yearbook, Part I: Child psychology* (pp. 1-20). Chicago: University of Chicago Press.

Samson, G. E. (1985). Effects of training in test-taking skills on achievement test performance: A quantitative synthesis. *Journal of Educational Research, 78*(5), 261-266.

Sapp, M. (1990a). Psychoeducational predictors of achievement for at-risk Milwaukee public school junior high school students. *The Wisconsin Counselor, 12*(2), 10-15.

Sapp, M. (1990b). Psychoeducational correlates of junior high at-risk students. *The High School Journal, 73*(4), 232-234.

Sapp, M. (1992). *Hypnosis techniques: Applications for academically at-risk middle school students.* Paper presented at the International Society for Professional Hypnosis Annual Conference.

Sapp, M. (1994a). Cognitive-behavioral counseling: Applications for African American middle school students who are academically at risk. *Journal of Instructional Psychology, 21*(2), 161–171.

Sapp, M. (1994b). The effects of guided imagery in reducing the worry and emotionality components of test anxiety. *Journal of Mental Imagery, 18*(3&4), 165–180.

Sapp, M. (1996a). Irrational beliefs that can lead to academic failure for African American middle school students who are academically at risk. *Journal of Rational-Emotive and Cognitive-Behavior Therapy, 14*(2), 123–134.

Sapp, M. (1996b). Three treatments for reducing the worry and emotionality components of test anxiety with undergraduate and graduate college students: cognitive-behavioral hypnosis, relaxation therapy, and supportive counseling. *Journal of College Student Development, 37*(1), 79-87.

Sapp, M., Durand, H., & Farrell, W. (1995). Measures of actual test anxiety in educationally and economically disadvantaged college students. *College Student Journal, 29*(1), 65–72.

Sapp, M., & Farrell, W. (1994). Cognitive-behavioral interventions: applications for academically at-risk and special education students. *Preventing School Failure, 39*(2), 19–24.

Sapp, M., Farrell, W., & Durand, H. (1995). The effects of mathematics, reading, and writing tests in producing worry and emotionality test anxiety with economically and educationally disadvantaged college students. *College Student Journal, 29*(1), 122–125.

Sarason, I. G. (1958). The effects of anxiety, reassurance, and meaningfulness of material to be learned on verbal learning. *Journal of Experimental Psychology, 56*, 472-477.

Sarason, I. G. (1972). Experimental approaches to test anxiety: Attention and uses of information. In C. D. Spielberger (Ed.), *Anxiety: Current trends in theory and research (Vol. 2).* New York: Academic Press.

Sarason, I. G. (1973). Test anxiety and cognitive modeling. *Journal of Personality and Social Psychology, 28*, 58-61.

Sarason, I. G. (1975). Anxiety and self-preoccupation. In I. G. Sarason & C. D. Spielberger (Eds.), *Stress and anxiety (Vol. 2)*. New York: Hemisphere/Hastead.

Sarason, I. G. (1980). Introduction to the study of test anxiety. In I. G. Sarason (Ed.), *Test anxiety: Theory, research and applications* (pp. 3-14). Hillsdale, NJ: Lawrence Erlbaum.

Sarason, I. G. (1984). Stress, anxiety, and cognitive interference: Reactions to tests. *Journal of Personality and Social Psychology, 46*, 929–938.

Sarason, I. G., & Ganzer, V. J. (1962). Anxiety, reinforcement and experimental instructions in a free verbal situation. *Journal of Abnormal and Social Psychology, 65*, 300-307.

Sarason, I. G., & Ganzer, V. J. (1973). Modeling and group discussion in the rehabilitation of juvenile delinquents. *Journal of Counseling Psychology, 20*, 442-449.

Sarason, S. B. (1966). The measurement of anxiety in children: Some questions and problems. In C. D. Spielberger (Ed.), *Anxiety and behavior* (pp. 469-478). New York: Academic Press.

Sarason, S. B., Davidson, K. S., Lighthall, F. F., Waite, R. R., & Ruebush, B. U. (1960). *Anxiety in elementary school children*. New York: Wiley.

Sarason, S. B., Hill, K. T., & Zimbardo, P. G. (1964). A longitudinal study of the relation of test anxiety to performance on intelligence and achievement tests. *Monographs of the Society for Research in Child Development, 29*(7, Serial No. 98).

Sarnacki, R. E. (1979). An examination of test-wiseness in the cognitive test domain. *Review of Educational Research, 4*(2), 252-279.

Schreiber, D. (1968). 700,000 dropouts. *American Education, 4*, 17-21.

Schunk, D. H. (1991). Self-efficacy and academic motivation. *Educational Psychologist, 26*(3 and 4), 207-231.

Schwarzer, R., & Schwarzer, C. (1996). A critical survey of coping instruments. In M. Zeidner & N. S. Endler (Eds.), *Handbook of coping: Theory, research, applications* (pp. 107–132). New York: Wiley.

Seipp, B., & Schwarzer, C. (1996). Cross-cultural anxiety research: A review. In C. Schwarzer & M. Zeidner (Eds.), *Stress, anxiety, and coping in academic settings* (pp. 13–68). Tubingen, Germany: Franke-Verlag.

Shavelson, R. J., & Bolus, R. (1982). Self-concept: The interplay of theory and methods. *Journal of Educational Psychology, 74*, 3-17.

Sieber, J. E. (1969). A paradigm for experimental modification of the effects of test anxiety on cognitive processes. *American Educational Research Journal, 6*, 46-66.

Sieber, J. E. (1980). Defining test anxiety: Problems and approaches. In I. G. Sarason (Ed.), *Test anxiety: Theory, research and applications* (pp. 15-42). Hillsdale, NJ: Lawrence Erlbaum.

Slavin, R. E. (1987). Mastery learning reconsidered. *Review of Educational Research, 57*, 175-213.

Slavin, R. E., Karweit, N. L., & Madden, N. A. (1989). *Effective programs for students at-risk.* Needham Heights, MA: Allyn and Bacon.

Smith, C. L., Sapp, M., Farrell, W., & Johnson, J. H. (1998). Psychoeducational correlates of achievement for high school seniors at a private school: The relationship among locus of control, self-esteem, academic achievement, and academic self-esteem. *The High School Journal, 81*(3), 161–167.

Spence, S. H., Duric, V., & Roeder, U. (1996). Performance realism in test-anxious students. *Anxiety, Stress, and Coping, 9*, 339–355.

Spielberger, C. D. (1980). *Test anxiety inventory.* Palo Alto, CA: Consulting Psychologists Press.

Spielberger, C. D., Anton, W. B., & Bedell, J. (1976). The nature and treatment of test anxiety. In M. Zuckerman & C. D. Spielberger (Eds.), *Emotions and anxiety: new concepts, methods and applications.* Hillsdale, NJ: Lawrence Erlbaum.

Spielberger, C. D., Gorsuch, R. L., Lushene, R., Vagg, P. R., & Jacobs, G. A. (1983). *Manual for the state-trait anxiety inventory.* Palo Alto, CA: Consulting Psychologists Press.

Spielberger, C. D., & Vagg, P. R. (Eds.). (1995). *Test anxiety: Theory, assessment, and treatment.* Washington, DC: Taylor and Francis.

Suinn, R. M. (1969). The STABS, a measure of test anxiety for behavior therapy: Normative data. *Behaviour Research and Therapy, 7*, 335-339.

Suinn, R. M., Edie, C. A., Nicoletti, J., & Spinelli, P. R. (1972). The MARS, a measure of mathematics anxiety: psychometric data. *Journal of Clinical Psychology, 28*, 373-375.

Thorkildsen, T. A., & Nicholls, J. G. (1991). Students' critiques of motivation. *Educational Psychology, 26*(3 and 4), 347-368.

Tobias, S. (1985). Test anxiety: Interference, defective skills and cognitive capacity. *Educational Psychologist, 20*(3), 135-142.

Vagg, P. R., Papsdorf, J. D. (1995). Cognitive therapy, study skills training, and biofeedback in the treatment of test anxiety. In C. D. Spielberger & P. R. Vagg (Eds.), *Test anxiety: Theory, assessment, and treatment* (pp. 183-194). Washington, DC: Taylor and Francis.

Well, A., & Matthews, G. (1994). *Attention and emotion: A clinical perspective.* Hillsdale, NJ: Erlbaum.

Weiner, B. (1990). History of motivational research in education. *Journal of Educational Psychology, 84*(4), 616-622.

Wessel, I., & Mersch, P. A. (1994). A cognitive behavioral group treatment for test-anxious adolescents. *Anxiety, Stress and Coping, 7*, 149-161.

West, C. K., Lee, J. F., & Anderson, T. H. (1969). The influence of test anxiety in the selection of relevant from irrelevant information. *The Journal of Educational Research, 63*, 51-52.

Wine, J. D. (1971). Test anxiety and direction of attention. *Psychological Bulletin, 76*, 92-104.

Wine, J. D. (1980). Cognitive-attentional theory of test anxiety. In I. G. Sarason (Ed.), *Test anxiety: Theory, research and applications* (pp. 349-385). Hillsdale, NJ: Lawrence Erlbaum.

Woolfolk, A. E., & Hoy, W. K. (1990). Prospective teachers' sense of efficacy and beliefs about control. *Journal of Educational Psychology, 52*(1), 81-91.

Yerkes, R. M., & Dodson, J. D. (1908). The relationship of strength of stimulus and rapidity of habit formation. *Journal of Comparative Neurology and Psychology, 18*, 459-492.

Zeidner, M. (1994). Personal and contextual determinants of coping and anxiety in an evaluative situation: A perspective study. *Personality and Individual Differences, 16*, 899-918.

Zeidner, M. (1995a). Adaptive coping with test situations: A review of literature. *Educational Psychologist, 30*, 123-133.

Zeidner, M. (1995b). Coping with examination stress: Resources, strategies, and outcomes. *Anxiety, Stress, and Coping, 8*, 279-298.

Zeidner, M. (1995c). Personality trait correlates of intelligence. In D. H. Saklofske & M. Zeidner (Eds.), *International handbook of personality and intelligence* (pp. 299-319). New York: Plenum Press.

Zeidner, M. (1996). How do high school and college students cope with test situations? *British Journal of Educational Psychology, 66,* 115–128.

Zeidner, M. (1998). *Test anxiety: The state of the art.* New York: Plenum Press.

Zeidner, M., & Saklofske, D. (1996). Adaptive and maladaptive coping. In M. Zeidner & N. S. Endler (Eds.), *Handbook of coping: Theory, research, applications* (pp. 505–531). New York: Wiley.

Zimmerman, B. J., & Martinez-Pons, M. (1990). Student differences in self-regulated learning: Relating grade, sex, and giftedness to self-efficacy and strategy use. *Journal of Educational Psychology, 82*(1), 51-59.

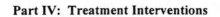

Part IV: Treatment Interventions

Chapter 11

CONTENTS

11.1 PSYCHOTHERAPY EFFICACY

There are several factors that determine the effectiveness of a given treatment (Strupp, 1986). This fact also applies to treatments for test anxiety. Using **meta-analysis,** a statistical technique summarizing the findings of 475 studies, Smith, Glass, and Miller (1980) found that **psychodynamic, gestalt, person-centered, transactional analysis, systematic desensitization, behavior modification, and cognitive-behavioral psychotherapy** were more effective than **untreated control groups.** In fact, Smith et al. concluded that all types of treatments were more effective than no treatment. Similarly, they found group psychotherapy to be as effective as individual therapy. Moreover, Smith et al. found that the effectiveness among different treatments was negligible.

Reanalyzing Smith et al. (1980) studies, using only subjects who were diagnosed neurotic from Smith et al. data, Andrews and Harvey (1981) found that behavioral psychotherapies had a higher average effect size than psychoanalytic psychotherapies. Most authorities agree that overall it cannot be determined from the research evidence that one form of treatment is more effective than another (Stiles, Shapiro, & Elliott, 1986). Paul (1967) proposed a more important series of questions concerning psychotherapy: **What treatment and by whom under what conditions is effective for which kinds of clients with what kinds of specific concerns?**

As Paul suggests, the effectiveness of psychotherapy research should be limited to a specific therapy and a certain technique; because many practitioners function differently depending on the client, the setting, and the conceptualization of the problem. Due to the complexity of psychotherapy, not enough information can be provided from comparisons of various approaches. Some factors that do influence the outcome of psychotherapy are client-therapist factors, client factors, therapist factors, and treatment factors (Frank, 1986).

In terms of **client-therapist factors,** there is evidence that a positive therapeutic alliance between the client and therapist is associated with treatment gains (Gendlin, 1986; Marziali, Marmar, & Krupnick, 1981).

Luborsky, Singer, and Luborsky (1980) found that **client factors** were better predictors of therapy outcome than therapist characteristics, client-therapist match characteristics, and treatment characteristics. For example, the client's age, gender, level of intelligence, educational level, marital status, and social class have all been researched as possible predictors of psychotherapy outcomes.

Garfield (1978, 1987, 1994) found that **age** was not actually related to therapy outcome or length of stay in treatment. Similarly, Luborsky et al. (1980) found no clear relationship between gender and therapy outcome or length of stay in treatment. Furthermore, Luborsky, Singer, and Luborsky (1971) found that **higher levels of intelligence** were correlated with better therapy outcomes. For verbal therapies and insight-oriented therapies, intelligence is an important factor. Also, Garfield (1978) found that **higher levels of education** were correlated with **increased therapy outcomes** and **increased levels of satisfaction**.

Bootzin, Bower, Zajonc, and Hall (1986, p. 560) reported **no relationship** between marital status and **therapy outcome**, even though **marital status** appears to have a relationship upon the **development of emotional disturbances**. Specifically, married individuals are less likely to have psychological disorders. Nevertheless, once divorce occurs, an individual is likely to experience an emotional disturbance. *Mental disorders can be ranked in terms of marital status. For example, mental disorders are highest among separated and divorced individuals, followed by single persons and widows and widowers.*

Frank (1974) reported the difficulties that clients from lower socioeconomic backgrounds have in terms of receiving psychotherapy. **First**, instead of being referred for psychotherapy, often these individuals are given **medical treatment**, are more apt to be assigned to **neophyte** therapists, and are more likely to receive the most **severe diagnosis**. If clients from the lower class remain in therapy, they actually do almost as well as middle class clients.

Therapist factors are associated with therapeutic outcome (Yalom, 1975). Bergin (1971) and Auerback and Johnson (1977) presented evidence that the **experience of the therapist** is associated with the client having more **success** in therapy. Also, greater experience in therapy is also associated with a **decrease** in therapy **dropout rates**. Furthermore, Cormier and Cormier (1991, pp. 11-39) describe many ingredients important for effective helping relationships. Vandenbos (1986) discusses what constitutes therapeutic change and the methods by which it comes about. *Finally, see Sapp (1997b) for a detailed discussion of effect size measures (differences between group means that are expressed in standard deviation units) for various forms of psychotherapy.*

Theoretically, cognitive-behavioral strategies should be effective in reducing test anxiety. These strategies would include and not be limited to the **BASIC-ID of multimodal behavior therapy, techniques from reality therapy (Radtke, Sapp, & Farrell, 1997), social-learning theories, rational-emotive behavior therapy, cognitive therapy, cognitive-behavior modification, personal constructs psychotherapy, transactional analysis, systematic desensitization, anxiety management training, aversive conditioning, covert desensitization, covert modeling, flooding, implosive therapy, positive self-reinforcement, negative self-reinforcement, differential self-reinforcement, Premack principle, self-punishment, self-control strategies, bibliotherapy, guided imagery, relaxation therapy, and hypnosis.** See Sapp (1997b) for a thorough discussion of cognitive-behavioral techniques.

11.2 RESEARCH SUPPORTING TREATMENT SCRIPTS FOR TEST ANXIETY

Becker (1982) reported that **overlearning,** that is, learning material to the point of mastery is an effective treatment to combat test anxiety. Overlearning can result in less worry and emotionality levels.

Sarason (1981) found that social support was an effective strategy for reducing test anxiety. Specifically, test preparation with a supportive friend can help one manage test anxiety. Another form of therapy related to social support, developed by Carl Rogers and has been found to be effective in reducing test anxiety in graduate students is person-centered therapy (Sapp, 1988b, 1996b). Ricketts and Galloway (1984) found that relaxation therapy was effective in treating test anxiety. Similarly, Dykeman (1992) found that increasing students' levels of self-efficacy resulted in a decrease in test anxiety.

Cormier and Cormier (1991, p. 482) reported that **systematic desensitization** was effective in reducing test anxiety. In addition, Suinn (1970), Suinn, Edie, and Spinelli (1970), Suinn and Hall (1970), and Hall and Hinkle (1972) also reported the effectiveness of systematic desensitization in reducing test anxiety. Systematic desensitization is probably the most researched treatment for test anxiety (Deluga, 1981). Wilson and Rotter (1986) found that anxiety management training significantly reduces test anxiety in middle school students.

Meichenbaum (1972) found that **cognitive therapy** and **cognitive-behavioral modification** were effective in reducing test anxiety. Harris and Johnson (1980, 1983) noted that **covert modeling** combined with study skills counseling was effective in alleviating test anxiety and in improving academic performance.

Hypnosis has shown to be effective in treating test anxiety. See Sapp (1997) for a detailed discussion of hypnosis. In fact, Sapp (1986) described the many applications that hypnosis has for the field of education. Sapp (1988a) reported how hypnosis can be used to reduce test anxiety. Similarly, Sapp (1989a) performed a **meta-analysis** on studies employing hypnosis to treat test anxiety, and he concluded that hypnosis was an effective method of treating test anxiety. Moreover, Sapp (1992a, 1994a, 1994b, 1996b) reported the effects of hypnosis in reducing test anxiety and improving achievement in college students.

Lieberman, Fisher, Russell, and King (1969) conducted an experimental study that indicated the effectiveness of hypnotic recorded techniques in removing students from academic probation. Also, Gibbons, Kilbourne, Saunders, and Castle (1970) conducted a **quasi-experimental** study using student volunteers divided equally into three experimental groups. These researchers reported that students who participated in hypnosis showed a statistically significant reduction in test anxiety. Further, Melnick and Russell (1976) reported a significant test anxiety reduction by treatment interaction with 27 subjects randomly assigned to a hypnosis, systematic desensitization, and a contact no-treatment control group. In an experimental study, Boutin and Tosi (1983) reported that hypnosis significantly reduced test anxiety.

Many qualitative studies have investigated the effects of hypnosis on test anxiety. For example, Boutin (1978) used a case study to demonstrate the effectiveness of rational stage-directed hypnosis in treating first-year nursing students for test anxiety. Moreover, Cohen (1982) presented an excellent narrative description in which hypnosis was utilized at a counseling center to treat clients who had test anxiety and academic difficulties. Further, Cercio (1983) combined hypnosis with fantasy relaxation technique to treat test anxiety. Finally, Herbert (1984) discussed how hypnosis was effective in treating test anxiety in medical students and residents.

In summary, cognitive-behavioral strategies have been shown to be effective in treating test anxiety (Spielberger, 1980). For example, relaxation therapy is effective in treating test anxiety (Ricketts & Galloway, 1984). Moreover, systematic desensitization has been shown to effectively treat the emotionality component of test anxiety but not the worry component (Deluga, 1981). This is also the case for **relaxation therapy**. Theoretically, cognitive therapies should be more effective in treating the worry component of test anxiety (Harris & Johnson, 1980, 1983) and behavioral strategies should be more effective in treating the emotionality components.

Recently, Sapp (1989, 1991, 1996b) described hypnosis and test anxiety as **cognitive-behavioral constructs** and demonstrated experimentally that cognitive-behavioral hypnosis was effective in reducing test anxiety and in improving academic achievement in college students. Moreover, Sapp (1994a) investigated the effects of **guided imagery** in reducing the **worry** and **emotionality components** of test anxiety. *He found a greater reduction in the worry component than the emotionality component of test anxiety.* In terms of reduced worry and emotionality and improved achievement, treatment gains were maintained at a 6-week follow-up.

In summary, both **cognitive and behavioral techniques** and **cognitive-behavioral strategies** are useful for reducing test anxiety; however, counseling for the improvement of study skills alone has not been shown to reduce test anxiety (Sapp, 1996a, 1996b). Nevertheless, it is recommended that a **combinational strategy** for reduction of test anxiety may be more effective than a **single strategy**. In addition, Sapp, Ioannidis, and Farrell (1995) found that test anxiety correlated significantly with other anxiety disorders such as posttraumatic stress disorder (Sapp, Farrell, Johnson, & Ioannidis, 1997). For example, combining a cognitive or behavioral technique (cognitive-behavioral) with study skills counseling has been shown to be a powerful combination for reducing test anxiety and for improving academic achievement. *Finally, one should always assess the level of study skills and test-wiseness of anyone experiencing test anxiety.*

11.3 APPROPRIATE CLIENTELE AND QUALIFICATIONS FOR TREATMENT SCRIPTS

The treatment scripts that will follow are applicable for middle school students through college or adult clients; however, with some modification the scripts could easily be adapted for elementary students. Because there has been little empirical investigation of treatment applications for elementary students or younger clients, the treatment scripts in this text reflect the existing empirical data that is specifically designed for middle school through adulthood clients.

The qualifications needed to apply the treatment scripts that will follow depend upon the script employed. The relaxation therapy script, study skills counseling script, and supportive counseling script can be employed by anyone carefully following the instructions provided. The cognitive-behavioral hypnosis and the systematic desensitization scripts should only be employed by advanced graduate students in the helping professions such as psychology, education, social work, and so on. In fact, the cognitive-behavioral hypnosis and systematic desensitization scripts have the greatest potential for putting a client at-risk. Thus, anyone who does not have advanced training in the helping professions should use the foregoing scripts only with extreme care and with supervision (Sapp, 1989b).

11.4 INTRODUCTION TO THE
STUDY SKILLS COUNSELING SCRIPT

The purpose of this study counseling script is to serve as a standardized treatment procedure for study skills training. It was designed to show clients effective ways of studying. In **session one**, the use of study time is covered in detail. For example, a method for teaching clients how to schedule their time is presented. This helps clients determine the actual time spent towards study. **Session two** focuses on shaping study behavior. During **session three,** the **SQ3R method** for studying is presented: **scan, question, read, recite**, and **review** study material. The last study session deals with recording lecture notes and preparing for examinations. In summary, there are four study counseling sessions covering a wide range of basic study skills.

11.5 STUDY SKILLS COUNSELING SESSION 1
(Adapted from Harris & Johnson, 1980)
Instructions

This first session is an introduction to the **rationale of study-effectiveness training**. Your performance as a therapist during this part of the treatment is important. You can initiate the introduction by identifying yourself to your client, by giving your name and educational background or any other pertinent information. At this time, communicate to the client that you will provide four study sessions.

You should describe to the client that test anxiety is probably linked to his or her past experiences that were unpleasant in terms of test taking. In addition, as the therapist, you should discuss the client's emotions and feelings associated with test taking and how they can result in feelings of anxiety. Tell the client that during the next few weeks the topic of study will be discussed.

The therapist should convey the following: "Today, we will discuss what study is and present a method that will be useful in helping you estimate the time you need for accomplishing the objectives set forth in your courses and to determine if you are using your time effectively."

Using a lecture or discussion format, you should convey the important points that follow:

Helpful Hints for Effective Study

Study is a vague, nonspecific concept that cannot be defined without reference to the objectives of each particular course. You can elaborate by stating that the course objectives are presented in the course syllabus during the first class period. Also, the course objectives include the types of exams given and the remarks made by the instructor. It is extremely important for you to state that the first step in beginning to study efficiently is planning study time from a general to an increasingly specific schedule.

Specific scheduling can be set up in a series of steps. **First,** work out a weekly schedule. Have the client write out a weekly schedule. Ask the client to label class time activities, free time, and job commitments on this schedule. **Second,** have the client estimate the average amount of time needed to study each subject in order to obtain a grade of B or better. **Third,** have the client schedule blocks of free time between classes, and assign these blocks for study of a particular subject. **Fourth,** ask the client to write down what he or she does while studying. For example, have the client note such behavior as breaks, headaches, nervousness, and so on. Also, ask the client to note the length of time it takes to get started on the assignment. If the client has any questions about the instructions, answer them freely. Emphasize that **monitoring of behavior** can lead to change. Plus, recording information can provide a valuable source of data, which can point to areas of strengths or weaknesses. Finally, ask the client to bring his or her time schedule to the next session.

11.6 STUDY SKILLS COUNSELING SESSION 2
Shaping Study Behavior

The following information should be communicated to the client: A researcher, Allen (1971), gave several students enrolled in an introductory psychology class at his university a questionnaire designed to measure their study habits. He used their responses to predict their grades and found that students obtaining higher grades reported the following about themselves:

1. **Although the students did not assign themselves a specific time to study each individual subject, they did set aside a specific time every day for study.**
2. **They usually studied during the day (often between classes) and made enjoyable activities contingent upon completing a definite assignment.**
3. **They studied alone.**
4. **They studied one subject continuously for at least one hour, rather than skipping from subject to subject.**
5. **They began working on long range assignments long before they were due.**
6. **They obtained at least three to six hours of exercise each week.**
7. **They spent less time studying material specific to psychology than students receiving lower grades.**

In summary, the students who were more efficient in using their allotted time received higher grades than did students who were not as efficient in using their study time.

After reading or discussing the shaping of study behavior, entertain any questions the client may have.

11.7 STUDY SKILLS COUNSELING SESSION 3
SQ3R Method

As naturally as possible, communicate the following information to the client: Efficient reading involves a transfer of material from the written page to memory. The process involves five steps: scan, question, read, recite, and review.

1. **Scan** - Look over the entire chapter, attempting to gain a general understanding of what the author is saying. Look especially at the major headings and the relationships among them. If the chapter has a summary, read this first because it can provide a general overview of what the author believes is most important. This procedure should take only about five minutes, and you should have picked out five to seven major points that are important. Research indicates that authors generally cover five to six major points per chapter.

2. **Question** - What are you about to read? What are you reading? What is the author attempting to communicate? Turn major and minor headings into questions. It is often helpful to write these questions down in a notebook. Such questions serve the function of allowing one to quickly review by using a problem solving frame of reference. Also, this allows you to quickly assess areas of strengths and weaknesses when reviewing for an exam. If there are questions you cannot answer, additional reviewing is necessary. Three types of questions are important:
   a. Definitions - Many test questions are of this type. For example, "What is psychology?"
   b. Similarities and Differences - This type of question is useful in determining whether the student can state the essential components of a concept. Similarly, this form of questioning helps one to distinguish how two or more concepts are related. For example, "How is counterconditioning and operant conditioning similar and different?"
   c. Examples - Questions of this type applies a learned definition or concept to a new situations. For example, "Which of these three examples is most like covert conditioning?"
3. **Read and Mark** - You should now read the text carefully in order to find answers to the questions you have written down. You should not waste time underlining. Rather, two efficient options are possible:
   a. You may work out a personal notational system to use in the margin. This allows you to quickly find relevant material during a review. For example, you may use I=important, S=summary, and VI=very important.
   b. You can write the answer to each question in a notebook immediately after the question. This has the advantage of consolidating all relevant material for review purposes. Your answers need not be lengthy. In fact, it is more important to pick out key phrases that will trigger recitation of entire concepts. Since all textbooks are the product of an outline, it is important to pay attention to four major places:
      (1) The first sentence of a paragraph. The rest of the paragraph often serves to elaborate the main idea presented in the first sentence.

    (2) In textbooks, graphs, table, and charts typically signify important material. In fact, they often serve to summarize key concepts that would otherwise require many pages of written material.

    (3) Key phrases to explain important information is likely to follow phrases such as "first, second, finally, and summary."

    (4) In chapter summaries.

4. **Recite** answers to questions after reading the entire chapter. Reciting aloud results is a rapid method of learning since you receive information from both verbal and auditory channels. If you can successfully memorize all main points and verbalize these without a prompt, you will do well on an exam covering this material because test questions will act as prompts.

5. **Review** - Review the material covered immediately after finishing all the questions in the chapter. Take no more than five minutes to reanswer all questions in the chapter from memory. You should follow this general rule: If material cannot be verbalized, it is not known. Since a great deal of information is covered during this session, allow plenty of time for the client to ask questions.

11.8 STUDY SKILLS COUNSELING SESSION 4

Tell the client that this is the last study session, and ask if there are any areas that need additional discussion. Communicate to the client that this session will involve the recording of lecture notes and preparation for exams. In terms of recording lecture notes cover the following main points:

1. **Many one hour lectures contain three to six main points.**

2. **Many instructors take pride in their work and attempt to present organized and informative lectures to students. Instructors will usually organize the lecture around the following:**

    a. **Present a broad overview of the material that will be covered.**

    b. **Outline how material will be covered.**

    c. **State the main points and label them as important.**

3. **If you have an instructor who is a poor lecturer, you must be aggressive in asking questions. For example, where are we going? What is the major point? Usually instructors will find this flattering and view the questions as a sign of interest.**

4. **Personal interests of the instructor will usually appear on the exam, be aware of what they are.**
5. **Seek out the instructor's philosophy of testing. For example, terms like "understanding" and "integrating material" usually indicate a preference for essay exams. In addition, terms like "being able to apply what you learn" indicates a preference for problems and analogy questions. Also, terms like "knowing the basics" indicate an emphasis for short answer questions involving similarities and differences.**
6. **The lecture itself will provide pertinent information that will appear on the exam. There are two important sources of information.**
    a. **Handouts may contain information that was not sufficiently covered in the text or lecture.**
    b. **If items are written on the board, they are probably important.**
7. **Always organize lecture notes after you take them.**
8. **After the lecture you should do the following:**
    a. **Take several minutes to skim over lecture notes.**
    b. **Write down a few sentences that summarize the main points of the lecture.**
    c. **Write down any information that may need clarification during the next lecture.**

How to Prepare for an Exam

The therapist should emphasize the following points:

1. **The importance of review.**
2. **Distribution of review time.**
3. **Relaxation in the examination situation.**

The therapist should stress that there is no easy way to study and that it involves effort and time. Essentially, one cannot get something for nothing.

Review is important in order to get information in the memory. The first review should occur as part of the original study process: scanning your lecture notes after the lecture, reciting material and answering questions about what you have read are review methods. Also, systematic review allows you to focus on areas that are not well-known and to skip ones that were mastered. In conclusion, if material is recited aloud, three sensory modalities are being employed sight, hearing and speech, which can result in increased speed of learning and retention.

Distribution of review time. The following points will be useful in conducting an efficient review:

1. **Space the reviews over time.** Research supports the notion that spaced reviews are superior to reviewing a mass of material at once. In addition, spaced reviews can lengthen retention time. It is important to review material as soon as possible after a class. Also, it is important to review each subject, each week, since constant repetition makes the material easier to verbalize under stressful exam conditions. This type of review need take no more time than 15 minutes per subject. You will find that not as much time is required to review material after several repetitions. So begin a concentrated review several days before an exam, and use questions to guide the directions of the review. In conclusion, reviews should be kept task-oriented rather than time-oriented.

Although a certain amount of anxiety is necessary in order to perform well, the client should be somewhat relaxed for the exam. Below are four procedures he or she can use to help manage anxiety when preparing to take an examination:

Four Procedures That Can Help You Manage Anxiety While Preparing to Take an Examination.

1. **Arrive early at the testing place.**
2. **Bring the proper materials.**
3. **Avoid discussions with others about possible questions and answers.**
4. **If suddenly you cannot recall some material during the exam, try not to panic.**

11.9 SUPPORTIVE COUNSELING SCRIPT
Rationale

Supportive counseling is based on the work of Carl Rogers' (1957) person-centered theory. Rogers consistently stated in the literature that three basic conditions necessary to promote change. **First**, the therapist must be genuine or real. That is, the therapist's external behavior matches his or her internal feelings. Essentially, the therapist is not wearing a facade, but displays realness. **Second**, the therapist must show acceptance of and a caring attitude towards the client. In other words, the therapist should be warm and accept the client the way he or she is.

Rogers described this **second component** as **unconditional positive regard** and acceptance. The caring is unconditional in that it is not based on any evaluative procedure such as judgment of the client's feelings, thoughts, behavior and so on. In summary, the therapist accepts the clients without any stipulations.

The **third component** that is necessary for change is deep understanding or accurate empathic understanding. The therapist is to understand clients' experiences and feelings as they are displayed during the therapeutic interaction. There is an implication behind this concept that the therapist will sense the client's feelings as if they were his or her own, but without becoming lost in these feelings.

The **ultimate phase of person-centered counseling is trying to see the world through the eyes of the client which suggests that empathy is more than reflection of feeling or content.** Nevertheless, your job as the therapist is to use empathy as much as possible by reflecting feelings and content.

In conclusion, person-centered therapy emphasizes the therapist's role to create a **supportive environment**. Unconditional positive regard or acceptance, along with clarification of concerns, are the major techniques. Finally, the goal of person-centered therapy is the hope that the client will achieve insight into himself and herself and about his/her personal concerns.

Purpose of Person-Centered Counseling

The therapist says the following: The purpose of this counseling is to **support your struggle with test anxiety**. I will assist you in clarifying your concerns, and I will facilitate your insights in discussing test taking and anxiety. As an endorser of self-support, I believe that everyone inherently has the ability to solve problems on his or her own. My goal will be to help you solve your problems related to test taking.

"At times, people become blocked and cannot resolve their concerns; so in order to assist you to overcome this block, I will help you explore your feelings related to test taking. One reason people become blocked is they attempt to solve problems without discussing them with someone. So, by explaining your concerns to me, you are also explaining them to yourself. This can help you develop different perspectives, and see things from various perspectives."

Instructions for Therapist

When using person-centered counseling, your role is just to listen to the client, and at times to reflect back statements and themes. **Reflection** has two aspects: You can reflect on the content the client is discussing, or you can reflect on feelings stated. The ideal is to reflect feelings. This model of therapy is based on that of Rogers, where the therapist does not attempt to give advice or to resolve the client's concerns. Instead, the therapist uses contact to assist the client to resolve concerns.

Underlying Theory

From this theoretical framework, it is assumed that the client has within himself or herself the **resources to resolve particular concerns**. Therefore, your job as therapist is to listen and at times to reflect the content stated or, ideally, the feelings given in the message. Remember not to try resolving any concerns or to give advice.

As a therapist, it is very difficult not to be in the role of telling clients how to resolve his or her concerns in terms of test anxiety. Rather, you can assist by asking open-ended questions and by being warm and accepting.

Always remember not to give advice about how to resolve any concerns. You may be surprised how the client progresses through the hour without receiving any advice.

If you are warm, empathic, and accepting of the client, he or she will move towards dealing with his or her concerns. In this case test anxiety is the major concern.

Method for Handling Questions

At times, clients may ask your opinion about an issue. If that occurs, ask, "What do you think about this?" In order to keep discussion moving, you may say things such as, "Can you tell me more about that?" If you can think of other ways to encourage discussion, feel free to do so; but remember that your job is to listen and to serve as a facilitator. In summary, as a therapist, you should urge the client to discover ideas to help resolve his or her own concerns about test anxiety. But do not give advice or offer solutions. Instead, allow the client to solve his or her own problems.

Number of Sessions

The literature shows that **four or more sessions** are helpful for getting clients to explore their feelings towards test anxiety. The first session can be opened by asking a general question, such as, "What do you think from the past contributed to your test anxiety?" Other questions may be as follows: "What effect has test anxiety had on your life?" "What have you tried that helped you with test anxiety?" "Do you think anything else could help?"

Handling Silence

You will find that sometimes a client is silent, but do not let this affect you. At this point, pose questions, ask how the client feels or rephrase points made earlier. Remember that silence can be a useful therapeutic tool.

Examples of Empathy

Here are some examples of reflecting feelings. **"You feel upset when you start studying for an exam. "You feel depressed when you do not do as well as you planned for an exam." "It is frustrating to panic on an exam." Cormier and Cormier (1991, p. 97) noted that affect range from weak to moderate to strong and are expressed by one of the following: anger, fear, uncertainty, sadness, happiness, strength or weakness.** On the next page is a list of some common emotions associated with individuals experiencing test anxiety.

List of Affect Words			
anger	lonely	betrayed	exhausted
threatened	defeated	misunderstood	restricted
sad	crushed	closed	jealous
worried	helpless	frustrated	energized
shame	calm	powerless	competent
confused	depressed	lost	incompetent
listless	stymied	odd	weak
stuck	powerful	cowardly	inadequate
rejected	weird	courageous	ashamed
frightened	strange	disturbed	discouraged
hurt	irritated	uncertain	nervous
pessimistic	assertive	embarrassed	happy
optimistic	confident	scared	

11.10 INTRODUCTION TO THE
RELAXATION THERAPY SCRIPT

The **relaxation script** is designed to instruct clients in relaxing their bodies and relieving tension. This will be achieved by first teaching clients to produce tension in muscle groups, followed by instructions on how to relieve tension. During the first session, the therapist will explain to clients the rationale underlying relaxation therapy. After the rationale is given, you will read a script to the client. Remember to read each script slowly in a, soft relaxed tone of voice.

There are **four sessions of relaxation therapy**. In the **first session**, subjects will be taught to sequentially tense and subsequently relax twenty muscle groups. In **session two**, the twenty muscle groups will be reduced to a combination of six muscle groups, which decreases the amount of time needed to produce relaxation. In **session three**, the muscle groups will be reduced from six to a combination of three. During **session four**, the client is taught to bring attention to tension in a particular muscle group.   Subsequently, he or she is taught to **recall** the feelings of relaxation that were associated with relaxation that occurred earlier by literally tensing and relaxing muscles. This involves what is called a recall procedure, which does not implement muscular tension. At the end of each of the four sessions, there is a debriefing period for the client. Take care to insure that the client does not tense muscles to the point of producing pain.

INSTRUCTIONS
(Adapted from Cormier & Cormier, 1991)

1. Verbal Set

    Therapist provides an explanation of relaxation therapy. The therapist can say something such as the following:

    "This therapy is called relaxation therapy which, is used to treat many concerns, such as insomnia, high blood pressure, and general anxiety as well as for test anxiety. Relaxation therapy can help you relieve tension. It will also help you to dissolve tension that interferes with effective functioning in daily activities as well as for test anxiety and performance anxiety."

2. The therapist gives an overview of how the therapy works. The following overview can be presented:

    "You will be taught to tense and relax various muscle groups. Some tension is necessary in the body in order to stand, sit or move, but at times you have too much tension. Once you learn to tense and relax the body, you will become aware of the difference between tension and relaxation. You will become trained to send messages to muscle groups to relax whenever unnecessary anxiety sets in."

3. The therapist describes relaxation therapy as a skill. Emphasize that relaxation training takes practice to learn well and that a great deal of repetition and training is required to perfect the skill.

4. The therapist instructs clients about the freedom to move around if uncomfortable feelings set in. Describe the internal feelings may occur.

    Tell the client that he or she is free to move around in order to relax or maintain relaxation. Also, indicate to the client that he or she may feel heavy sensations while going through the exercises and that these sensations are natural.

5. Client's Dress

    Instruct clients to wear comfortable clothing during each session. The therapist should indicate that certain contact lenses may cause irritation. Because the exercises will require clients to close his or her eyes, the therapist should inquire if the client wears the type of contact lenses that may cause irritation. If so, the client should remove the lenses prior to the session or wear eyeglasses on that day.

6. The therapist should model the exercises in order to get the client started initially.

For example, the therapist may say the following: "I am going to show you the exercises we will use during relaxation therapy. Let me demonstrate relaxation therapy.

First, I will tense my dominant hand and forearm and then relax it. This is how the exercise is performed, just tensing muscles for about five seconds and then relaxing for about ten seconds."

11.11 RELAXATION THERAPY SESSION 1
Adapted from the method used by Bernstein and Borkovec (1973)

Rationale
Communicate to the client that **practicing relaxation therapy** at least **twice a day** will help build confidence and increase motivation in the client's ability to reduce general anxiety and specifically the anxiety related to effective study and testing situations. The following rationale can be reemphasized. One purpose of relaxation therapy is to help the client understand the difference between tension and relaxation. Basically, tension is the opposite of relaxation. If one can learn to relax during these sessions, he or she will be able to relax during a test situation and perform at his or her optimal level.

Once the rationale is restated, ask the client if there are any questions. Tell the client that various muscle groups throughout the body will play a part in this exercise. If there are no questions at this point, begin the script.

Instructions
Each time you ask the client to tense a muscle group, **allow five to seven seconds** for the tension to build, and allow about a ten second pause before preceding to the next muscle group. Constantly reassure the client by using positive reinforcement: That's good, or you are doing fine. Maintain a positive attitude throughout the treatment. Finally, slowly read the script in a soft voice.

SCRIPT: Session 1
Remember I said that I would ask you to tense and relax certain muscles in the body. Let us begin! Please get into a relaxed position in the chair (this can be worded to fit the position the client is in). Close your eyes! We will begin with the muscles of the hand. Which is your dominant hand? That's the hand we will start with. I want you to tense

the muscles of that hand... Tense them really tightly. It is not necessary to tense the muscles until there is pain. Tense them just below the level of feeling pain. As you tense them, notice how they feel. Feel the tension move over your knuckles and through your lower arm. Now relax.

Bend back the wrist of your dominant hand. Steady the tension... Relax! Now, let us do the same thing for the arm. Tense the forearm. Steady the tension; now; relax. Now we will move to the muscles of the biceps. I want you to tense the biceps of the dominant arm by pushing the elbow down against the arm of the chair. Notice the feeling of tension in your biceps. Now, let the tension go, and relax the biceps.

Let's move to the nondominant hand. We will perform the same procedure of tension and relaxation. Now tense the nondominant hand... mobilize all of the tension from the day into that hand. That's it! Now, relax that hand. Bend the wrist backwards. Feel the tension... Now relax... Tense the forearm of the same hand... now... relax. Now we will relax the muscles of the biceps the same as we did it for the other arm.

Tense the muscles of the biceps of the nondominant arm. Push your arm down against the arm of the chair (Modify this statement to fit client's seating arrangement). Now, relax! Notice how different your left and right arms feel. Bring your attention to the two relaxed arms... Notice the difference in feeling.

Let's move to the muscles of the upper face. Tense the muscles of the forehead. Steady that tension; now release it. Now we will move to other parts of the face. Wrinkle up your entire face. Make a very ugly face with wrinkles. That's it; make a very wrinkled face. Steady the tension. Now relax. We can now move to the lips. Pucker your lips. Steady that tension. Now release it. Close your eyes. Close them very tightly.

Squint your eyes very tightly and simultaneously wrinkle your nose. This will build tension in the central part of the face. Steady the tension; now release it. Let your face relax. Now let's move to the inside of your mouth. Push your tongue against the roof of your mouth. Steady that tension. Now release it! Feel the relaxation moving through your face.

We will go to the back of the head and neck. Try to touch the back of your head to the back of your neck. Steady the tension... Now relax. Let the tension go.

Pull your chin downward toward your chest. Steady that tension... Now, you can relax this group of muscles. Let's go to the shoulders and upper back. Try to bring your shoulders up to your ears. Steady the tension. Now relax. Now we will move to the back. Push your back against the chair (Again adjust the wording to fit the sitting arrangement). Steady the tension; then relax.

Now we will proceed by tensing the muscles of the stomach. Draw in the stomach muscles. Try to draw the muscles in your stomach towards your spine. Really draw these muscles in. Now relax. Tense the muscles of the buttocks. Steady the tension... now relax.

Now we will tense the muscles of the dominant leg. Also, point the dominant foot towards the ceiling in order to tense it; now relax. Notice the relaxation in your dominant foot and leg. Notice how different it feels being relaxed as opposed to being tense. Let's tense the nondominant leg and foot. Point the foot towards the ceiling while tensing it. Simultaneously, tense the leg. Steady the tension. Now relax... Feel the relaxation... Notice it. Allow the relaxation to move from your arms to your legs and feet.

Now extend both legs out in front of your body. Steady the tension. Now you can relax. Now point the dominant foot downward, this will stretch the calf. Steady the tension... now relax. Let's move to the nondominant foot. Point it downward. Steady the tension... and let it go. Curl the toes of your dominant foot. Steady the tension. Now you can release it.

Let us move to the other foot. Curl the toes. Steady the tension. Now relax. Now we will return to certain muscles. Let's move back to the face. I want you to wrinkle up your face. Please do not feel embarrassed; just wrinkle it up as much as possible; then let it relax. Let's do this again. Make a big frown... now relax. (It is not uncommon for clients to laugh at this point). Now close your eyes. Close your eyes extremely tight, now relax. If you did not keep your eyes closed, you can close them for the rest of the exercises. Now we will move to the neck. Push your head towards the back of your neck, now relax. Let's do this again... now relax. Now tense the front muscles of the neck by pressing the chin towards your chest... Now, relax the front of the neck. Feel the relaxation that is moving through the relaxed parts of your body. We will now concentrate on the chest and shoulder muscles. Stick out your chest... Really stick out your chest... Make it extremely tense. Now, let it relax. Push your shoulders towards the back of the chair (Make adjustments for the clients seating position). Push as hard as you can, but of course, not to the point of producing pain. Now you can relax... Notice the feeling of relaxation. Now tense the muscles of your stomach.

Draw the muscles of your stomach in tightly. Really tense these muscles. Feel the tension. Now relax.

Bring your attention to the breathing motion of your stomach. Notice as it goes in and out how you become more and more relaxed. Pay attention to your breathing, and become more and more relaxed. Now, let's tense the muscles of the buttocks.

Tense the muscles of the buttocks... now relax. You can now feel the relaxation move throughout all of your body. Be aware of the relaxation that is present throughout your entire body.

If there is any tension left in your body, notice it and let it go as you relax. You can do this by comparing any tension to relaxed parts of your body. Now, I am going to go through the muscle groups we have relaxed. These muscles were the hands, biceps, arms, the face... the mouth... the neck... the chest, the shoulders... the stomach, the buttocks... the thighs... the calves and the feet.

State to the client that it is now time to start terminating the relaxation session. The client should be informed that the therapist will count from one to five.

After the explanation of termination, the therapist can say the following: One... Two... You feel... calm and relaxed, just as if you had a pleasant nap. Tonight or whenever you go to sleep, you will get a restful and peaceful sleep. Three... four... and five...

Questioning

As a means of terminating the session, the therapist should ask the clients, "How do you feel?" Allow the client to comment about his or her feelings about the experience. The therapist can gain additional information by asking "Did you have difficulty getting certain muscles to relax?" Asking the client to describe what relaxation was like for him or her can provide useful information for the next session. If the client disliked certain things, be sure to exclude them from subsequent sessions. Some clients will ask if it is necessary to memorize all the muscle groups. Simply, reassure them that the goal of the therapy is to learn relaxation process and not to memorize specific muscle groups. Rather, explain that the muscle groups are merely a guide for learning. Reassure the client that the important aspects of this treatment will be remembered due to practice.

End the session by stressing the importance of practice, and encourage the client to keep a homework log sheet for each practice session. Emphasize that practice sessions can be brief: approximately 15 to 20 minutes twice a day. The client can also give his or her reactions to relaxation therapy on a ten point scale, where one is extremely relaxed and ten is extremely tense.

11.12 RELAXATION THERAPY
Session 2

This session will begin the execution of a series of procedures designed to reduce the amount of time and physical exertion necessary to achieve relaxation. Session two is designed to decrease the number of muscle groups from **nineteen** to **six**.

Rationale

It is important to explain the rationale of this **new procedure** to a client. First, this added technique will result in less time needed in order to relax. Second, eventually a client will be able to produce relaxation throughout the body **without any observable muscular tension**. This will demonstrate to him or her that relaxation can occur without reclining in a chair or lying down. In addition, relaxation will become a skill that the client can carry around with him or her and use in any stressful situation, such as test anxiety. This skill can result in more confidence in taking tests and in entering tense situations.

Instructions

First review the muscle groups that were used in previous week's session. One way to accomplish this is to ask the client which muscles were tensed and relaxed in the last session.
A brief summary of the muscles is as follows:
1. Hands and wrists
2. Forearms
3. Biceps
4. Head
5. Eyes
6. Mouth
7. Lips
8. Nose
9. Neck
10. Throat
11. Stomach

12. Chest
13. Buttocks
14. Thighs
15. Legs
16. Ankles
17. Calves
18. Feet
19. Toes

Communicate to the client that the original extensive muscle group will be reduced to a combination of **six muscles**. The six muscle groups are as follows:

1. The muscles of the dominant arm, which includes the hand, wrist, forearms and biceps.
2. The muscles of the nondominant arm, which includes the hand, wrist, forearm and biceps.
3. The face muscles, which includes the head, eyes, mouth, lips and nose.
4. The neck muscles, which include the front and back muscles of the neck and throat.
5. The stomach muscles.
6. The leg muscles, which include both legs and buttock muscles, the thighs, ankles, calves, feet and toes.

Tell the client that the muscle groups will be tensed and relaxed just like the individual groups of muscles were the previous week.

RELAXATION SCRIPT: SESSION 2

Please close your eyes. Extend your dominant arm. Extend it out in front of your body. Now, I want you to tense the muscles in this arm. Remember you do not have to produce pain while tensing these muscles. While you are tensing these muscles, also tense the hand, wrist, forearm and biceps. Now relax this arm. Let's go through the same procedure again. Tense the dominant arm... Make sure you also tense the hand muscles, wrist, forearm and biceps. Now, relax. I want you to note the difference between tension and relaxation. Be aware of this difference. I want you to now extend the nondominant arm out. Tense this arm. Simultaneously, tense the hand, wrist, forearm and biceps. Now relax; let's do it again. Tense this arm, making sure to notice the tension in the hand, wrist, forearm and biceps. Steady the tension; now relax. Can you notice the difference between tension and relaxation?

We will now move to the facial muscles. I want you to wrinkle your face. You should produce tension while doing this wrinkling. Steady the tension. Now relax. We will do this again, but this time making sure we include the muscles in the back of the head. Bend our head backwards. That's it; bend your head backwards. Feel the tension... Steady the tension, now relax. Let's go through this procedure again, but this time making sure we put some emphasis on the eyes, mouth, lips and nose. Tense your face again, making sure you feel tension in your eyes... mouth... lips... and nose. Steady the tension. Now relax.

Now, if your eyes are not closed, please close them. Notice the feeling of relaxation in your hands, wrist, forearms, biceps, head, eyes, mouth, lips and nose.

Let's move to the neck muscles. Tense the neck muscles. Steady the tension. That's good; now relax. Let's repeat this procedure. Tense the neck muscles, but make sure you include the front of the neck, the throat and the back of the neck. Steady the tension... Now relax... Note the difference between tension and relaxation. That's good. Be aware of the difference.

We will now move to the stomach muscles. I want you to draw the stomach muscles in very tightly. Draw in the stomach muscles... as though you were trying to touch the back of your spine with your stomach. Steady the tension... Now relax. Note the difference in your breathing. Notice how your breathing is slow and regular. Be aware of your breathing as you relax more and more by noting the difference between tension and relaxation.

We will now move to the leg muscles. Extend both legs. While you are extending them, point the toes toward the ceiling. Steady the tension in the thighs, legs, ankles, calves, feet and toes. Now relax. Let's do it again; extend the legs. Steady the tension in the buttocks... thighs... legs... ankles... calves... feet... and toes. Now relax. Note the difference between tension and relaxation.

Notice how your body felt when it was tense, and how it feels now while it is relaxed. Bring your attention to your breathing, and be aware of the feeling of relaxation move throughout your entire body. Feel the relaxation moving through your hands... wrist... forearms... biceps... head... eyes... mouth... lips... nose... neck... throat... stomach... buttocks... thighs... legs... ankles... calves... feet... and toes. Notice the difference between tension and relaxation. That's it! Be aware of the difference.

It is now time to start terminating this session by counting from one to five. One... Two... Be aware of the feelings of relaxation, knowing that whenever you go to sleep you will experience a restful sleep. Just like the one you had a long time ago. Three... When you come out of this deep relaxation exercise, you will feel alert, refreshed and comfortable. Four... Five... It is up to you at your own rate and pace.

Termination

Be sure to ask the client how he or she feels. The therapist may also ask, "How was it?" and "Did you feel as relaxed as the last time?" Note that some clients will not feel as relaxed this time as compared to the first session. Emphasize that it is important for the client to practice in order to feel the full benefits of this technique. Reassure the client by noting that, with practice, even more relaxation can be achieved; and, with practice, relaxation will become easier and easier. Be aware of the possibility of setbacks at each point in the transition of the relaxation training program. Be sure to emphasize to the client that practice is the only way to master these techniques.

11.13 RELAXATION THERAPY SESSION 3
Instructions

Inquire if the client has any questions or feedback from the second session. Then repeat the six groups of muscles covered during the previous week. A brief summary of the muscles is as follows:

1. The muscles of the dominant arm, which included the hand, wrist, forearm and biceps.
2. The muscles of the nondominant arm, which included the hand, wrist, forearm and biceps.
3. The face muscles, which included the head, eyes, mouth, lips and nose.
4. The neck muscles, which included the front and back muscles of the neck and the throat.
5. The stomach and chest muscles.
6. The leg muscles, which included both legs, the buttocks, the thighs, ankles, calves, feet and toes.

    The therapist should state to the clients that the six muscle groups will be reduced to a combination of three muscle groups, which are as follows:

1. The muscles of both arms.

2.   The muscles of the center of the body, which include the face, neck and stomach muscles.

3.   Both legs, which include the buttocks, thighs, ankles, calves, feet and toes.

Explain to the client that these three muscle groups will be tensed and relaxed. Consequently, since the number of muscle groups will be reduced, it will take less time for relaxation to occur.

11.13 RELAXATION THERAPY SCRIPT: SESSION 3

We will again use a shorter version of the relaxation training program. Get into a relaxed position. Close your eyes. We will start with the muscles of your arms. There are two ways you can do this. First, you can extend both arms out in front of you, or you can bend both arms at the elbow while resting them on the chair (adjust this statement to fit the client's seating arrangement). Now, I want you to tense both arms. Bring tension to both arms. Feel the tension in the hands... wrist... forearms... and biceps. Steady the tension... Now you can relax the tension. Let's do this again; tense both arms... Notice how the tension builds up. Now relax. Notice the relaxation in both arms. Feel the relaxation. Pay attention to the relaxation. Notice the difference between tension and relaxation.

Now we will move to the center of the body. First, if your eyes are not closed, please close them. I want you to tense the muscles of the face. You now know how to do this by wrinkling the face, head, mouth, nose and lips. In addition, you have to tense the neck, chest and stomach at the same time. Tense the muscles in the center of the body. Remember these muscles include the face, eyes, mouth, lips, nose, throat and stomach. That's it... draw in these muscles... especially in the stomach. Steady the tension in the center of the body. Now, relax the center of the body. Let's do it again. Tense the muscles towards the center of the body. Hold that tension; now release it.

Notice the difference between tension and relaxation. Allow the relaxation to move throughout the arms and the center of the body. That's good; feel the relaxation.

Now we will move to the legs. Extend both legs and bring tension to the legs, buttocks, thighs... calves... ankles... feet... and toes. Steady the tension in the legs. Now relax. Let's do this again. Steady the tension in the legs. Feel the tension build in your legs, buttocks, calves, feet and toes. Now relax. Feel the relaxation move throughout your entire body.

Notice the relaxation in the hands..., wrists..., forearm..., biceps..., head..., eyes..., mouth..., lips..., nose..., neck..., throat..., stomach..., buttocks..., thighs..., legs..., ankles..., calves..., feet and toes. That's it; feel the relaxation move throughout the entire body. Bring your attention to your breathing. Notice as you inhale and exhale that you become more and more relaxed. Be aware of your breathing, and notice the relaxation. That's it. Feel the relaxation throughout your entire body. With each breath you take, feel the relaxation. It is time to terminate this session. I will count from one to five.

As I count, you will continue to feel relaxed and refreshed, and when you go to sleep you will get a good rest and wake up feeling better than you have felt in a long, long time. Now, One... Two... Three... Four... Five... It is up to you at your own rate and pace.

Termination
Ask the client, "How do you feel?" or "How was it this time for you?" Remember that some clients may indicate they were not as relaxed as last week or the week before. It is important to continue to state that practice is important. The therapist should continue to state that he or she has confidence in the ability of the client to master the relaxation training. Always be reassuring to the client. For example, say, "I see that you are improving and it is getting easier and easier."

11.14 RELAXATION THERAPY: SESSION 4
Instructions
It is important to notify the client that this is the last session. Ask the client if he or she has had any reactions to the treatment. Review the procedures for the three muscle groups, which are as follows:
1.   Both arms.
2.   The center of the body, which included the muscles of the head, eyes, mouth, lips, nose, neck, throat, chest and stomach.
3.   Both legs, which included the muscles of buttocks, thighs, ankles, calves, feet and toes.

Description of New Procedure
Inform the client that the procedure this week is different. Explained to the client that he or she will be asked to **bring attention to tension in particular muscle groups without producing muscular tension**, and to recall the feelings associated with the release of tension by thinking of

feelings of relaxation associated with previous sessions. The point to emphasize is that muscular tension will not be employed in this session.

Relaxation Therapy SCRIPT: Session 4

Get into a relaxed position. The session this week is different. We will not be tensing muscles. Instead, we will just bring attention to tensed parts of the body and remember what it felt like when tension was released sometime earlier. Yes, what it felt like when tension was released sometime earlier. Close your eyes. Let's start with the three muscle groups we used last week. I would like you to focus your attention on the muscles of your arms. Notice any tension or feelings of tightness in your arms. Be aware of what they are like. Now, I want you to relax by remembering what it felt like last week to release the tension once relaxation occurred. Recall what it was like to release the tension in these muscles of the arms. Just allow them to become deeply relaxed. That's it, allowing them to become deeply relaxed. Yes, this is very similar to the regular tension and relaxation exercises, but the only difference is the actual production of muscular tension is eliminated. Again, focus your attention on both arms. If there is any tension, notice, be aware, and finally let it go. Relax and release the tension. If there is any tension in your hands... wrist... forearms... release it by recalling what it felt like last time when you relaxed the tension out of the muscles.

Focus all of your attention on the center of your body. Notice if there is any tension in your head, eyes, lips, nose, neck, throat and stomach. If so, release it by recalling what is was like to release the tension last week or at some earlier period. Relax the center of the body very deeply. Experience this relaxation (pause). Feel relaxation in the hands, wrists, biceps, head, eyes, mouth, lips, nose, neck, throat and stomach. I want you to again bring your attention to the center of your body, and if there is any tension, release it. That's it, good!

Now we will move to the legs. Notice both of your legs. Be aware of any tension that is in them. Release the tension by recalling what it was like to relax... That's it. Feel the relaxation in the thighs... legs... ankles... calves... feet... and toes. Again, bring your attention to your legs... Notice if there is any tension... Now relax the muscles in your legs by remembering what is was like to relax these muscles last week or at some earlier time period. That's good. Be aware of the relaxation that is moving through your entire body. Good... Feel the deep level of relaxation... That's good... easier and easier... as you relax. In a few minutes. I will count from one to five as a means of terminating this session. As I count, you will continue to feel relaxed, calm and refreshed as though you have experienced a deep and peaceful sleep. When you go to bed you will experience a restful and peaceful sleep like the one you had a long time ago. Now, One... Two... Three... Four... Five... It's up to you at your own rate and pace. Good.

Termination
Ask, "How was that?" or "Did you experience any difference this time?" If the client has any questions, deal with them and reassure the client that practice will lead to mastery of this relaxation exercise. Always appear confident about the ability of the client to learn this skill. If a client has specific difficulties, indicate that those difficulties will probably disappear with practice.

11.15 SYSTEMATIC DESENSITIZATION
Systematic desensitization (SD) is a cognitive-behavioral technique that can be used to treat test anxiety and other anxieties such as speech and various phobias. Developed by psychiatrist **Joseph Wolpe**, SD can be used if the client is capable of **mental imagery**. SD is similar to other cognitive-behavioral methods such as **relaxation therapy** and **hypnosis**.

There are three steps to SD. **First**, the therapist trains the client in deep muscle relaxation (see the relaxation therapy script). **Second**, the therapist and client construct a test hierarchy—a list of situations that produce test anxiety, ranked from the least anxious to the most anxious. Third, after the client relaxes, the therapist describes the scene from the test anxiety hierarchy that produces the least anxiety and asks the client to imagine that scene. Once the client can do this without any anxiety, the therapist moves to the next scene on the hierarchy and asks the client to imagine it. The **SD procedure is repeated until the client is able to imagine the scene on the test anxiety hierarchy** that previously produced the most anxiety **without experiencing any increased anxiety**.

Rationale of SD Presented to the Client
It is important to present a **rationale of SD to the client**. It can be communicated that SD is a procedure used to help the client overcome test anxiety. Furthermore, it can be stated that SD is based on the fact that a client cannot be anxious and relaxed at the same time.

At this point, it is important to describe the three steps of SD. For example, communicate to the client that he or she will **first learn to relax**. **Second**, communicate that you will assist the client in constructing a test anxiety hierarchy that will be used for **guided imagery exercises**. Specifically, communicate to the client that you will describe the least to the most anxiety producing item or scene from the test anxiety hierarchy until there is no reported anxiety. At this point, it is important to entertain questions.

As previously stated, there are three steps to SD. The first step is **teaching relaxation**. The relaxation therapy script is employed for this purpose. After the client learns deep muscle relaxation, the next step is **constructing a test anxiety hierarchy**. A good lead into the hierarchy is explaining to the client how to rate levels of test anxiety on a ten-point scale, where 1 is the lowest level of test anxiety and 10 is the highest level of test anxiety.

Therapists may find that the construction of a test anxiety hierarchy is the most challenging feature of SD. As previously stated, a hierarchy is a list of stimulus situations that a client responds to with graded amounts of test anxiety or other emotional reaction. Cormier and Cormier (1991, p. 487) describe three types of hierarchies, spatiotemporal, thematic and personal.

A **spatiotemporal hierarchy** is constructed by using items that present physical or time dimensions. For example, imaging yourself sitting in an examination room five minutes before the start of a major examination. This would be an example of a spatiotemporal test anxiety hierarchy item.

Thematic hierarchies consists of exposing the client to a variety of components or parameters that make up test anxiety. For example, activities such as studying and receiving criticism. Another example of a thematic hierarchy would be, "I have failed this exam; how are my parents going to react?" Essentially, the therapist is looking for major themes that underlie test anxiety with a given client. Personal hierarchies are used with clients who report test anxiety that occurred with a certain individual in his or her past, such as a mathematics or science teacher.

Items from the STABS are also useful for constructing a test anxiety hierarchy. It is recommended that the therapist use from 10 to 20 items on the hierarchy. Also, it is important to include some control items at the bottom of the hierarchy list. For example, "Imagine yourself waking on the beach on a warm spring day." Control items are scenes in which the client does not have any anxiety. They can be useful for producing relaxation.

In terms of ranking items on the test anxiety hierarchy, it is important to **explain to the client how items are ranked on the ten-point scale**, with control and lower ranked items at the bottom of the hierarchy. Items on the hierarchy may be initially categorized as low, medium and high test anxiety items. From this categorization, a numerical rating can be attached to each test anxiety scene on the hierarchy.

Sometimes it is important for a client to write out items to be included in the hierarchy at home. Then these items can be discussed and written on a 3" x 5" index card. The therapist should ensure that the items on the hierarchy are as evenly spaced as possible. In addition, it is important to be flexible in terms of changing items on the hierarchy to fit the needs of the client.

SAMPLE TEST ANXIETY HIERARCHY

1. Listening to your teacher describe what may be on an exam.
2. Thinking about an exam the day before it is to be given.
3. Listening to the other students describe items that may appear on the exam that you have not studied.
4. While taking an exam, worrying that you will run out of time.
5. Finding yourself confused while taking a difficult exam.

Once the hierarchy system is established, it is important to discuss a **signaling system**. During the presentation of hierarchy scenes, there are several times when the therapist and client need to communicate. Cormier and Cormier (1991, pp. 487-498) described several ways that a client can signal whether he or she is in a relaxed or tense state. One method is to have the client raise his or her left index finger one inch to signal that a clear image is formed.

Afterwards, the scene is presented for about ten seconds. The client is asked to rate the level of anxiety felt during visualization on the point scale discussed earlier, where one is the least amount of anxiety and ten is the greatest amount. This process of signaling and rating each scene occurs for each item on the test anxiety hierarchy. Each scene should be preceded with a relaxation response.

After a relaxation response, it is important to have the client rate his or her level of anxiety to ensure that it is below five on a ten point scale. **A rating of 1-3 is more preferable**. Once the client reports a low rating of anxiety, the therapist can continue presenting items from the test anxiety hierarchy.

During each session the therapist starts with the first item on the test anxiety hierarchy. Presentation of subsequent scenes should always begin with the last item successfully completed from the previous session. This ensures a smooth transition from one session to the next and facilitates learning. Similarly, starting with the last successfully completed item on the test anxiety hierarchy can prevent spontaneous recovery of the test anxiety response. It is important for the therapist to be prepared for the possibility of occasional relapses between test anxiety scene presentations.

When presenting items from the test anxiety hierarchy, the therapist should first describe the item and then ask the client to visualize or imagine it.

The **image should be presented between 20 to 40 seconds or longer**. Even if the client quickly signals test anxiety, continue having him or her imagine the scene for at least 20 seconds before saying the word "stop." If a client imagines a scene from the test anxiety hierarchy and does not report any anxiety, it is still appropriate to have him or her relax using the relaxation response. In addition, pausing 40 to 60 seconds between scenes is useful; however, Cormier and Cormier (1991, p. 498) reported that some clients may need several minutes between scenes. If it is important to make sure that a client has successfully coped with an item on the test anxiety hierarchy before proceeding to subsequent items. If a client reports anxiety after several exposures to the same item on the test anxiety hierarchy, the therapist may want to replace this item with one that is less intense or expose the client to the item for a shorter period of time.

Also, **it may be necessary to check what is happening in terms of the client's imagery.** This is important to ensure that the client is visualizing the image described. Each imagined item on the test anxiety hierarchy should be preceded by relaxation.

SD Script

First, I am going to review the relaxation training with you. Remember, the following test anxiety hierarchy we constructed? It consisted of the following five items:

1. **Listening to your teacher describe what may be on an exam.**
2. **Thinking about an exam the day before it is to be given.**

3. **Listening to the other students describe items that may appear on the exam that you have not studied.**
4. **While taking an exam, worrying that you will run out of time.**
5. **Finding yourself confused while taking a difficult exam.**

Let's start with the relaxation exercise. Close your eyes, and remember what it was like to relax before, especially when I asked you to tense and relax muscle groups earlier during treatment. Remember what it was like to relax—that is allowing your body to relax and letting any tension in your body leave. If you want, imagine being in a very relaxed place such as a beach or a vacation spot. (This is actually having the client imagine a control or nonanxiety producing item to ensure relaxation.) Now, I am going to describe the first item on your test anxiety hierarchy. If you experience any anxiety while imagining this scene, just raise your right index finger.

Now, I want you to imagine sitting in one of your classrooms, especially one in which you really fear taking an exam. It could also be a classroom where you are not doing very well. Imagine listening to your teacher describe items that may appear on an upcoming exam. (Allow the client to experience this scene for about 20-40 seconds, even if he or she signals anxiety immediately. If after 20 seconds the client does not signal any anxiety, have the client relax, pause for about 30 to 60 seconds, and proceed to the next item on the hierarchy.)

If the client signals anxiety, after about 20 seconds, have the client relax by having him or her imagine a relaxing scene or by having him or her perform the relaxation exercise. At this point, two things can occur; the same item can be repeated to the client, or the session can be terminated. During the next session, the same item can be attempted again following the previous instructions. (If after three or more attempts to imagine an item on the test anxiety hierarchy, the client still signals anxiety, it is important to make some adjustment on the hierarchy.)

All right, you can relax and clear the test anxiety hierarchy item from your mind. Relax now, by thinking of the last session of relaxation or a pleasant relaxing place or scene. (Pause 30 to 60 seconds.) I want you to imagine the same item again. That's it; imagine listening to your teacher describe items that may be on an exam. Imagine him or her describing as many items as possible. (Allow the client to experience this scene for about 20-40 seconds.) That's good, you can erase that scene from your mind and relax. Think about the last relaxation session or a favorite relaxing place. (Allow the client to relax for about 20-40 seconds.) (If two successive presentations of an item do not elicit anxiety, move to the next item on the test anxiety hierarchy and follow the same procedure used with item one.) When the session ends, it is important to have the client practice visualizing the items completed successfully during the treatment and to practice the relaxation procedure as it was used during SD.

11.16 SUMMARY OF COGNITIVE-BEHAVIORAL HYPNOSIS THERAPY SCRIPT

The introduction to this script presents an explanation of the treatment along with **dispelling misconceptions about hypnosis**. In addition, the topic of a test anxiety hierarchy is discussed. A **lever technique** is used for inducing a trance. This script can be repeated as many times as necessary for clients to make cognitive changes in terms of their test taking attitude. The literature suggests that clients report some changes in terms of test anxiety after participating in from **four to six sessions**.

Instructions

Cognitive-behavioral hypnosis (CBH) is a generic term for applying cognitive-behavioral techniques to hypnosis (Golden, Down, & Friedberg, 1987). CBH strategies are based on the assumption that many psychological disturbances are the result from **negative self-hypnosis**, a term coined by Araoz (1981, 1982, 1985). Negative self-hypnosis is similar to the principles advocated by Ellis (1985), who stated that many emotional disturbances are the result of **irrational thinking**. In particular, test anxiety would be the result of irrational thinking concerning test taking or evaluative situations.

Like other cognitive-behavioral methods, CBH employs the **scientific method**. Clients are taught to substantiate cognitions by using **empirical evidence**, which is part of the scientific method. Another feature of CBH is teaching clients to fully accept and tolerate themselves without any negative evaluations. This is a form of learning to cope in spite of the fact that things may be unpleasant. For example, clients must learn to accept themselves in spite of the fact that they have failed or not done well on an examination.   Also, clients are taught to recognize **self-defeating cognitions** and to substitute rational cognitions in place of irrational ones (Sapp, 1997a, 1997b).

From a CBH perspective, **rational cognitions** result in behaviors that are self-enhancing. Similarly, these behaviors are not based on what Dryden (1987) calls cognitive distortions. CBH teaches clients that it is permissible to make mistakes and that this is a natural part of life.

CBH assumes that **humans are fallible** and are **bound to err**. Another principle of CBH is taking what we often call dire needs, such as desires for love, approval, success and so on and turning these desires into their appropriate preferences. Furthermore, blame is viewed as a facilitator of self-defeating behavior within the CBH framework. In fact, CBH teaches clients to accept themselves and others without blaming anyone.

Another feature of CBH is teaching clients to **recognize dogmatic, rigid, "musts' and absolutistic "shoulds" in terms of thinking**. For example, it is irrational for a client to think on a cognitive level that "I must perform well on this examination and should do well or else. If I don't, I am a failure." Instead, CBH teaches the client to use more **flexible forms of thinking** such as "I would like to do well on this examination, and I will do the best I can. But if I fail, this does not make me a failure as a person. I just failed this particular examination."

Because CBH assumes that clients have many irrational cognitions that have been **internalized into a philosophy of life**, another one of its goals is to change a client's self-defeating philosophy of life. Ultimately, the goal of CBH is to change the clients immature, irrational, unrealistic and demanding ways of thinking into a logical, empirical and rational thought process. Finally, CBH assumes that a client must continue to work and practice in order to maintain cognitive change and as Ellis notes, it is constant work and practice in order to be minimally disturbed.

Misconceptions about CBH
It is important to deal with any misconceptions about CBH. for example, some clients believe they will lose consciousness during CBH. Others assume there is a weakening of the will and so on. Below is a list of some common misconceptions taken from *A Syllabus on Hypnosis* (1973)
1. Loss of consciousness
2. Weakening of the will
3. Requires a weak mind
4. Giving away of secrets
5. Gullibility confused with suggestibility

6.   Inability to dehypnotize

It is important to describe what CBH is and to indicate how it can be used as a treatment. For example, it is usually enough to say that CBH is a **form of relaxation** which involves suggestions that will be helpful in managing test anxiety. Let the client know that you expect this treatment to be beneficial. Rapport is important for creating a positive response set. Tell the client that humans have a great deal of untapped potential.

For example, the therapist can explain how it is possible to **control physiological** processes through CBH. In addition, the therapist should describe other interesting uses of CBH (e.g. pain, weight control, habit control and so). Finally, maintain a positive attitude, which will serve as a motivator and as a form of reassurance.

Adapted from Cormier and Cormier (1991). The following should also be communicated to subjects: One of the goals of this treatment is for you to become aware of factors that maintain test anxiety (whether it is math or performance-related anxiety and so). Once you learn some of the factors that are responsible for maintaining your anxiety, you can combat and change them. Surprisingly, one of the factors that contributes to anxiety is the thinking processes you go through in evaluative situations. Specifically, a **correlation** appears to exist between how anxious you are and the kinds of thoughts you are experiencing. More directly, the anxiety you experience in the test (math and so on) situation may be tied to the kinds of thoughts you had and where you choose to focus your attention.

You will be taught how to control your thinking and attention. Thinking is what we say to ourselves, **negative self-statements** and magical thinking. Just simply being aware of these facts is the first step towards change. You will learn how to control your thinking processes through cognitive-behavioral hypnosis. (Allow discussion at this time if the client chooses.)

Let us talk a little more about thoughts. Many feelings we have are based upon the way we think about social situations. Simply, it is not a given situation that produces anxiety, but rather it is the way we look at a certain situation. For example, students who have difficulty in school often tell themselves that negative things are bound to happen, that they are no good and must fail.

Cognitive-behavioral hypnotherapy will involve examining some of these unproductive thought patterns. In fact, research indicates if people can learn to get rid of unproductive and self-defeating thoughts, and to replace them with realistic, rational ones, then difficult situations become easier just by viewing things in a more positive light. Below is a checklist of the items the therapist should cover before administering the CBH script.

Outline

A Syllabus on Hypnosis (1973)
1. **Remove misconceptions.**
2. **Explain thoroughly to the client the focus of the treatment and the course of instructions that will be undertaken.**
3. **Stress that CBH is self-hypnosis.**
4. **Emphasize to the client that he or she will always be in control and that you will merely be a guide.**
5. **Emphasize that the role of the client is to learn self-hypnosis and to practice it outside of therapy sessions.**
6. **Just before the induction starts, ask the client if there are any questions. Remember to use a positive response set. For example, "I think it is good that you question whether or not you can utilize CBH because this is a sign of intelligence." If there are no questions, you may say, "That's good that there are no questions, because now we can begin."**

For several reasons, it is important for the therapist to **model behavior** during this initial session. **First**, modeling prepares the client for what to expect. **Second**, it will serve as a guiding part of the instructions, which may help lessen initial anxiety. **Finally**, modeling will demonstrate to the client that this is a collaborative approach.

Once the therapist begins reading the script, it is necessary to lower the voice. Also, it is important to reassure the client. This can be dealt with by modeling, in an unhurried fashion, a relaxed state and by indicating there is plenty of time.

Test Anxiety Hierarchy

At this point, it is important to explain to a client that CBH makes use of a **personalized test anxiety hierarchy**. The therapist should state that this test anxiety hierarchy consists of thinking about anxiety-arousing situations related to taking tests. Help the client organize a hierarchy, starting with events that arouse small amounts of anxiety to situations that evoke unmanageable anxiety.

Indicate to the clients that the test anxiety hierarchy should not be too long. To illustrate, three to five items is sufficient.

Sample Test Anxiety Hierarchy
(Adapted from Harris & Johnson, 1980; 1983)
1. **Studying materials for an exam.**
2. **Talking about an exam the day before it is to be given.**
3. **Listening to the professor describe items that may appear on the exam.**
4. **Seeing questions on an exam you cannot answer.**
5. **Seeing items on an exam that you did not study.**

CBH Induction
Now get into a relaxed position. I am going to show you how to use your arm as a level in order to enter a relaxed state (the therapist should model this behavior). Make a tight fist with either hand. I want you to make your fist as tight as possible. Extend your hand out in front of your body. Focus all the tension from the day into your hand. If you like, stare at the back of your hand. If anyone comes to the door, I will take care of it. If the phone rings, I will take care of it. For now, I just want you to pay attention to your hand. You may notice as you bring attention to your hand, you can almost feel the blood flow through it. It may feel warm and tingly. That's it, bring your attention to your hand. I know you can hear the sounds of other people in the next room; you may also be able to hear sounds in this room (refer to sounds in the environment). The only important thing now... is what I have to communicate to you.

As I said earlier, if anyone comes to the door, or if the phone rings, leave it to me. I know you can hear any sounds you wish; the sounds in this room, the sounds in the next room... Nevertheless, the most important thing for you now is the message I have to communicate to you.

You do not need to give any attention to anything in this room or the next room unless you have a particular interest in something in the room, or in certain sounds you may find interesting.

Whenever you are ready to enter a pleasant hypnotic state, simply with your arm raised, tightly mobilize that tension through your entire body right into your hand (Symbolically, this is a way of representing tension from the body into the hand).

I want you to feel that tension move from the tip of your head to the bottom of your toes. Let all the tension, energy, become focused in your shoulder, arm, and hand. That is right; begin to stare at your hand. While you are staring at it, notice what is happening as you experience yourself going into a deep hypnotic state. Your hand will tire from the struggle and loosen its grip, while you will feel this weariness spread throughout all of you. What was once steel will become like a hard stick of butter that will melt as you allow your arm to lower and experience yourself melting.

I do not know how much tension is in your body, or how long it will take to centralize it in your hand. There is plenty of time... plenty of time... like butter, melting into the chair, slowly at your own pace and rate. Whenever you are ready to start, remember, at your own pace and rate. You are the one who is in control.

Now, if you want to slowly relieve the tension, let your arm down like a lever. As your arm goes down, your level of relaxation will go up. That's it, slowly allowing your arm to go down. As your arm goes down, you can have a hypnotic experience. That's good! Relaxing more and more.

It is as though you were butter melting, but you can experience yourself melting in that chair (make adjustments to fit the client's seating arrangement). As you are sitting in the chair, you have probably realized that your breathing has changed. It is a slow comfortable good rhythm. Your entire body is changing to meet this new level of relaxation.

In a little while, I'm going to count from ten to one. As I count, you will feel your level of comfort increasing. Now, ten... nine... more and more relaxed. That's it... eight... at your own rate and pace... seven... six... five... halfway there... four... three... two... one.

(Adapted from Masters, 1978.) As you are sitting there in a relaxed state, I can talk to you in a special way. I can communicate things that you will process at a deep level. It may appear for the first time that someone is actually communicating to your true self. There are some things that I want you to remember. First, you need not be annoyed inwardly or outwardly. Second, you need not suppress your anger. What is needed is an observation of your impatience. You will see the need to overlook and make allowances right at that moment, not because you have to, but because you want to. Do not be afraid to speak up patiently. You may be surprised to see a lot of suppressed resentment bubbling to the surface.

Remember not to analyze these feelings... just observe and release them. You will realize that it is your resentment that hurts you more than the cruel things that others do or say to you. You will learn to overlook unimportant things and be outspoken on the spot about things that need to be dealt with. Probably the ones to make allowances for first are your loved ones. If you cannot do it for them, how is it possible to overlook unimportant things? You must learn not to have imaginary conversations with yourself about what you will say to people the next time you see them. Learn to have faith in yourself and be spontaneous.

If you can learn to be patient and discern people as they are without judging them, you will be better off. When you are calm and patient and not upset, it is not possible to hurt anyone with words or actions. Also, it is not possible to please everyone anyway... so stop trying. If you are not resentful and judgmental, you can be disagreeable without being obnoxious. Do not feel hurt about things which are said that are meant to hurt you. Criticism must roll off you like water falling off the back of a duck. It is not necessary to be excited by praise or criticism. Also, do not be too quick to criticize or give praise.

Now, I would like to explain something to you. I want you to enjoy feeling very comfortable. In fact, if you want to, you can enjoy yourself so much that you let your unconscious mind listen to me while your conscious mind relaxes... and you think comfortably about a very pleasant place, your favorite peaceful place.

Many of the things I want to assist you in accomplishing are governed by your unconscious mind. Continue as you are, at ease, in comfort; and at the proper time, you will become aware of how to take care of your problems. You will be able to deal with all your problems.

I am going to discuss your problem, and I will do it in this way. I will sketch it in general, and I want you to realize that I am going to ask of you only the things that are actually possible for you to do. There are many things that we can do. There are many things that we can do of which we are unaware. For example, we can attend a lecture and not be aware of the passing of time because we are so interested in what the lecturer is saying. Also, when a lecture is boring, we can feel the discomfort of the chair. Nevertheless, we can sit and listen to an interesting lecturer and never feel all the dullness and tiredness... and the hardness of the seat, but with a good lecturer you only hear a voice.

(Confusional technique) During this pleasant hypnotic experience, please listen to this voice. You are here to do certain important things. You have felt some things although you may have not felt other things because you did not pay special attention to them. Notice, how a voice would sound in a soundproof room. You have had extensive experience in forgetting things that would seem upon ordinary reasoning to be unreasonable.

(Age Regression) I remember sitting in school one day. Often I would daydream when I became tired of listening to the teacher. I liked sitting by the dollhouse so I could look inside and create whatever I wanted in my imagination. In my imagination, I could experience Christmas. As a matter of fact, I can remember one Christmas where I went to visit Grandma. It was a cold Christmas night... The stars were glittering in the sky. The north star was glaring straight in front of us. Once we arrived at Grandma's house. I can remember her telling us a story. It was a Christmas story! The story was about a boy, or maybe a girl, who was granted anything he or she wanted for Christmas. The boy, or was it a girl, was not sure of what to wish for. The boy envisioned receiving many boxes of gifts, while the girl pictured herself riding in a sleigh around the world. Finally, the boy and girl were given a gift from their grandmother. The girl's was in a large covered box with the most expensive decorated wrapping paper. The boy and girl struggled to get inside of the box in order to see the present. Once they got inside there was something... it was a bright light... It was the Star of Bethlehem... The light from the star was warm and pleasant like the warmth of a warm spring day. The light surfaced over the bodies of both the boy and girl, bringing about the warmest and most refreshing rays. It relaxed their head... face... neck... back... chest... stomach... legs... and feet. The boy and girl smiled at experiencing such a delightful present.

Today is an important day. It is important because you will notice differences in the levels of your anxiety. You will not feel as anxious, tense or upset as you felt sometime earlier. You will never experience the same level of anxiety again. Your anxiety will become less frequent and less severe... less frequent and severe... until it becomes moderate in level so you can cope with it. It will only be a level that motivates you to do the things you need to do... and things you ought to do. All this will happen... just as I say it will.

Now as you visualize a test-taking situation, think about your test anxiety hierarchy (pause), imagine the first item on the hierarchy (pause). You will remember that test anxiety stems from irrational beliefs and the inability to visualize or think about and use skills of competence from the past in current test situations. Imagine the second item on your test anxiety hierarchy. See it as clearly as you can in your mind. You may find that you have many irrational beliefs about test taking, such as, "I lose respect when I do poorly on exams," "I must get every item correct on the exam," "Others are watching me as I take exams." "The exam has just started, but I am running out of time," and when "I do poorly on exams, this makes me a failure as a person."

You will always be prepared for examinations. You will have read all materials and studied well. Remember, you must be well prepared for exams, and you feel confident and motivated.

Visualize the test-taking situation again (pause). As you visualize the test-taking situation, notice your emotional responses. Identify specific irrational thoughts.   Once you identify these thoughts, you must challenge, confront, and finally replace them with positive and rational self-talk. For example, it is not necessary to worry about the performance of others. You do not need to ruminate over alternatives. You feel adequate and competent, and you can succeed at the task at hand. You will remember the following: Even though exams are important, the results are not related to my self-worth as a person. I can do well on exams without getting every item correct. Instead of concentrating on others, I need to focus my attention on exams. I will budget my time carefully by not spending too much time on any one problem. Also, I will do easier items first and later return to the difficult ones. Finally, feel the benefits of cognitive-hypnosis every day.

(Adapted from John Hartland, 1973.) Every day your mind will become calmer, clearer... composed... placid... and more tranquil. You will become less easily worried... less fearful and apprehensive about studying and demonstrating your knowledge on tests.

(Adapted from Bassman, 1983.) Each day you will become and remain more relaxed, less tense, but with a moderate level of anxiety and a great deal of motivation to do well on exams. You will develop confidence in yourself. You will feel more confidence in your ability to study each day, and you will also have more confidence in your ability to do whatever you should to be able to do... without fear of failure... without fear of consequences... without unnecessary anxiety... and without uneasiness.

(Adapted from Hartland, 1973.) Every day... you will become physically stronger and, of course, fitter. You will find yourself being more alert... more energetic... more wide awake. You will become less easily tired... less easily fatigued... and less easily discouraged. Your nerves will become stronger and steadier. You will find yourself becoming so interested in what you are studying and other important things that are going on... that your mind will be less pre-occupied with yourself, and you will be less conscious of yourself and your feelings. Every day... your mind will become much calmer and clearer... more composed... placid... and tranquil. You will become less easily worried... less easily agitated... much less fearful, less apprehensive, and less easily upset.

Each day you will be able to think more clearly. You will be able to concentrate more easily. As your memory improves, you will be able to see things in their true perspective without blowing events out of proportion.

Every day you will become emotionally calmer.... more settled... less easily disturbed. Every day you will feel life has a purpose, and you will also have feelings of well-being. You will have feelings of personal safety, and security, which you may have not felt for a long time. Every day you will become and remain more and more relaxed... both mentally and physically. This will happen, just as I say it will. You are going to feel happier and more content, cheerful and optimistic... less easily discouraged, and less easily depressed.

(Adapted from Reardon, 1973.) Cognitive-behavioral hypnosis will give you all the courage and confidence to take the t out of can't and find out that you can and will. If you want positive things to happen, and you expect them to happen, they will happen. Cognitive-behavioral hypnosis will give you the power and ability to cope with the tension and stress of everyday living. You will find an ability within you to tolerate persons, places and things that used to annoy you. You will be able to modify yourself to the environment even if you cannot change structural constraints. As you control your body with your mind, you will be able to control the things you feel, think and say, which will help you stop worrying about the past and help you to stop feeling apprehensive about things that will occur in the future.

In a few moments, I will count from one to ten. As I am counting, you will raise your arm back to the same level you used to initiate this experience. When I say the number ten, you will return your arm to that starting position and come out of cognitive-behavioral hypnosis. When you come out of this self-absorption, you will feel refreshed and relaxed as if you had just experienced a very peaceful and comfortable nap.

Whenever you go to sleep, you will be able to enjoy the comfort of your bed. You will have a very deep and restful sleep like the one you had a long... long time ago. When it is time, you will awaken feeling calm and secure, rested, comfortable and confident. Yes, confident in your ability to easily go into and come out of cognitive-behavioral hypnosis, and to comfortably carry out this treatment. Good, easier and easier. Now, one... two... three... four... five... six... seven, eight, nine, and ten. Now, it is up to you at your own rate and pace.

Debriefing

Ask the client to describe his or her hypnotic experience. If the client has any questions, deal with them in a positive and reassuring manner. Once the client has described his or her experience, summarize the major features, and state that people have many kinds of experiences in hypnosis. Tell the client that he or she did an excellent job. Remember, this is extremely important for setting up a positive response set. Finally, tell the client that you expect even better performance the next session.

11.17 COGNITIVE-BEHAVIORAL THERAPY

Sapp (1994a, 1994b, 1996a, 1996b); Farrell, Sapp, Johnson, and Pollard (1994); Sapp and Farrell (1994); Sapp, McNeely, and Torres (1998); Smith, Sapp, Farrell, Johnson (1998); Radtke et al. (1997); Sapp, Farrell, and Durand (1995); Sapp, Durand, and Farrell (1995a, 1995b); and Sapp (1994a. 1994b) described cognitive-behavioral therapy as a school of behaviorism that combines cognitive and behavioral psychology. In fact, cognitive-behavioral strategies are effective in reducing test anxiety in children (Sapp, 1994a, 1994b; Sapp & Farrell, 1994), adolescents and adults (Sapp, 1996a, 1996b; Sapp, Durand, & Farrell, 1995a, 1995b).

Sapp (1997b) indicated that **rationale-emotive behavior therapy (REBT)** is the original cognitive-behavioral therapy. **REBT** postulates that test anxiety stems from students' self-defeating behavior and irrational beliefs. For example, test-anxious students tend to **reindoctrinate themselves with irrational beliefs** such as, "I must pass this test," "my life is based on succeeding on this test," and so on. The foundations for test-anxious students' irrational beliefs are initiated and continued on a cognitive level. Also, these students tend to have low levels of self-acceptance, and they tend to sabotage their plans that could lead to success on exams.

Sapp (1996a, 1996b) stated that test-anxious students tend to hold at least three irrational beliefs. **First,** many of these students believe they cannot succeed without being "A" students. **Second,** these students assume that it is easier to avoid exams and other academic situations than to face them. It can be emphasized to test-anxious students that being personally responsible can improve academic performance, but avoiding exams and other academic situations will increase one's sense of fear and anxiety. **Third,** these students tend to assume that it is the end of the world when they do not perform well on exams. It is important to teach test-anxious students that failures on exams are just that—failures, and they have nothing to do with one's personal self-worth. In addition, when a test-anxious student learns to tolerate his or her failure on exams, he or she tends to develop high levels of frustration tolerance and a decrease in test anxiety. And, eventually, his or her test performance will improve.

In using cognitive-behavioral therapy with test-anxious students, these students need to be aware of three insights. **First,** they need to be aware that test anxiety is the result of irrational thinking. **Irrational thoughts** are ones that tend to prevent students from achieving their goals. **Second,** constantly, test-anxious students tend to reindoctrinate themselves with irrational beliefs about test anxiety, and they seek historical causes of their irrational beliefs about test anxiety. This tends to help maintain their test anxiety. Test-anxious students can be taught to challenge and confront their irrational beliefs in the present and not to seek historical causes of their irrational beliefs about test anxiety. **Finally,** test-anxious students have to constantly work to change their irrational beliefs about test anxiety, and, over time, they can be minimally affected by tests; hence, there are not any magical or perfect cures for test anxiety.

References

Allen, G. J. (1971). *Desensitization study counseling manual.* Unpublished manual.

Andrews, G., & Harvey, R. (1981). Does psychotherapy benefit neurotic patients? A reanalysis of the Smith, Glass and Miller data. *Archives of General Psychiatry, 38,* 1203-1208.

A syllabus on hypnosis and a handbook of therapeutic suggestions. (1973). Des Plaines, IL: Education and Research Foundations, American Society of Clinical Hypnosis.

Araoz, D. L. (1981). Negative self-hypnosis. *Journal of Contemporary Psychotherapy, 12,* 45-52.

Araoz, D. L. (1982). *Hypnosis and sex therapy.* New York: Brunner/Mazel.

Araoz, D. L. (1985). *The new hypnosis.* New York: Brunner/Mazel.

Auerbach, A., & Johnson, M. (1977). Research on the therapist's level of experience. In A. Gurman & A. Razin (Eds.), *Effective psychotherapy* (pp. 10-50). New York: Pergamon Press.

Bassman, S. (1983). *The effects of indirect hypnosis, relaxation and homework on the primary and secondary psychological symptoms of women with muscle-contraction headache.* Unpublished doctoral dissertation, University of Cincinnati, Cincinnati, Ohio.

Becker, P. (1982). Fear reactions and achievement behavior of students approaching an examination. In H. W. Krohne & L. Laux (Eds.), *Achievement, stress and anxiety* (pp. 275-290). Washington, DC: Hemisphere.

Bergin, A. E. (1971). The evaluation of therapeutic outcomes. In A. E. Bergin & S. L. Garfield (Eds.), *Handbook of psychotherapy and behavior change: An empirical analysis.* New York: Wiley.

Bernstein, D., & Borkovec, T. (1973). *Progressive relaxation training: A manual for helping professions.* Chicago: Research Press.

Bootzin, R. R., Bower, G. H., Zajonc, R. B., & Hall, E. (1986). *Psychology today: An introduction* (6th ed.). New York: Random House.

Boutin, G. E. (1978). Treatment of test anxiety by rational stage directed hypnotherapy: A case study. *American Journal of Clinical Hypnosis, 21*, 52-57.

Boutin, G. E., & Tosi, D. J. (1983). Modifications of irrational ideas and test anxiety through rational stage directed hypnotherapy. *American Journal of Clinical Hypnosis, 39*(3), 382-391.

Cercio, J. E. (1983). The use of hypnotic elements and audio recordings with the fantasy relaxation technique. *Personnel and Guidance Journal, 61*(7), 436-437.

Cohen, H. A. (1982). *The use of clinical hypnosis in a college counseling center.* (ERIC Document Reproduction Service No. ED 222 804)

Cormier, W., & Cormier, L. (1991). *Interviewing strategies for helpers: A guide to assessment and evaluation* (3rd ed.). Pacific Grove, CA: Wadsworth.

Deluga, R. (1981). *The effects of rational behavior therapy upon law students' test anxiety and academic grade point average.*

Unpublished doctoral dissertation, University of Cincinnati, Cincinnati, Ohio.

Dryden, W. (1987). *Counseling individuals: The rational-emotive approach.* London: Taylor and Francis.

Dykeman, B. F. (1992). *The effects of motivational orientation, feedback condition, and self-efficacy on test anxiety.* Unpublished doctoral dissertation, University of Wisconsin-Milwaukee, Milwaukee, Wisconsin.

Ellis, A. (1985). *Overcoming resistance: Rational-emotive therapy with difficult clients.* New York: Springer.

Farrell, W., Sapp, M., Johnson, J., & Pollard, D. (1994). Assessing college aspirations among at-risk high school students: A principal component analysis. *The High School Journal, 77*(4), 294–303.

Frank, J. D. (1974). Therapeutic components of psychotherapy: A 25-year progress report of research. *Journal of Nervous and Mental Disease, 159,* 325-342.

Frank, J. D. (1986). What is psychotherapy? In S. Bloch (Ed.), *An introduction to psychotherapy* (pp. 5-45). New York: Oxford University Press.

Garfield, S. L. (1978). Research on client variables in psychotherapy. In S. L. Garfield & A. E. Bergin (Eds.), *Handbook of psychotherapy and behavior change: Empirical analysis* (pp. 20-75). New York: Wiley.

Garfield, S. L. (1987). Ethical issues in research on psychotherapy. *Counseling and Values, 31,* 115-125.

Garfield, S. L. (1994). Research on client variables in psychotherapy. In A. E. Bergin & S. L. Garfield (Eds.), *Handbook of psychotherapy and behavior change* (4th ed., pp. 1909–228). New York: Wiley.

Gendlin, E. T. (1986). What comes after traditional psychotherapy research? *American Psychologist, 41,* 131-136.

Gibbons, D., Kilbourne, L., Saunders, A., & Castles, C. (1970). The cognitive control of behavior: A comparison of systematic desensitization and hypnotically-induced "directed experience" technique. *American Journal of Clinical Hypnosis, 12*(3), 141-143.

Golden, W. L., Dowd, E. T., & Friedberg, F. (1987). *Hypnotherapy: A modern approach.* New York: Pergamon Press.

Hall, R. A., & Hinkle, J. E. (1972). Vicarious desensitization of test anxiety. *Behaviour Research and Therapy, 10,* 407-410.

Harris, G., & Johnson, S. B. (1980). Comparison of individualized covert modeling, self-control desensitization, and study skills training for alleviating test anxiety. *Journal of Consulting and Clinical Psychology, 48*, 186-194.

Harris, G., & Johnson, S. B. (1983). Coping imagery and relaxation instructions in covert modeling treatment for test anxiety. *Behavior Therapy, 14*, 144-157.

Hartland, J. (1973). *A syllabus on hypnosis and a handbook of therapeutic suggestions.* Des Plaines, IL: American Society of Clinical Hypnosis, Education and Research Foundations.

Herbert, S. V. (1984). A simple hypnotic approach to treat test anxiety in medical students and residents. *Journal of Medication Education, 59*(10), 841-842.

Lieberman, L. R., Fisher, J. R., Russell, T., & King, W. B. (1968). Use of tape recorded suggestions as an aid to probation students. *American Journal of Clinical Hypnosis, 2*(1), 341-343.

Luborsky, L., Singer, B., & Luborsky, L. (1971). Factors influencing the outcome of psychotherapy: A review of quantitative research. *Psychological Bulletin, 75*, 145-185.

Luborsky, L., Singer, B., & Luborsky, L. (1980). Predicting the outcome of psychotherapy: Findings of the Penn psychotherapy project. *Archives of General Psychiatry, 37*, 471-481.

Marziali, E., Marmar, C., & Krupnick, J. (1981). Therapeutic alliance scales: Development and relationship to psychotherapy outcome. *American Journal of Psychiatry, 138*, 361-364.

Masters, R. (1978). *How your mind can keep you well.* Los Angeles: Foundations of Human Understanding.

Meichenbaum, D. (1972). Cognitive modification of test anxious college students. *Journal of Consulting and Clinical Psychotherapy, 39*, 370-380.

Melnick, J., & Russell, R. W. (1976). Hypnosis versus systematic desensitization in the treatment of test anxiety. *Journal of Counseling Psychology, 23*(4), 291-295.

Paul, G. L. (1967). Outcome research in psychotherapy. *Journal of Consulting Psychotherapy, 31*, 109-188.

Radtke, L., Sapp, M., & Farrell, W. (1997). Reality therapy: A meta-analysis. *The Journal of Reality Therapy, 17*(1), 4–9.

Reardon, W. T. (1973). In *A syllabus on hypnosis and a handbook of therapeutic suggestions.* Des Plaines, IL: Education and Research Foundation, American Society of Clinical Hypnosis.

Ricketts, M. S., & Galloway, R. E. (1984). Effects of three one-hour single-session treatments for test anxiety. *Psychological Reports, 54,* 113-119.

Rogers, C. R. (1957). The necessary and sufficient conditions of therapeutic personality change. *Journal of Consulting Psychology, 21,* 95-103.

Sapp, M. (1986, October). Hypnotherapy: Its place in education. *Hypnotherapy Today,* pp. 1, 5.

Sapp, M. (1988a, March). Hypnotherapy and test anxiety: A look at the literature. *Hypnotherapy Today,* pp. 1-2.

Sapp, M. (1988b). *The effects of three treatments for test anxiety: Autosuggestion therapy combined with study skills training, relaxation therapy combined with study skills counseling and nondirective therapy.* Unpublished doctoral dissertation, University of Cincinnati, Cincinnati, Ohio.

Sapp, M. (1989a). Hypnotherapy in treatment of test anxiety [letter to the editor]. *The Behavior Therapist, 2*(9), 210.

Sapp, M. (1989b). Some possible negative aftereffects of hypnosis. *The International Journal of Professional Hypnosis, 5*(1), 6-8.

Sapp, M. (1991). Hypnotherapy and test anxiety: Two cognitive-behavior constructs the effects of hypnosis in reducing test anxiety and improving academic achievement in college students. *The Australian Journal of Clinical Hypnotherapy and Hypnosis, 12*(1), 25-33.

Sapp, M. (1992a). Relaxation and hypnosis in reducing anxiety and stress. *The Australian Journal of Clinical Hypnotherapy and Hypnosis, 13*(2), 39-55.

Sapp, M. (1992b). The effects of hypnosis in reducing test anxiety and improving academic achievement in college students. *The International Journal of Professional Hypnosis, 6*(1), 20-22..

Sapp, M. (1994a). The effects of guided imagery in reducing the worry and emotionality components of test anxiety. *Journal of Mental Imagery, 18*(3&4), 165-180.

Sapp, M. (1994b). Cognitive-behavioral counseling: Applications for African American middle school students who are academically at risk. *Journal of Instructional Psychology, 21*(2), 161-171.

Sapp, M. (1996a). Irrational beliefs that can lead to academic failure for African American middle school students who are academically at risk. *Journal of Rational-Emotive and Cognitive-Behavior Therapy, 14*(2), 123–134.

Sapp, M. (1996b). Three treatments for reducing the worry and emotionality components of test anxiety with undergraduate and graduate college students: Cognitive-behavioral hypnosis, relaxation therapy, and supportive counseling. *Journal of College Student Development, 37*(1), 79–87.

Sapp, M. (1997a). Theories of hypnosis. *The Australian Journal of Clinical Hypnotherapy and Hypnosis, 18*(2), 43–54.

Sapp, M. (1997b). *Counseling and psychotherapy: Theories, associated research, and issues.* Lanham, MD: University Press of America.

Sapp, M., Durand, H., & Farrell, W. (1995). Measures of actual test anxiety in educationally and economically disadvantaged college students. *College Student Journal, 29*(1), 65–72.

Sapp, M., & Farrell, W. (1994). Cognitive-behavioral interventions: Applications for academically at-risk and special education students. *Preventing School Failure, 38*(2), 19–24.

Sapp, M., Farrell, W., & Durand, H. (1995a). Cognitive-behavioral therapy: Applications for African American middle school at-risk students. *Journal of Instructional Psychology, 22*(2), 169–177.

Sapp, M., Farrell, W., & Durand, H. (1995b). The effects of mathematics, reading, and writing tests in producing worry and emotionality test anxiety with economically and educationally disadvantaged college students. *College Student Journal, 29*(1), 122–125.

Sapp, M., Farrell, W., Johnson, J., & Ioannidis, G. (1997). Utilizing the PK Scale of the MMPI-2 to detect posttraumatic stress disorder in college students. *Journal of Clinical Psychology, 53*(8), 1–6.

Sapp, M., Ioannidis, G., & Farrell, W. C. (1995). Posttraumatic stress disorder, imaginative involvement, hypnotic susceptibility, anxiety and depression. *The Australian Journal of Clinical Hypnotherapy and Hypnosis, 16*(2), 75–87.

Sapp, M., McNeely, R. L., & Torres, J. B. (1998). Death and dying of aged African Americans. *Journal of Human Behavior in the Social Environment, 1*(2/3), 229–315.

Sarason, I. G. (1981). Test anxiety, stress and social support. *Journal of Personality, 41*, 101–114.

Smith, C. L., Sapp, M., Farrell, W., & Johnson, J. H. (1998). Psychoeducational correlates of achievement for high school seniors at a private school: The relationship among locus of control, self-esteem, academic achievement, and academic self-esteem. *The High School Journal, 81*(3), 161–167.

Smith, M. L., Glass, G. V., & Miller, T. I. (1980). *The benefits of psychotherapy*. Baltimore: Johns Hopkins Press.

Speilberger, C. D. (1980). *Test anxiety inventory*. Palo Alto, CA: Consulting Psychologist Press.

Stiles, W. B., Shapiro, D. A., Elliott, R. (1986). Are all psychotherapies equivalent? *American Psychologist, 41*, 165-180.

Strupp, H. H. (1986). Psychotherapy: Research, practice, and public policy (How to avoid dead ends). *American Psychologists, 41*, 120-130.

Suinn, R. M. (1970). Short-term desensitization therapy. *Behaviour Research and Therapy, 8*, 383-384.

Suinn, R. M., Edie, C. A., & Spinelli, P. R. (1970). Accelerated massed desensitization: Innovation in short term treatment. *Behavior Therapy, 1*, 303-311.

Suinn, R. M., & Hall, R. (1970). Marathon desensitization groups: An innovative technique. *Behavior Research and Therapy, 8*, 97-98.

Vandenbos, G. R. (1986). Psychotherapy research: A special issue. *American Psychologist, 41*, 111-112.

Wilson, N. H., & Rotter, J. C. (1986). Anxiety management training and study skills counseling for students on self esteem and test anxiety and performance. *The School Counselor, 34*(1), 18-31.

Yalom, I. D. (1975). *The theory and practice of group psychotherapy*. New York: Basic Books.

Appendix

Table A	Percent Area Under the Normal Curve Between the Mean and Z
Table B	Critical Values of t
Table C	Critical Values for F
Table D	Percentage Points of the Studentized Range
Table E	Critical Values for Bryant-Paulson Procedure
Table F	The Hartley F-Max Test for Homogeneity of Variances
Table G	Critical Values for Dunnett's Test
Table H	Critical Values of Pearson r
Table I	Critical Values of r_s (Spearman Rank-Order Correlation Coefficient)
Table J	Critical Values of Chi-Square
Table K	A Table of Random Numbers

Table A

Percent Area Under the Normal Curve Between the Mean and z*

z	.00	.01	.02	.03	.04	.05	.06	.07	.08	.09
0.0	00.00	00.40	00.80	01.20	01.60	01.99	02.39	02.79	03.19	03.59
0.1	03.98	04.38	04.78	05.17	05.57	05.96	06.36	06.75	07.14	07.53
0.2	07.93	08.32	08.71	09.10	09.48	09.87	10.26	10.64	11.03	11.41
0.3	11.79	12.17	12.55	12.93	13.31	13.68	14.06	14.43	14.80	15.17
0.4	15.54	15.91	16.28	17.00	17.00	17.36	17.72	18.08	18.44	18.79
0.5	19.15	19.50	19.85	20.19	20.54	20.88	21.23	21.57	21.90	22.24
0.6	22.57	22.91	23.24	23.57	23.89	24.22	24.54	24.86	25.17	25.49
0.7	25.80	26.11	26.42	26.73	27.04	27.34	27.64	27.94	28.23	28.52
0.8	28.81	29.10	29.39	29.67	29.95	30.23	30.51	30.78	31.06	31.33
0.9	31.59	31.86	32.12	32.38	32.64	32.89	33.15	33.40	33.65	33.89
1.0	34.13	34.38	34.61	34.85	35.08	35.31	35.54	35.77	35.99	36.21
1.1	36.43	36.65	36.86	37.08	37.29	37.49	37.70	37.90	38.10	38.30
1.2	38.49	38.69	38.88	39.07	39.25	39.44	39.62	39.80	39.97	40.15
1.3	40.32	40.49	40.66	40.82	40.99	41.15	41.31	41.47	41.62	41.77
1.4	41.92	42.07	42.22	42.36	42.51	42.65	42.79	42.92	43.06	43.19
1.5	43.32	43.45	43.57	43.70	43.82	43.94	44.06	44.18	44.29	44.41
1.6	44.52	44.63	44.74	44.84	44.95	45.05	45.15	45.25	45.35	45.45
1.7	45.54	45.64	45.73	45.82	45.91	45.99	46.08	46.16	46.25	46.33
1.8	46.41	46.49	46.56	46.64	46.71	46.78	46.86	46.93	46.99	47.06
1.9	47.13	47.19	47.26	47.32	47.38	47.44	47.50	47.56	47.61	47.67
2.0	47.72	47.78	47.83	47.88	47.93	47.98	48.03	48.08	48.12	48.17
2.1	48.21	48.26	48.30	48.34	48.38	48.42	48.46	48.50	48.54	48.57
2.2	48.61	48.64	48.68	48.71	48.75	48.78	48.81	48.84	48.87	48.90
2.3	48.93	48.96	48.98	49.01	49.04	49.06	49.09	49.11	49.13	49.16
2.4	49.18	49.20	49.22	49.25	49.27	49.29	49.31	49.32	49.34	49.36
2.5	49.38	49.40	49.41	49.43	49.45	49.46	49.48	49.49	49.51	49.52
2.6	49.53	49.55	49.56	49.57	49.59	49.60	49.61	49.62	49.63	49.64
2.7	49.65	49.66	49.67	49.68	49.69	49.70	49.71	49.72	49.73	49.74
2.8	49.74	49.75	49.76	49.77	49.77	49.78	49.79	49.79	49.80	49.81
2.9	49.81	49.82	49.82	49.83	49.84	49.84	49.85	49.85	49.86	49.86
3.0	49.87									
3.5	49.98									
4.0	49.997									
5.0	49.99997									

*Reproduced with permission of the Trustees of Biometrika.

Table B

Critical Values of t*

	Level of significance for one-tailed test					
	.10	.05	.025	.01	.005	.0005
	Level of significance for two-tailed test					
df	.20	.10	.05	.02	.01	.001
1	3.078	6.314	12.706	31.821	63.657	636.619
2	1.886	2.920	4.303	6.965	9.925	31.598
3	1.638	2.353	3.182	4.541	5.841	12.941
4	1.533	2.132	2.776	3.747	4.604	8.610
5	1.476	2.015	2.571	3.365	4.032	6.859
6	1.440	1.943	2.447	3.143	3.707	5.959
7	1.415	1.895	2.365	2.998	3.449	5.405
8	1.397	1.860	2.306	2.896	3.355	5.041
9	1.383	1.833	2.262	2.821	3.250	4.781
10	1.372	1.812	2.228	2.764	3.169	4.587
11	1.363	1.796	2.201	2.718	3.106	4.437
12	1.356	1.782	2.179	2.681	3.055	4.318
13	1.350	1.771	2.160	2.650	3.012	4.221
14	1.345	1.761	2.145	2.624	2.977	4.140
15	1.341	1.753	2.131	2.602	2.947	4.073
16	1.337	1.746	2.120	2.583	2.921	4.015
17	1.333	1.740	2.110	2.567	2.898	3.965
18	1.330	1.734	2.101	2.552	2.878	3.922
19	1.328	1.729	2.093	2.539	2.861	3.883
20	1.325	1.725	2.086	2.528	2.845	3.850
21	1.323	1.721	2.080	2.518	2.831	3.819
22	1.321	1.717	2.074	2.508	2.819	3.792
23	1.319	1.714	2.069	2.500	2.807	3.767
24	1.318	1.711	2.064	2.492	2.797	3.745
25	1.316	1.708	2.060	2.485	2.787	3.725

Table B (Continued)

	Level of significance for one-tailed test					
	.10	.05	.025	.01	.005	.0005
	Level of significance for two-tailed test					
df	.20	.10	.05	.02	.01	.001
26	1.315	1.706	2.056	2.479	2.779	3.707
27	1.314	1.703	2.052	2.473	2.771	3.690
28	1.313	1.701	2.048	2.467	2.763	3.674
29	1.311	1.699	2.045	2.462	2.756	3.659
30	1.310	1.697	2.042	2.457	2.750	3.646
40	1.303	1.684	2.021	2.423	2.704	3.551
60	1.296	1.671	2.000	2.390	2.660	3.460
120	1.289	1.658	1.980	2.358	2.617	3.373
∞	1.282	1.645	1.960	2.326	2.576	3.291

*Table B is taken from Table III of R. A. Fisher and F. Yates (1963), "Statistical Tables for Biological Agricultural and Medical Research" (6th ed.). Oliver and Boyd, Edinburgh. Reproduced by permission of the authors and publishers.

Test Anxiety: Appendix

Table C

Critical Values for F

		df for Numerator							
df error	α	1	2	3	4	5	6	8	12
1	.01	4052	4999	5403	5625	5764	5859	5981	6106
	.05	161.45	199.50	215.71	224.58	230.16	233.99	238.88	243.91
	.10	39.86	49.50	53.59	55.83	57.24	58.20	59.44	60.70
	.20	9.47	12.00	13.06	13.73	14.01	14.26	14.59	14.90
2	.01	98.49	99.00	99.17	99.25	99.30	99.33	99.36	99.42
	.05	18.51	19.00	19.16	19.25	19.30	19.33	19.37	19.41
	.10	8.53	9.00	9.16	9.24	9.29	9.33	9.37	9.41
	.20	3.56	4.00	4.16	4.24	4.28	4.32	4.36	4.40
3	.001	167.5	148.5	141.1	137.1	134.6	132.8	130.6	128.3
	.01	34.12	30.81	29.46	28.71	28.24	27.91	27.49	27.05
	.05	10.13	9.55	9.28	9.12	9.01	8.94	8.84	8.74
	.10	5.54	5.46	5.39	5.34	5.31	5.28	5.25	5.22
	.20	2.68	2.89	2.94	2.96	2.97	2.97	2.98	2.98
4	.001	74.14	61.25	56.18	53.44	51.71	50.53	49.00	47.41
	.01	21.20	18.00	16.69	15.98	15.52	15.21	14.80	14.37
	.05	7.71	6.94	6.59	6.39	6.26	6.16	6.04	5.91
	.10	4.54	4.32	4.19	4.11	4.05	4.01	3.95	3.90
	.20	2.35	2.47	2.48	2.48	2.48	2.47	2.47	2.46
5	.001	47.04	36.61	33.20	31.09	29.75	28.84	27.64	26.42
	.01	16.26	13.27	12.06	11.39	10.97	10.67	10.29	9.89
	.05	6.61	5.79	5.41	5.19	5.05	4.95	4.82	4.68
	.10	4.06	3.78	3.62	3.52	3.45	3.40	3.34	3.27
	.20	2.18	2.26	2.25	2.24	2.23	2.22	2.20	2.18
6	.001	35.51	27.00	23.70	21.90	20.81	20.03	19.03	17.99
	.01	13.74	10.92	9.78	9.15	8.75	8.47	8.10	7.72
	.05	5.99	5.14	4.76	4.53	4.39	4.28	4.15	4.00
	.10	3.78	3.46	3.29	3.18	3.11	3.05	2.98	2.90
	.20	2.07	2.13	2.11	2.09	2.08	2.06	2.04	2.02
7	.001	29.22	21.69	18.77	17.19	16.21	15.52	14.63	13.71
	.01	12.25	9.55	8.45	7.85	7.46	7.19	6.84	6.47
	.05	5.59	4.74	4.35	4.12	3.97	3.87	3.73	3.57
	.10	3.59	3.26	3.07	2.96	2.88	2.83	2.75	2.67
	.20	2.00	2.04	2.02	1.99	1.97	1.96	1.93	1.91
8	.001	25.42	18.49	15.83	14.39	13.49	12.86	12.04	11.19
	.01	11.26	8.65	7.59	7.01	6.63	6.37	6.03	5.67
	.05	5.32	4.46	4.07	3.84	3.69	3.58	3.44	3.28
	.10	3.46	3.11	2.92	2.81	2.73	2.67	2.59	2.50
	.20	1.95	1.98	1.95	1.92	1.90	1.88	1.86	1.83

Table C (Continued)

| df error | α | \multicolumn{8}{c}{df for Numerator} |
		1	2	3	4	5	6	8	12
9	.001	22.86	16.39	13.90	12.56	11.71	11.13	10.37	9.57
	.01	10.56	8.02	6.99	6.42	6.06	5.80	5.47	5.11
	.05	5.12	4.26	3.86	3.63	3.48	3.37	3.23	3.07
	.10	3.36	3.01	2.81	2.69	2.61	2.55	2.47	2.38
	.20	1.91	1.94	1.90	1.87	1.85	1.83	1.80	1.76
10	.001	21.04	14.91	12.55	11.28	10.48	9.92	9.20	8.45
	.01	10.04	7.56	6.55	5.99	5.64	5.39	5.06	4.71
	.05	4.96	4.10	3.71	3.48	3.33	3.22	3.07	2.91
	.10	3.28	2.92	2.73	2.61	2.52	2.46	2.38	2.28
	.20	1.88	1.90	1.86	1.83	1.80	1.78	1.75	1.72
11	.001	19.69	13.81	11.56	10.35	9.58	9.05	8.35	7.63
	.01	9.65	7.20	6.22	5.67	5.32	5.07	4.74	4.40
	.05	4.84	3.98	3.59	3.36	3.20	3.09	2.95	2.79
	.10	3.23	2.86	2.66	2.54	2.45	2.39	2.30	2.21
	.20	1.86	1.87	1.83	1.80	1.77	1.75	1.72	1.68
12	.001	18.64	12.97	10.80	9.63	8.89	8.38	7.71	7.00
	.01	9.33	6.93	5.95	5.41	5.06	4.82	4.50	4.16
	.05	4.75	3.88	3.49	3.26	3.11	3.00	2.85	2.69
	.10	3.18	2.81	2.61	2.48	2.39	2.33	2.24	2.15
	.20	1.84	1.85	1.80	1.77	1.74	1.72	1.69	1.65
13	.001	17.81	12.31	10.21	9.07	8.35	7.86	7.21	6.52
	.01	9.07	6.70	5.74	5.20	4.86	4.62	4.30	3.96
	.05	4.67	3.80	3.41	3.18	3.02	2.92	2.77	2.60
	.10	3.14	2.76	2.56	2.43	2.35	2.28	2.20	2.10
	.20	1.82	1.83	1.78	1.75	1.72	1.69	1.66	1.62
14	.001	17.14	11.78	9.73	8.62	7.92	7.43	6.80	6.13
	.01	8.86	6.51	5.56	5.03	4.69	4.46	4.14	3.80
	.05	4.60	3.74	3.34	3.11	2.96	2.85	2.70	2.53
	.10	2.10	2.73	2.52	2.39	2.31	2.24	2.15	2.05
	.20	1.81	1.81	1.76	1.73	1.70	1.67	1.64	1.60
15	.001	16.59	11.34	9.34	8.25	7.57	7.09	6.47	5.81
	.01	8.68	6.36	5.42	4.89	4.56	4.32	4.00	3.67
	.05	4.54	3.68	3.29	3.06	2.90	2.79	2.64	2.48
	.10	3.07	2.70	2.49	2.36	2.27	2.21	2.12	2.02
	.20	1.80	1.79	1.75	1.71	1.68	1.66	1.62	1.58
16	.001	16.12	10.97	9.00	7.94	7.27	6.81	6.19	5.55
	.01	8.53	6.23	5.29	4.77	4.44	4.20	3.89	3.55
	.05	4.49	3.63	3.24	3.01	2.85	2.74	2.59	2.42
	.10	3.05	2.67	2.46	2.33	2.24	2.18	2.09	1.99
	.20	1.79	1.78	1.74	1.70	1.67	1.64	1.61	1.56

Table C (Continued)

df error	α	1	2	3	4	5	6	8	12
					df for Numerator				
17	.001	15.72	10.66	8.73	7.68	7.02	6.56	5.96	5.32
	.01	8.40	6.11	5.18	4.67	4.34	4.10	3.79	3.45
	.05	4.45	3.59	3.20	2.96	2.81	2.70	2.55	2.38
	.10	3.03	2.64	2.44	2.31	2.22	2.15	2.06	1.96
	.20	1.78	1.77	1.72	1.68	1.65	1.63	1.59	1.55
18	.001	15.38	10.39	8.49	7.46	6.81	6.35	5.76	5.13
	.01	8.28	6.01	5.09	4.58	4.25	4.01	3.71	3.37
	.05	4.41	3.55	3.16	2.93	2.77	2.66	2.51	2.34
	.10	3.01	2.62	2.42	2.29	2.20	2.13	2.04	1.93
	.20	1.77	1.76	1.71	1.67	1.64	1.62	1.58	1.53
19	.001	15.08	10.16	8.28	7.26	6.61	6.18	5.59	4.97
	.01	8.18	5.93	5.01	4.50	4.17	3.94	3.63	3.30
	.05	4.38	3.52	3.13	2.90	2.74	2.63	2.48	2.31
	.10	2.99	2.61	2.40	2.27	2.18	2.11	2.02	1.91
	.20	1.76	1.75	1.70	1.66	1.63	1.61	1.57	1.52
20	.001	14.82	9.95	8.10	7.10	6.46	6.02	5.44	4.82
	.01	8.10	5.85	4.94	4.43	4.10	3.87	3.56	3.23
	.05	4.35	3.49	3.10	2.87	2.71	2.60	2.45	2.28
	.10	2.97	2.59	2.38	2.25	2.16	2.09	2.00	1.89
	.20	1.76	1.75	1.70	1.65	1.62	1.60	1.56	1.51
21	.001	14.59	9.77	7.94	6.95	6.32	5.88	5.31	4.70
	.01	8.02	5.78	4.87	4.37	4.04	3.81	3.51	3.17
	.05	4.32	3.47	3.07	2.84	2.68	2.57	2.42	2.25
	.10	2.96	2.57	2.36	2.23	2.14	2.08	1.98	1.88
	.20	1.75	1.74	1.69	1.65	1.61	1.59	1.55	1.50
22	.001	14.38	9.61	7.80	6.81	6.19	5.76	5.19	4.58
	.01	7.94	5.72	4.82	4.31	3.99	3.76	3.45	3.12
	.05	4.30	3.44	3.05	2.82	2.66	2.55	2.40	2.23
	.10	2.95	2.56	2.35	2.22	2.13	2.06	1.97	1.86
	.20	1.75	1.73	1.68	1.64	1.61	1.58	1.54	1.49
23	.001	14.19	9.47	7.67	6.69	6.08	5.65	5.09	4.48
	.01	7.88	5.66	4.76	4.26	3.94	3.71	3.41	3.07
	.05	4.28	3.42	3.03	2.80	2.64	2.53	2.38	2.20
	.10	2.94	2.55	2.34	2.21	2.11	2.05	1.95	1.84
	.20	1.74	1.73	1.68	1.63	1.60	1.57	1.53	1.49
24	.001	14.03	9.34	7.55	6.59	5.98	5.55	4.99	4.39
	.01	7.82	5.61	4.72	4.22	3.90	3.67	3.36	3.03
	.05	4.26	3.40	3.01	2.78	2.62	2.51	2.36	2.18
	.10	2.93	2.54	2.33	2.19	2.10	2.04	1.94	1.83
	.20	1.74	1.72	1.67	1.63	1.59	1.57	1.53	1.48

Table C (Continued)

df error	α	\multicolumn{8}{c}{df for Numerator}
		1	2	3	4	5	6	8	12
25	.001	13.88	9.22	7.45	6.49	5.88	5.46	4.91	4.31
	.01	7.77	5.57	4.68	4.18	3.86	3.63	3.32	2.99
	.05	4.24	3.38	2.99	2.76	2.60	2.49	2.34	2.16
	.10	2.92	2.53	2.32	2.18	2.09	2.02	1.93	1.82
	.20	1.73	1.72	1.66	1.62	1.59	1.56	1.52	1.47
26	.001	13.74	9.12	7.36	6.41	5.80	5.38	4.83	4.24
	.01	7.72	5.53	4.64	4.14	3.82	3.59	3.29	2.96
	.05	4.22	3.37	2.98	2.74	2.59	2.47	2.32	2.15
	.10	2.91	2.52	2.31	2.17	2.08	2.01	1.92	1.81
	.20	1.73	1.71	1.66	1.62	1.58	1.56	1.52	1.47
27	.001	13.61	9.02	7.27	6.33	5.73	5.31	4.76	4.17
	.01	7.68	5.49	4.60	4.11	3.78	3.56	3.26	2.93
	.05	4.21	3.35	2.96	2.73	2.57	2.46	2.30	2.13
	.10	2.90	2.51	2.30	2.17	2.07	2.00	1.91	1.80
	.20	1.73	1.71	1.66	1.61	1.58	1.55	1.51	1.46
28	.001	13.50	8.93	7.19	6.25	5.66	5.24	4.69	4.11
	.01	7.64	5.45	4.57	4.07	3.75	3.53	3.23	2.90
	.05	4.20	3.34	2.95	2.71	2.56	2.44	2.29	2.12
	.10	2.89	2.50	2.29	2.16	2.06	2.00	1.90	1.79
	.20	1.72	1.71	1.65	1.61	1.57	1.55	1.51	1.46
29	.001	13.39	8.85	7.12	6.19	5.59	5.18	4.64	4.05
	.01	7.60	5.42	4.54	4.04	3.73	3.50	3.20	2.87
	.05	4.18	3.33	2.93	2.70	2.54	2.43	2.28	2.10
	.10	2.89	2.50	2.28	2.15	2.06	1.99	1.89	1.78
	.20	1.72	1.70	1.65	1.60	1.57	1.54	1.50	1.45
30	.001	13.29	8.77	7.05	6.12	5.53	5.12	4.58	4.00
	.01	7.56	5.39	4.51	4.02	3.70	3.47	3.17	2.84
	.05	4.17	3.32	2.92	2.69	2.53	2.42	2.27	2.09
	.10	2.88	2.49	2.28	2.14	2.05	1.98	1.88	1.77
	.20	1.72	1.70	1.64	1.60	1.57	1.54	1.50	1.45
40	.001	12.61	8.25	6.60	5.70	5.13	4.73	4.21	3.64
	.01	7.31	5.18	4.31	3.83	3.51	3.29	2.99	2.66
	.05	4.08	3.23	2.84	2.61	2.45	2.34	2.18	2.00
	.10	2.84	2.44	2.23	2.09	2.00	1.93	1.83	1.71
	.20	1.70	1.68	1.62	1.57	1.54	1.51	1.47	1.41
60	.001	11.97	7.76	6.17	5.31	4.76	4.37	3.87	3.31
	.01	7.08	4.98	4.13	3.65	3.34	3.12	2.82	2.50
	.05	4.00	3.15	2.76	2.52	2.37	2.25	2.10	1.92
	.10	2.79	2.39	2.18	2.04	1.95	1.87	1.77	1.66
	.20	1.68	1.65	1.59	1.55	1.51	1.48	1.44	1.38

Table C (Continued)

df error	α	\multicolumn{8}{c}{df for Numerator}							
		1	2	3	4	5	6	8	12
120	.001	11.38	7.31	5.79	4.95	4.42	4.04	3.55	3.02
	.01	6.85	4.79	3.95	3.48	3.17	2.96	2.66	2.34
	.05	3.92	3.07	2.68	2.45	2.29	2.17	2.02	1.83
	.10	2.75	2.35	2.13	1.99	1.90	1.82	1.72	1.60
	.20	1.66	1.63	1.57	1.52	1.48	1.45	1.41	1.35
∞	.001	10.83	6.91	5.42	4.62	4.10	3.74	3.27	2.74
	.01	6.64	4.60	3.78	3.32	3.02	2.80	2.51	2.18
	.05	3.84	2.99	2.60	2.37	2.21	2.09	1.94	1.75
	.10	2.71	2.30	2.08	1.94	1.85	1.77	1.67	1.55
	.20	1.64	1.61	1.55	1.50	1.46	1.43	1.38	1.32

Table D

Percentage Points of the Studentized Range*

Error df	α	\multicolumn{10}{c}{Number of Means (p) or Number of Steps Between Ordered Means (r)}
		2	3	4	5	6	7	8	9	10	11
2	.05	6.08	8.33	9.80	10.9	11.7	12.4	13.0	13.5	14.0	14.4
	.01	14.0	19.0	22.3	24.7	26.6	28.2	29.5	30.7	31.7	32.6
3	.05	4.50	5.91	6.82	7.50	8.04	8.48	8.85	9.18	9.46	9.72
	.01	8.26	10.6	12.2	13.3	14.2	15.0	15.6	16.2	16.7	17.8
4	.05	3.93	5.04	5.76	6.29	6.71	7.05	7.35	7.60	7.83	8.03
	.01	6.51	8.12	9.17	9.96	10.6	11.1	11.5	11.0	12.3	12.6
5	.05	3.64	4.60	5.22	5.67	6.03	6.33	6.58	6.80	6.99	7.17
	.01	5.70	6.98	7.80	8.42	8.91	9.32	9.67	9.97	10.24	10.48
6	.05	3.46	4.34	4.90	5.30	5.63	5.90	6.12	6.32	6.49	6.65
	.01	5.24	6.33	7.03	7.56	7.97	8.32	8.61	8.87	9.10	9.30
7	.05	3.34	4.16	4.68	5.06	5.36	5.61	5.82	6.00	6.16	6.30
	.01	4.95	5.92	6.54	7.01	7.37	7.68	7.94	8.17	8.37	8.55
8	.05	3.26	4.04	4.53	4.89	5.17	5.40	5.60	5.77	5.92	6.05
	.01	4.75	5.64	6.20	6.62	6.96	7.24	7.47	7.68	7.86	8.03
9	.05	3.20	3.95	4.41	4.76	5.02	5.24	5.43	5.59	5.74	5.87
	.01	4.60	5.43	5.96	6.35	6.66	6.91	7.13	7.33	7.49	7.65
10	.05	3.15	3.88	4.33	4.65	4.91	5.12	5.30	5.46	5.60	5.72
	.01	4.48	5.27	5.77	6.14	6.43	6.67	6.87	7.05	7.21	7.36
11	.05	3.11	3.82	4.26	4.57	4.82	5.03	5.20	5.35	5.49	5.61
	.01	4.39	5.15	5.62	5.97	6.25	6.48	6.67	6.84	6.99	7.13
12	.05	3.08	3.77	4.20	4.51	4.75	4.95	5.12	5.27	5.39	5.51
	.01	4.32	5.05	5.50	5.84	6.10	6.32	6.51	6.67	6.81	6.94
13	.05	3.06	3.73	4.15	4.45	4.69	4.88	5.05	5.19	5.32	5.43
	.01	4.26	4.96	5.40	5.40	5.73	6.19	6.37	6.53	6.67	6.79
14	.05	3.03	3.70	4.11	4.41	4.64	4.83	4.99	5.13	5.25	5.36
	.01	4.21	4.89	5.32	5.63	5.88	6.08	6.26	6.41	6.54	6.66
15	.05	3.01	3.67	4.08	4.37	4.59	4.78	4.94	5.08	5.20	5.31
	.01	4.17	4.84	5.25	5.56	5.80	5.99	6.16	6.31	6.44	6.55
16	.05	3.00	3.65	4.05	4.33	4.56	4.74	4.90	5.03	5.15	5.26
	.01	4.13	4.79	5.19	5.49	5.72	5.92	6.08	6.22	6.35	6.46
17	.05	2.98	3.63	4.02	4.30	4.52	4.70	4.86	4.99	5.11	5.21
	.01	4.10	4.74	5.14	5.43	5.66	5.85	6.01	6.15	6.27	6.38
18	.05	2.97	3.61	4.00	4.28	4.49	4.67	4.82	4.96	5.07	5.17
	.01	4.07	4.70	5.09	5.38	5.60	5.79	5.94	6.08	6.20	6.31
19	.05	2.96	3.59	3.98	4.25	4.47	4.65	4.79	4.92	5.04	5.14
	.01	4.05	4.67	5.05	5.33	5.55	5.73	5.89	6.02	6.14	6.25

Table D (Continued)

Error df	α	\multicolumn{10}{c}{Number of Means (p) or Number of Steps Between Ordered Means (r)}
		2	3	4	5	6	7	8	9	10	11
20	.05	2.95	3.58	3.96	4.23	4.45	4.62	4.77	4.90	5.01	5.11
	.01	4.02	4.64	5.02	5.29	5.51	5.69	5.84	5.97	6.09	6.19
24	.05	2.92	3.53	3.90	4.17	4.37	4.54	4.68	4.81	4.92	5.01
	.01	3.96	4.55	4.91	5.17	5.37	5.54	5.69	5.81	5.92	6.02
30	.05	2.89	3.49	3.85	4.10	4.30	4.46	4.60	4.72	4.82	4.92
	.01	3.89	4.45	4.80	5.05	5.24	5.40	5.54	5.65	5.76	5.85
40	.05	2.86	3.44	3.79	4.04	4.23	4.39	4.52	4.63	4.73	4.82
	.01	3.82	4.37	4.70	4.93	5.11	5.26	5.39	5.50	5.60	5.69
60	.05	2.83	3.40	3.74	3.98	4.16	4.31	4.44	4.55	4.65	4.73
	.01	3.76	4.28	4.59	4.82	4.99	5.13	5.25	5.36	5.45	5.53
120	.05	2.80	3.36	3.68	3.92	4.10	4.24	4.36	4.47	4.56	4.64
	.01	3.70	4.20	4.50	4.71	4.87	5.01	5.12	5.21	5.30	5.37
∞	.05	2.77	3.31	3.63	3.86	4.03	4.17	4.29	4.39	4.47	4.55
	.01	3.64	4.12	4.40	4.60	4.76	4.88	4.99	5.08	5.16	5.23

Table D (Continued)

Error df	α	\multicolumn{9}{c}{Number of Means (p) or Number of Steps Between Ordered Means (r)}
		12	13	14	15	16	17	18	19	20
2	.05	14.7	15.1	15.4	15.7	15.9	16.1	16.4	16.6	16.8
	.01	33.4	34.1	34.8	35.4	36.0	36.5	37.0	37.5	37.9
3	.05	9.72	10.2	10.3	10.5	10.7	10.8	11.0	11.1	11.2
	.01	17.5	17.9	18.2	18.5	18.8	19.1	19.3	19.5	19.8
4	.05	8.21	8.37	8.52	8.66	8.79	8.91	9.03	9.13	9.23
	.01	12.8	13.3	13.1	13.5	13.7	13.9	14.1	14.2	14.4
5	.05	7.32	7.47	7.60	7.72	7.83	7.93	8.03	8.12	8.21
	.01	10.70	10.89	11.08	11.24	11.40	11.55	11.68	11.81	11.93
6	.05	6.79	6.92	7.03	7.14	7.24	7.34	7.43	7.51	7.59
	.01	9.48	9.65	9.81	9.95	10.08	10.21	10.32	10.43	10.54
7	.05	6.43	6.55	6.66	6.76	6.85	6.94	7.02	7.10	7.17
	.01	8.71	8.86	9.00	9.12	9.24	9.35	9.46	9.55	9.65
8	.05	6.18	6.29	6.39	6.48	6.57	6.65	6.73	6.80	6.87
	.01	8.18	8.31	8.44	8.55	8.66	8.76	8.85	8.94	9.03
9	.05	5.98	6.09	6.19	6.28	6.36	6.44	6.51	6.58	6.64
	.01	7.78	7.91	8.03	8.13	8.23	8.33	8.41	8.49	8.57
10	.05	5.83	5.93	6.03	6.11	6.19	6.27	6.34	6.40	6.47
	.01	7.49	7.60	7.71	7.81	7.91	7.99	8.08	8.15	8.23
11	.05	5.71	5.81	5.90	5.98	6.06	6.13	6.20	6.27	6.33
	.01	7.25	7.36	7.46	7.56	7.65	7.73	7.81	7.88	7.95
12	.05	5.61	5.71	5.80	5.88	5.95	6.02	6.09	6.15	6.21
	.01	7.06	7.17	7.26	7.36	7.44	7.52	7.59	7.66	7.73
13	.05	5.53	5.63	5.71	5.79	5.86	5.93	5.99	6.05	6.11
	.01	6.90	7.01	7.10	7.19	7.27	7.35	7.42	7.48	7.55
14	.05	5.46	5.55	5.64	5.71	5.79	5.85	5.91	5.97	6.03
	.01	6.77	6.87	6.96	7.05	7.13	7.20	7.27	7.33	7.39
15	.05	5.40	5.49	5.57	5.65	5.72	5.78	5.85	5.90	5.96
	.01	6.66	6.76	6.84	6.93	7.00	7.07	7.14	7.20	7.26
16	.05	5.35	5.44	5.52	5.59	5.66	5.73	5.79	5.84	5.90
	.01	6.56	6.66	6.74	6.82	6.90	6.97	7.03	7.09	7.15
17	.05	5.31	5.39	5.47	5.54	5.61	5.67	5.73	5.79	5.84
	.01	6.48	6.57	6.66	6.73	6.81	6.87	6.94	7.00	7.05
18	.05	5.27	5.35	5.43	5.50	5.57	5.63	5.69	5.74	5.79
	.01	6.41	6.50	6.58	6.65	6.73	6.79	6.85	6.91	6.97
19	.05	5.23	5.31	5.39	5.46	5.53	5.59	5.65	5.70	5.75
	.01	6.34	6.43	6.51	6.58	6.65	6.72	6.78	6.84	6.89
20	.05	5.20	5.28	5.36	5.43	5.49	5.55	5.61	5.66	5.71
	.01	6.28	6.37	6.45	6.52	6.59	6.65	6.71	6.77	6.82

Test Anxiety: Appendix

Table D (Continued)

Error df	α	Number of Means (p) or Number of Steps Between Ordered Means (r)								
		12	13	14	15	16	17	18	19	20
24	.05	5.10	5.18	5.25	5.32	5.38	5.44	5.49	5.55	5.59
	.01	6.11	6.19	6.26	6.33	6.39	6.45	6.51	6.56	6.61
30	.05	5.00	5.08	5.15	5.21	5.27	5.33	5.38	5.43	5.47
	.01	5.93	6.01	6.08	6.14	6.20	6.26	6.31	6.36	6.41
40	.05	4.90	4.98	5.04	5.11	5.16	5.22	5.27	5.31	5.36
	.01	5.76	5.83	5.90	5.96	6.02	6.07	6.12	6.16	6.21
60	.05	4.81	4.88	4.94	5.00	5.06	5.11	5.15	5.20	5.24
	.01	5.60	5.67	5.73	5.78	5.84	5.89	5.93	5.97	6.01
120	.05	4.71	4.78	4.84	4.90	4.95	5.00	5.04	5.09	5.13
	.01	5.44	5.50	5.56	5.61	5.66	5.71	5.75	5.79	5.83
∞	.05	4.62	4.68	4.74	4.80	4.85	4.89	4.93	4.97	5.01
	.01	5.29	5.35	5.40	5.45	5.49	5.54	5.57	5.61	5.65

*Reproduced with permission of the Trustees of *Biometrika*.

Table E

Critical Values for Bryant-Paulson Procedure*

C = Number of Covariates

Error df	C	α	Number of Groups										
			2	3	4	5	6	7	8	10	12	16	20
3	1	.05	5.42	7.18	8.32	9.17	9.84	10.39	10.86	11.62	12.22	13.14	13.83
		.01	10.28	13.32	15.32	16.80	17.98	18.95	19.77	21.12	22.19	23.82	25.05
	2	.05	6.21	8.27	9.60	10.59	11.37	12.01	12.56	13.44	14.15	15.22	16.02
		.01	11.97	15.56	17.91	19.66	21.05	22.19	23.16	24.75	26.01	27.93	29.38
	3	.05	6.92	9.23	10.73	11.84	12.72	13.44	14.06	15.05	15.84	17.05	17.95
		.01	13.45	17.51	20.17	22.15	23.72	25.01	26.11	27.90	29.32	31.50	33.13
4	1	.05	4.51	5.84	6.69	7.32	7.82	8.23	8.58	9.15	9.61	10.30	10.82
		.01	7.68	9.64	10.93	11.89	12.65	13.28	13.82	14.70	15.40	16.48	17.29
	2	.05	5.04	6.54	7.51	8.23	8.80	9.26	9.66	10.31	10.83	11.61	12.21
		.01	8.69	10.95	12.43	13.54	14.41	15.14	15.76	16.77	17.58	18.81	19.74
	3	.05	5.51	7.18	8.25	9.05	9.67	10.19	10.63	11.35	11.92	12.79	13.45
		.01	9.59	12.11	13.77	15.00	15.98	16.79	17.47	18.60	19.50	20.87	21.91
5	1	.05	4.06	5.17	5.88	6.40	6.82	7.16	7.45	7.93	8.30	8.88	9.32
		.01	6.49	7.99	8.97	9.70	10.28	10.76	11.17	11.84	12.38	13.20	13.83
	2	.05	4.45	5.68	6.48	7.06	7.52	7.90	8.23	8.76	9.18	9.83	10.31
		.01	7.20	8.89	9.99	10.81	11.47	12.01	12.47	13.23	13.84	14.77	15.47
	3	.05	4.81	6.16	7.02	7.66	8.17	8.58	8.94	9.52	9.98	10.69	11.22
		.01	7.83	9.70	10.92	11.82	12.54	13.14	13.65	14.48	15.15	16.17	16.95
6	1	.05	3.79	4.78	5.40	5.86	6.23	6.53	6.78	7.20	7.53	8.04	8.43
		.01	5.83	7.08	7.88	8.48	8.96	9.36	9.70	10.25	10.70	11.38	11.90
	2	.05	4.10	5.18	5.87	6.37	6.77	7.10	7.38	7.84	8.21	8.77	9.20
		.01	6.36	7.75	8.64	9.31	9.85	10.29	10.66	11.28	11.77	12.54	13.11
	3	.05	4.38	5.55	6.30	6.84	7.28	7.64	7.94	8.44	8.83	9.44	9.90
		.01 ·	6.85	8.36	9.34	10.07	10.65	11.13	11.54	12.22	12.75	13.59	14.21
7	1	.05	3.62	4.52	5.09	5.51	5.84	6.11	6.34	6.72	7.03	7.49	7.84
		.01	5.41	6.50	7.20	7.72	8.14	8.48	8.77	9.26	9.64	10.24	10.69
	2	.05	3.87	4.85	5.47	5.92	6.28	6.58	6.83	7.24	7.57	8.08	8.46
		.01	5.84	7.03	7.80	8.37	8.83	9.21	9.53	10.06	10.49	11.14	11.64
	3	.05	4.11	5.16	5.82	6.31	6.70	7.01	7.29	7.73	8.08	8.63	9.03
		.01	6.23	7.52	8.36	8.98	9.47	9.88	10.23	10.80	11.26	11.97	12.51
8	1.	.05	3.49	4.34	4.87	5.26	5.57	5.82	6.03	6.39	6.67	7.10	7.43
		.01	5.12	6.11	6.74	7.20	7.58	7.88	8.15	8.58	8.92	9.36	9.87
	2	.05	3.70	4.61	5.19	5.61	5.94	6.21	6.44	6.82	7.12	7.59	7.94
		.01	5.48	6.54	7.23	7.74	8.14	8.48	8.76	9.23	9.61	10.19	10.63
	3	.05	3.91	4.88	5.49	5.93	6.29	6.58	6.83	7.23	7.55	8.05	8.42
		.01	5.81	6.95	7.69	8.23	8.67	9.03	9.33	9.84	10.24	10.87	11.34
10	1	.05	3.32	4.10	4.58	4.93	5.21	5.43	5.63	5.94	6.19	6.58	6.87
		.01	4.76	5.61	6.15	6.55	6.86	7.13	7.35	7.72	8.01	8.47	8.82
	2	.05	3.49	4.31	4.82	5.19	5.49	5.73	5.93	6.27	6.54	6.95	7.26
		.01	5.02	5.93	6.51	6.93	7.27	7.55	7.79	8.19	8.50	8.99	9.36
	3	.05	3.65	4.51	5.05	5.44	5.75	6.01	6.22	6.58	6.86	7.29	7.62
		.01	5.27	6.23	6.84	7.30	7.66	7.96	8.21	8.63	8.96	9.48	9.88

Table E (Continued)

Error df	C	α	\multicolumn{11}{c}{Number of Groups}
			2	3	4	5	6	7	8	10	12	16	20
12	1	.05	3.22	3.95	4.40	4.73	4.98	5.19	5.37	5.67	5.90	6.26	6.53
		.01	4.54	5.31	5.79	6.15	6.43	6.67	6.87	7.20	7.46	7.87	8.18
	2	.05	3.35	4.12	4.59	4.93	5.20	5.43	5.62	5.92	6.17	6.55	6.83
		.01	4.74	5.56	6.07	6.45	6.75	7.00	7.21	7.56	7.84	8.27	8.60
	3	.05	3.48	4.28	4.78	5.14	5.42	5.65	5.85	6.17	6.43	6.82	7.12
		.01	4.94	5.80	6.34	6.74	7.05	7.31	7.54	7.90	8.20	8.65	9.00
14	1	.05	3.15	3.85	4.28	4.59	4.83	5.03	5.20	5.48	5.70	6.03	6.29
		.01	4.39	5.11	5.56	5.89	6.15	6.36	6.55	6.85	7.09	7.47	7.75
	2	.05	3.26	3.99	4.44	4.76	5.01	5.22	5.40	5.69	5.92	6.27	6.54
		.01	4.56	5.31	5.78	6.13	6.40	6.63	6.82	7.14	7.40	7.79	8.09
	3	.05	3.37	4.13	4.59	4.93	5.19	5.41	5.59	5.89	6.13	6.50	6.78
		.01	4.72	5.15	6.00	6.36	6.65	6.89	7.09	7.42	7.69	8.10	8.41
16	1	.05	3.10	3.77	4.19	4.49	4.72	4.91	5.07	5.34	5.55	5.87	6.12
		.01	4.28	4.96	5.39	5.70	5.95	6.15	6.32	6.60	6.83	7.18	7.45
	2	.05	3.19	3.90	4.32	4.63	4.88	5.07	5.24	5.52	5.74	6.07	6.33
		.01	4.42	5.14	5.58	5.90	6.16	6.37	6.55	6.85	7.08	7.45	7.73
	3	.05	3.29	4.01	4.46	4.78	5.03	5.23	5.41	5.69	5.92	6.27	6.53
		.01	4.56	5.30	5.76	6.10	6.37	6.59	6.77	7.08	7.33	7.71	8.00
18	1	.05	3.06	3.72	4.12	4.41	4.63	4.82	4.98	5.23	5.44	5.75	5.98
		.01	4.20	4.86	5.26	5.56	5.79	5.99	6.15	6.42	6.63	6.96	7.22
	2	.05	3.14	3.82	4.24	4.54	4.77	4.96	5.13	5.39	5.60	5.92	6.17
		.01	4.32	5.00	5.43	5.73	5.98	6.18	6.35	6.63	6.85	7.19	7.46
	3	.05	3.23	3.93	4.35	4.66	4.90	5.10	5.27	5.54	5.76	6.09	6.34
		.01	4.44	5.15	5.59	5.90	6.16	6.36	6.54	6.83	7.06	7.42	7.69
20	1	.05	3.03	3.67	4.07	4.35	4.57	4.75	4.90	5.15	5.35	5.65	5.88
		.01	4.14	4.77	5.17	5.45	5.68	5.86	6.02	6.27	6.48	6.80	7.04
	2	.05	3.10	3.77	4.17	4.46	4.69	4.88	5.03	5.29	5.49	5.81	6.04
		.01	4.25	4.90	5.31	5.60	5.84	6.03	6.19	6.46	6.67	7.00	7.25
	3	.05	3.18	3.86	4.28	4.57	4.81	5.00	5.16	5.42	5.63	5.96	6.20
		.01	4.35	5.03	5.45	5.75	5.99	6.19	6.36	6.63	6.85	7.19	7.45
24	1	.05	2.98	3.61	3.99	4.26	4.47	4.65	4.79	5.03	5.22	5.51	5.73
		.01	4.05	4.65	5.02	5.29	5.50	5.68	5.83	6.07	6.26	6.56	6.78
	2	.05	3.04	3.69	4.08	4.35	4.57	4.75	4.90	5.14	5.34	5.63	5.86
		.01	4.14	4.76	5.14	5.42	5.63	5.81	5.95	6.21	6.41	6.71	6.95
	3	.05	3.11	3.76	4.16	4.44	4.67	4.85	5.00	5.25	5.45	5.75	5.98
		.01	4.22	4.86	5.25	5.54	5.76	5.94	6.10	6.35	6.55	6.87	7.11
30	1	.05	2.94	3.55	3.91	4.18	4.38	4.54	4.69	4.91	5.09	5.37	5.58
		.01	3.96	4.54	4.89	5.14	5.34	5.50	5.64	5.87	6.05	6.32	6.53
	2	.05	2.99	3.61	3.98	4.25	4.46	4.62	4.77	5.00	5.18	5.46	5.68
		.01	4.03	4.62	4.98	5.24	5.44	5.61	5.75	5.98	6.16	6.44	6.66
	3	.05	3.04	3.67	4.05	4.32	4.53	4.70	4.85	5.08	5.27	5.56	5.78
		.01	4.10	4.70	5.06	5.33	5.54	5.71	5.85	6.08	6.27	6.56	6.78

Table E (Continued)

Error df	C	α	Number of Groups										
			2	3	4	5	6	7	8	10	12	16	20
40	1	.05	2.89	3.49	3.84	4.09	4.29	4.45	4.58	4.80	4.97	5.23	5.43
		.01	3.88	4.43	4.76	5.00	5.19	5.34	5.47	5.68	5.85	6.10	6.30
	2	.05	2.93	3.53	3.89	4.15	4.34	4.50	4.64	4.86	5.04	5.30	5.50
		.01	3.93	4.48	4.82	5.07	5.26	5.41	5.54	5.76	5.93	6.19	6.38
	3	.05	2.97	3.57	3.94	4.20	4.40	4.56	4.70	4.92	5.10	5.37	5.57
		.01	3.98	4.54	4.88	5.13	5.32	5.48	5.61	5.83	6.00	6.27	6.47
60	1	.05	2.85	3.43	3.77	4.01	4.20	4.35	4.48	4.69	4.85	5.10	5.29
		.01	3.79	4.32	4.64	4.86	5.04	5.18	5.30	5.50	5.65	5.89	6.07
	2	.05	2.88	3.46	3.80	4.05	4.24	4.39	4.52	4.73	4.89	5.14	5.33
		.01	3.83	4.36	4.68	4.90	5.08	5.22	5.35	5.54	5.70	5.94	6.12
	3	.05	2.90	3.49	3.83	4.08	4.27	4.43	4.56	4.77	4.93	5.19	5.38
		.01	3.86	4.39	4.72	4.95	5.12	5.27	5.39	5.59	5.75	6.00	6.18
120	1	.05	2.81	3.37	3.70	3.93	4.11	4.26	4.38	4.58	4.73	4.97	5.15
		.01	3.72	4.22	4.52	4.73	4.89	5.03	5.14	5.32	5.47	5.69	5.85
	2	.05	2.82	3.38	3.72	3.95	4.13	4.28	4.40	4.60	4.75	4.99	5.17
		.01	3.73	4.24	4.54	4.75	4.91	5.05	5.16	5.35	5.49	5.71	5.88
	3	.05	2.84	3.40	3.73	3.97	4.15	4.30	4.42	4.62	4.77	5.01	5.19
		.01	3.75	4.25	4.55	4.77	4.94	5.07	5.18	5.37	5.51	5.74	5.90

*Reproduced with permission of the trustees of *Biometrika*.

Test Anxiety: Appendix

Table F

The Hartley F-Max Test for Homogeneity of Variances*

df = n-1**	α	Number of Variances										
		2	3	4	5	6	7	8	9	10	11	12
2	.05	39.0	87.5	142	202	266	333	403	475	550	626	704
	.01	199	448	729	1036	1362	1705	2063	2432	2813	3204	3605
3	.05	154	27.8	39.2	50.7	62.0	72.9	83.5	93.9	104	114	124
	.01	47.5	85	120	151	184	216	249	281	310	337	361
4	.05	9.60	15.5	20.6	25.2	29.5	33.6	37.5	41.4	44.6	48.0	51.4
	.01	23.2	37.	49.	59.	69.	79.	89.	97.	106.	113.	120
5	.05	7.15	10.8	13.7	16.3	18.7	20.8	22.9	24.7	26.5	28.2	29.9
	.01	14.9	22.	28.	33.	38.	42.	46.	50.	54.	57	60
6	.05	5.82	8.38	10.4	12.1	13.7	15.0	16.3	17.5	18.6	19.7	20.7
	.01	11.1	15.5	19.1	22.	25.	27.	30.	32.	34.	36	37
7	.05	4.99	6.94	8.44	9.70	10.8	11.8	12.7	13.5	14.3	151	15.8
	.01	8.89	12.1	14.5	16.5	18.4	20.	22.	23.	24.	26	27
8	.05	4.43	6.00	7.18	8.12	9.03	9.78	10.5	11.1	11.7	12.2	12.7
	.01	7.50	9.9	11.7	13.2	14.5	15.8	16.9	17.9	18.9	19.8	21
9	.05	4.03	5.34	6.31	7.11	7.80	8.41	8.95	9.45	9.91	10.3	10.7
	.01	6.54	8.5	9.9	11.1	12.1	13.1	13.9	14.7	15.3	16.0	16.6
10	.05	3.72	4.85	5.67	6.34	6.92	7.42	7.87	8.28	8.66	9.01	9.34
	.01	5.85	7.4	8.6	9.6	10.4	11.1	11.8	12.4	12.9	13.4	13.9
12	.05	3.28	4.16	4.79	5.30	5.72	6.09	6.42	6.72	7.00	7.25	7.48
	.01	4.91	6.1	6.9	7.6	8.2	8.7	9.1	9.5	9.9	10.2	10.6
15	.05	2.86	3.54	4.01	4.37	4.68	4.95	5.19	5.40	5.59	5.77	5.93
	.01	4.07	4.9	5.5	6.0	6.4	6.7	7.1	7.3	7.5	7.8	8.0

*Table F (continued)

df n-1**	α	Number of Variances										
		2	3	4	5	6	7	8	9	10	11	12
20	.05	2.46	2.95	3.29	3.54	3.76	3.94	4.10	4.24	4.37	4.49	4.59
	.01	3.32	3.8	4.3	4.6	4.9	5.1	5.3	5.5	5.6	5.8	5.9
30	.05	2.07	2.40	2.61	2.78	2.91	3.02	3.12	3.21	3.29	3.36	3.39
	.01	2.63	3.0	3.3	3.4	3.6	3.7	3.8	3.9	4.0	4.1	4.2
60	.05	1.67	1.85	1.96	2.04	2.11	2.17	2.22	2.26	2.30	2.33	2.36
	.01	1.96	2.2	2.3	2.4	2.4	2.5	2.5	2.6	2.6	2.7	2.7
∞	.05	1.00	1.00	1.00	1.00	1.00	1.00	1.00	1.00	1.00	1.00	1.00
	.01	1.00	1.00	1.00	1.00	1.00	1.00	1.00	1.00	1.00	1.00	1.00

*Reproduced with permission of the Trustees of *Biometrika*.
**If group sizes are unequal, employ harmonic mean.

Table G

Critical Values for Dunnett's Test

Error df	α	Two-Tailed Comparisons k = number of treatment means, including control								
		2	3	4	5	6	7	8	9	10
5	0.05	2.57	3.03	3.29	3.48	3.62	3.73	3.82	3.90	3.97
	0.01	4.03	4.63	4.98	5.22	5.41	5.56	5.69	5.80	5.89
6	0.05	2.45	2.86	3.10	3.26	3.39	3.49	3.57	3.64	3.71
	0.01	3.71	4.21	4.51	4.71	4.87	5.00	5.10	5.20	5.28
7	0.05	2.36	2.75	2.97	3.12	3.24	3.33	3.41	3.47	3.53
	0.01	3.50	3.95	4.21	4.39	4.53	4.64	4.74	4.82	4.89
8	0.05	2.31	2.67	2.88	3.02	3.13	3.22	3.29	3.35	3.41
	0.01	3.36	3.77	4.00	4.17	4.29	4.40	4.48	4.56	4.62
9	0.05	2.26	2.61	2.81	2.95	3.05	3.14	3.20	3.26	3.32
	0.01	3.25	3.63	3.85	4.01	4.12	4.22	4.30	4.37	4.43
10	0.05	2.23	2.57	2.76	2.89	2.99	3.07	3.14	3.19	3.24
	0.01	3.17	3.53	3.74	3.88	3.99	4.08	4.16	4.22	4.28
11	0.05	2.20	2.53	2.72	2.84	2.94	3.02	3.08	3.14	3.19
	0.01	3.11	3.45	3.65	3.79	3.89	3.98	4.05	4.11	4.16
12	0.05	2.18	2.50	2.68	2.81	2.90	2.98	3.04	3.09	3.14
	0.01	3.05	3.39	3.58	3.71	3.81	3.89	3.96	4.02	4.07
13	0.05	2.16	2.48	2.65	2.78	2.87	2.94	3.00	3.06	3.10
	0.01	3.01	3.33	3.52	3.65	3.74	3.82	3.89	3.94	3.99
14	0.05	2.14	2.46	2.63	2.75	2.84	2.91	2.97	3.02	3.07
	0.01	2.98	3.29	3.47	3.59	3.69	3.76	3.83	3.88	3.93
15	0.05	2.13	2.44	2.61	2.73	2.82	2.89	2.95	3.00	3.04
	0.01	2.95	3.25	3.43	3.55	3.64	3.71	3.78	3.83	3.88
16	0.05	2.12	2.42	2.59	2.71	2.80	2.87	2.92	2.97	3.02
	0.01	2.92	3.22	3.39	3.51	3.60	3.67	3.73	3.78	3.83
17	0.05	2.11	2.41	2.58	2.69	2.78	2.85	2.90	2.95	3.00
	0.01	2.90	3.19	3.36	3.47	3.56	3.63	3.69	3.74	3.79
18	0.05	2.10	2.40	2.56	2.68	2.76	2.83	2.89	2.94	2.98
	0.01	2.88	3.17	3.33	3.44	3.53	3.60	3.66	3.71	3.75
19	0.05	2.09	2.39	2.55	2.66	2.75	2.81	2.87	2.92	2.96
	0.01	2.86	3.15	3.31	3.42	3.50	3.57	3.63	3.68	3.72
20	0.05	2.09	2.38	2.54	2.65	2.72	2.80	2.86	2.90	2.95
	0.01	2.85	3.13	3.29	3.40	3.48	3.55	3.60	3.65	3.69
24	0.05	2.06	2.35	2.51	2.61	2.70	2.76	2.81	2.86	2.90
	0.01	2.80	3.07	3.22	3.32	3.40	3.47	3.52	3.57	3.61
30	0.05	2.04	2.32	2.47	2.58	2.66	2.72	2.77	2.82	2.86
	0.01	2.75	3.01	3.15	3.25	3.33	3.39	3.44	3.49	3.52
40	0.05	2.02	2.29	2.44	2.54	2.62	2.68	2.73	2.77	2.81
	0.01	2.70	2.95	3.09	3.19	3.26	3.32	3.37	3.41	3.44
60	0.05	2.00	2.27	2.41	2.51	2.58	2.64	2.69	2.73	2.77
	0.01	2.66	2.90	3.03	3.12	3.19	3.25	3.29	3.33	3.37
120	0.05	1.98	2.24	2.38	2.47	2.55	2.60	2.65	2.69	2.73
	0.01	2.62	2.85	2.97	3.06	3.12	3.18	3.22	3.26	3.29
∞	0.05	1.96	2.21	2.35	2.44	2.51	2.57	2.61	2.65	2.69
	0.01	2.58	2.79	2.92	3.00	3.06	3.11	3.15	3.19	3.22

Reproduced from: Dunnett, C. W. (1964). New tables for multiple comparisons with a control. *Biometric, 20*, 482-491.
Permission granted by the Biometric Society.

Table H

Critical Values of the Pearson r*

df (=N-2; N=number of pairs)	Level of significance for one-tailed test			
	.05	.025	.01	.005
	Level of significance for two-tailed test			
	.10	.05	.02	.01
1	.988	.997	.9995	.9999
2	.900	.950	.980	.990
3	.805	.878	.934	.959
4	.729	.811	.882	.917
5	.669	.754	.833	.874
6	.622	.707	.789	.834
7	.582	.666	.750	.798
8	.549	.632	.716	.765
9	.521	.602	.685	.735
10	.497	.576	.658	.708
11	.476	.553	.634	.684
12	.458	.532	.612	.661
13	.441	.514	.592	.641
14	.426	.497	.574	.623
15	.412	.482	.558	.606
16	.400	.468	.542	.590
17	.389	.456	.528	.575
18	.378	.444	.516	.561
19	.369	.433	.503	.549
20	.360	.423	.492	.537
21	.352	.413	.482	.526
22	.344	.404	.472	.515
23	.337	.396	.462	.505
24	.330	.388	.453	.496
25	.323	.381	.445	.487

Table H (Continued)

df (=N-2; N=number of pairs)	Level of significance for one-tailed test			
	.05	.025	.01	.005
	Level of significance for two-tailed test			
	.10	.05	.02	.01
26	.317	.374	.437	.479
27	.311	.367	.430	.471
28	.306	.361	.423	.463
29	.301	.355	.416	.456
30	.296	.349	.409	.449
35	.275	.325	.381	.418
40	.257	.304	.358	.393
45	.243	.288	.228	.372
50	.231	.273	.322	.354
60	.211	.250	.295	.325
70	.195	.232	.274	.302
80	.183	.217	.256	.283
90	.173	.205	.242	.267
100	.164	.195	.230	.254

*From R. A. Fisher and F. Yates (1963). "Statistical Tables for Biological, Agricultural and Medical Research" (6th ed.). Oliver and Boyd, Edinburgh. Reproduced by permission of authors and publishers.

Table I

Critical Values of r_s (Spearman Rank-Order Correlation Coefficient)*

No. of pairs (N)	Level of significance for one-tailed test			
	.05	.025	.01	.005
	Level of significance for two-tailed test			
	.10	.05	.02	.01
5	.900	1.000	1.000	---
6	.829	.886	.943	1.000
7	.714	.786	.893	.929
8	.643	.738	.833	.881
9	.600	.683	.783	.833
10	.564	.648	.746	.794
12	.506	.591	.712	.777
14	.456	.544	.645	.715
16	.425	.506	.601	.665
18	.399	.475	.564	.625
20	.377	.450	.534	.591
22	.359	.428	.508	.562
24	.343	.409	.485	.537
26	.329	.392	.465	.515
28	.317	.377	.448	.496
30	.306	.364	.432	.478

*From Zar, J. H. (1972). Significant testing of Spearman rank correlation coefficient. *Journal of the American Statistical Association, 67*, 578-580. Reproduced with permission from the *Journal of the American Statistical Association*.

Table J

Critical Values of Chi-Square*

df**	Level of significance					
	.20	.10	.05	.02	.01	.001
1	1.64	2.71	3.84	5.41	6.63	10.83
2	3.22	4.61	5.99	7.82	9.21	13.82
3	4.64	6.25	7.82	9.84	11.34	16.27
4	5.99	7.78	9.49	11.67	13.28	18.46
5	7.29	9.24	11.07	13.39	15.09	20.52
6	8.56	10.64	12.59	15.03	16.81	22.46
7	9.80	12.02	14.07	16.62	18.48	24.32
8	11.03	13.36	15.51	18.17	20.09	26.12
9	12.24	14.68	16.92	19.68	21.67	27.88
10	13.44	15.99	18.31	21.16	23.21	29.59
11	14.63	17.28	19.68	22.62	24.71	31.26
12	15.81	18.55	21.03	24.05	26.22	32.91
13	16.98	19.81	22.36	25.47	27.69	34.53
14	18.15	21.06	23.68	26.87	29.14	36.12
15	19.31	22.31	25.00	28.26	30.58	37.70
16	20.46	23.54	26.30	29.63	32.00	39.25
17	21.62	24.77	27.59	31.00	33.41	40.79
18	22.76	25.99	28.87	32.35	34.81	42.31
19	23.90	27.20	30.14	33.69	36.19	43.82
20	25.04	28.41	31.41	25.02	37.57	45.32
21	26.17	29.62	32.67	36.34	38.93	46.80
22	27.30	30.81	33.92	37.66	40.29	48.27
23	28.43	32.01	35.17	38.97	41.64	49.73
24	29.55	33.20	36.42	40.27	42.98	51.18
25	30.68	34.38	37.65	41.57	44.31	52.62

Table J (continued)

	Level of significance					
df**	.20	.10	.05	.02	.01	.001
26	31.80	35.56	38.89	42.86	45.64	54.05
27	32.91	36.74	40.11	44.14	46.96	55.48
28	34.03	37.92	41.34	45.42	48.28	56.89
29	35.14	39.09	42.56	46.69	49.59	58.30
30	36.25	40.26	43.77	47.96	50.89	59.70

*From R. A. Fisher and F. Yates (1963). "Statistical Tables for Biological, Agricultural and Medical Research" (6th ed.). Oliver and Boyd, Edinburgh. Reproduced by permission of the authors and publishers.

**For df greater than 30, the value obtained from the expression

$$\sqrt{2\chi^2} - \sqrt{2df - 1}$$

may be used as a t ratio.

Test Anxiety: Appendix

Table K

A Table of Random Numbers

Row	1	2	3	4	5	6	7	8	9	10	11	12	13	14	15	16	17	18	19	20	21	22	23	24	25	26	27	28	29	30	31	32
													Column Number																			
1	2	7	8	9	4	0	7	2	3	2	5	4	2	6	7	1	6	8	5	9	1	3	5	4	0	3	6	6	7	6	5	1
2	2	2	6	0	4	1	7	7	3	8	7	3	6	7	9	4	2	1	3	8	9	0	3	4	9	0	2	6	3	0	9	8
3	9	1	6	6	3	9	4	9	1	0	5	1	5	2	2	7	5	2	5	3	4	1	3	9	5	8	1	3	8	2	9	2
4	7	0	5	5	9	2	7	5	7	8	0	8	8	5	0	6	0	5	9	0	5	7	4	5	2	0	6	1	6	4	2	0
5	4	7	3	6	6	3	9	8	2	1	7	9	7	6	4	2	4	9	6	0	3	6	3	5	3	9	9	1	8	5	1	3
6	8	2	0	2	8	7	7	6	0	2	2	3	1	1	1	6	4	8	5	2	2	3	4	2	2	6	5	2	2	4	9	6
7	0	8	7	5	3	3	6	4	2	6	8	3	1	6	5	0	0	5	5	7	8	1	0	1	2	9	1	4	3	4	7	6
8	9	4	1	9	0	8	4	6	6	8	6	3	3	2	2	3	7	4	7	5	1	5	7	6	3	7	9	4	5	5	3	5
9	5	0	0	6	7	4	0	0	0	1	9	5	9	9	1	8	1	4	7	4	9	8	7	2	4	3	0	8	6	4	2	7
10	1	9	5	4	1	5	2	6	2	9	4	1	1	5	8	4	4	4	6	1	8	7	8	6	4	8	7	4	4	0	5	8
11	5	6	4	4	1	8	7	2	8	3	6	1	5	9	8	6	2	2	9	1	9	0	4	8	1	0	1	3	5	3	4	4
12	7	9	2	5	1	9	7	9	3	1	8	6	8	7	7	6	6	5	0	3	8	1	1	2	4	7	8	9	1	7	5	2
13	3	3	3	5	9	5	1	4	0	8	2	5	6	3	5	4	6	5	7	2	6	7	8	9	9	9	8	0	9	1	5	3
14	1	9	0	4	0	0	9	9	5	7	4	1	5	9	4	7	6	4	8	2	6	4	4	1	8	8	1	5	4	3	8	0
15	5	4	4	7	2	0	3	7	9	1	0	9	6	2	9	7	4	7	6	1	1	6	1	2	2	9	5	8	4	4	8	6
16	2	9	8	2	5	5	9	3	2	0	4	9	0	6	4	4	2	1	5	7	3	6	5	5	4	5	7	9	6	6	4	0
17	9	7	6	2	6	7	7	3	3	3	1	7	5	0	9	6	1	1	3	9	2	1	1	0	0	1	3	7	7	3	7	3
18	5	8	2	4	3	3	0	8	5	3	5	7	5	8	3	5	9	3	4	5	4	6	3	9	2	7	1	1	4	9	1	3
19	4	3	4	9	5	0	3	6	2	9	7	4	6	2	5	6	9	8	3	6	1	4	0	3	5	9	7	1	8	0	6	9
20	1	1	9	8	4	8	0	6	7	0	9	7	9	6	9	9	4	0	6	0	0	5	9	6	5	1	4	2	0	4	1	9
21	6	9	1	8	3	3	7	5	9	6	6	7	7	6	0	4	5	3	4	5	7	3	0	6	1	0	3	0	0	3	5	0
22	7	0	0	3	8	1	3	4	7	9	5	2	6	9	9	7	3	2	5	0	2	3	5	3	9	7	4	8	9	4	1	5
23	3	7	2	0	8	1	5	6	9	0	1	7	8	9	6	6	6	0	7	8	1	9	6	7	4	8	9	6	3	6	5	1
24	2	7	0	0	0	6	5	0	6	5	6	0	3	2	9	3	1	7	2	2	8	4	9	0	4	3	2	4	5	5	1	2
25	3	0	7	0	7	8	4	9	4	2	8	2	4	7	4	9	6	0	4	3	8	1	7	7	0	9	8	4	6	3	1	2

Table K (continued)

Row		Column Number																													
	1	2	3	4	5	6	7	8	9	10	11	12	13	14	15	16	17	18	19	20	21	22	23	24	25	26	27	28	29	30	31	32
26	6	2	9	3	3	1	7	7	5	2	2	3	4	6	4	2	2	4	7	5	4	4	4	1	7	1	6	7	1	2	6	8
27	5	4	9	2	1	4	8	5	7	0	9	6	4	7	2	1	8	9	7	8	1	3	3	4	6	6	5	9	0	7	0	3
28	0	3	7	0	1	7	3	8	0	3	6	2	3	1	0	9	5	5	2	5	9	2	0	2	8	7	7	2	0	2	7	2
29	9	3	6	6	2	2	0	9	7	2	3	9	2	8	7	3	1	0	7	0	8	9	3	8	8	5	3	1	3	1	0	9
30	2	9	5	6	9	9	5	8	9	8	2	8	0	0	4	4	8	8	5	7	2	1	3	4	9	5	2	6	8	3	6	6
31	8	5	7	2	9	2	6	5	9	3	9	7	1	8	3	5	6	6	1	2	1	5	5	5	6	1	7	1	5	7	5	9
32	8	4	5	7	7	9	9	5	1	4	5	5	0	9	5	3	1	3	9	3	7	8	1	4	0	5	4	1	5	4	4	0
33	8	7	9	8	1	8	4	1	4	3	7	7	0	9	1	9	4	6	1	3	8	6	5	9	2	2	8	1	6	9	0	1
34	7	3	2	5	1	8	6	3	2	8	5	8	6	9	3	4	5	2	6	1	9	0	8	9	0	5	4	6	8	0	3	2
35	8	9	9	0	1	8	8	8	9	5	7	5	0	4	1	1	6	0	3	1	3	0	3	5	8	9	2	7	8	8	7	1
36	0	2	9	7	8	8	1	7	6	1	6	7	6	4	2	5	0	5	8	3	2	4	7	7	2	2	6	2	6	8	6	0
37	0	5	2	3	2	3	8	1	8	8	1	6	2	3	0	7	3	0	1	2	6	2	6	8	3	7	4	4	3	8	9	9
38	2	2	6	8	1	6	9	6	2	6	7	9	1	7	8	0	2	4	8	0	4	7	3	3	8	4	4	8	4	3	3	8
39	0	7	8	4	9	5	8	8	0	7	2	1	8	1	7	5	3	0	7	4	1	0	3	2	0	1	2	8	6	5	9	4
40	4	8	0	7	0	5	9	9	4	9	6	9	8	2	0	6	4	0	7	8	1	1	4	2	1	6	7	0	7	3	1	2
41	9	2	0	1	6	7	2	8	3	9	8	8	3	4	7	8	4	0	5	1	6	8	7	8	3	5	4	5	0	4	0	6
42	0	8	8	3	4	0	9	5	2	8	4	5	0	4	8	2	6	2	9	2	1	9	8	5	3	1	0	7	8	5	3	9
43	2	0	6	9	7	5	2	8	2	5	5	4	0	7	7	1	7	8	6	8	5	1	3	7	8	2	7	1	9	3	6	3
44	3	1	8	6	8	3	5	6	3	2	7	4	1	8	9	4	5	6	8	0	6	4	6	4	1	0	9	1	9	8	1	4
45	0	0	8	6	1	7	5	0	8	5	6	5	0	8	2	7	1	1	6	3	4	6	0	0	9	4	7	9	2	4	8	7
46	3	3	2	9	4	2	5	3	3	8	2	4	2	6	2	5	2	9	0	1	3	7	6	5	9	1	4	6	0	1	0	1
47	8	4	7	4	0	4	5	1	2	1	0	4	2	5	7	7	9	4	6	5	8	3	3	8	1	0	3	7	7	7	8	6
48	0	2	4	3	0	2	0	7	2	8	8	0	8	4	1	6	0	2	3	5	9	7	5	1	3	6	3	2	8	7	5	8
49	4	-6	5	6	3	0	4	5	2	0	1	5	2	7	9	5	3	0	2	2	1	6	1	1	0	0	9	1	6	1	7	7
50	3	4	8	3	4	5	8	7	5	9	7	1	6	3	9	9	0	9	4	2	5	8	9	5	3	3	3	6	4	5	2	0

Author Index

Subject Index